NINE CHOICES

JOHNNY CASH

NINE CHOICES

AND AMERICAN CULTURE

JONATHAN SILVERMAN

 University of Massachusetts Press
Amherst & Boston

Copyright © 2010 by University of Massachusetts Press
All rights reserved
Printed in the United States of America

LC 2010014697
ISBN 978-1-55849-827-3 (paper); 826-6 (library cloth)

Designed by Sally Nichols
Set in Minion Pro
Printed and bound by Thomson-Shore, Inc.

Library of Congress Cataloging-in-Publication Data

Silverman, Jonathan, 1965–
Nine choices : Johnny Cash and American culture / Jonathan Silverman.
    p. cm.
Includes bibliographical references and index.
ISBN 978-1-55849-827-3 (pbk. : alk. paper)
— ISBN 978-1-55849-826-6 (library cloth : alk. paper)
1. Cash, Johnny. 2. Country musicians—United States—Biography. I. Title.
ML420.C265S55 2010
782.421642092—dc22
[B]
                    2010014697

British Library Cataloguing in Publication data are available.

CONTENTS

PREFACE

In the spring of 2005, I took a photograph of an East Village store window, where three Johnny Cash T-shirts were prominently displayed. Surrounding them were legions of other T-shirts featuring the bands AC/DC, Sonic Youth, Led Zeppelin, Ratt, Poison, and Metallica, among others, as well as such iconic figures as John Lennon and David Bowie. None of those bands and artists could be counted as "country," a primary signifier of Johnny Cash, so on the surface there seems little to connect them. After all, Cash is hardly rock and roll, even if he is in the Rock and Roll Hall of Fame. Yet there is a connection: the artists are all familiar to onlookers, and each is, to at least some audience, iconic—and cool. By his presence as the single country performer in the window, Cash suggests his transcendence into a category beyond country. Whether that window display was aimed at a particular audience or multiple audiences is an open question, but Cash's presence suggests a wide audience. To drive traffic inside the store, a T-shirt has to have currency with audiences who have an interest in purchasing it. What we do not know is what audience that was. Did the store owner place it there to bring in southern or international tourists? Was he or she from the South? Or had Cash made it to so different a level that such concerns did not matter? We do know the T-shirt is a commodity, but these were tied explicitly to celebrity and achievement. Unlike many forms of recognition, one cannot apply to be immortalized on a T-shirt; one has to earn that fame in ways too complex to seek deliberately.

The second picture is taken from the road in front of Cash's boyhood home in the farming community of Dyess, Arkansas. Cash spent his childhood on a farm that grew cotton; he ended up on a cotton T-shirt far in time, place, and function from those fields. This situational irony of Cash's connection to cotton fields and cotton clothing also suggests a link between different types of commodity—a raw, unshaped one and those that are manufactured and processed. Making a product for public consumption involves taking the raw material, processing it, and converting it to a commercial idea. Such a process describes Cash's career, too; he started as an unknown son of a farmer and became an international icon through his own efforts but also through the efforts of producers, managers, record companies, and journalists. The difference between the man and his T-shirt is that stars like Cash possess agency, whereas shirts do not.

The two photos taken together serve as a number of metaphors, one of which clearly delineates the literal and symbolic distance from rural Arkansas to a New York City T-shirt shop. Another is that although Cash became a big star, his southern and farming upbringing gave him the perceived authenticity that drove so much of his appeal.

The two photos also stand in for the role of the interpreter in helping us understand Cash. Johnny Cash is not on those T-shirts or in the land in front of his childhood home—*images* of Johnny Cash are on the T-shirts, and his history lies abstractly in the land. I took both photos, placed them near one another, and then explained their juxtaposition. Such a process marks Cash's entire career; people have their own ideas about what Cash means, including media members or academics as well as audiences. I wrote about the links I saw between T-shirts and Cash; others might have focused on the artistry of the shirts or the musical umbrella (or window in this case) that seemed to cover all those musicians. Some might think these photos have little to say about Cash; audiences bring their own ideas and interpretation to this or any other text. The man, the images, my interpretation, a reader's reaction—all help constitute the way we now understand Johnny Cash. What this book does is focus on how these components add up to the Johnny Cash we think we know.

My own story with Johnny Cash begins some two decades before the publication of this book, when I moved for graduate school to a mixing pot of musical styles: Austin, Texas. Everyone I knew seemed to love Cash, despite only minimal play on the radio before Rick Rubin relaunched his career. And Cash was a rich text even then, a person who seemed worth understanding. How one approaches texts is a question many of us undertook to address as graduate students in American studies at the University of Texas at Austin. American studies is an interdisciplinary discipline that often focuses on trying put ideas, people, places, movements, and so on in context, depending on the text involved.

Using a contextual approach, I explore Cash and the forces that helped make him a star (and a T-shirt) through the frame of the choices he made. Cash made his decisions in a period that was changing rapidly, and in which new contexts, audiences, and musical styles all appeared. I argue that despite a sound, appearance, and persona that now seems unchanging, Cash negotiated these new developments with a variety of strategies, some seemingly well planned, others less so. That is to say, though he made many career and life-changing decisions, we cannot know precisely his process but only the landscape that produced them. Thus, I have tried to ground my speculation about Cash in available historical sources as well as interviews I have done. By analyzing his songs, autobiographies, interviews, and also works about him such as movies, biographies, and other media constructions, I seek to provide a broad cultural perspective on Cash.

I am also interested in the way Cash actively participated in his own career. As many have observed, public figures are both real people and images, the latter created by a combination of media attention, audience expectations, and personal choice; they perform in public, and any "private" glimpse we get tends also to be performance. So finding out not only who the real Johnny Cash was but also why he made the decisions he did—and who else participated—is a difficult task. This work, then, is speculative, but frankly no more speculative or tentative than other interpretations or recounting—we have to accept that we will know only part of Johnny Cash. Finally, I'm also interested in the way audiences received him. He had many fans, fans who liked not just country but many different types of music. What was it about Cash that seemed to transcend genre? What does it say about genres that Cash was able to work within so many?

Nine Choices is a study done through the lenses of biography, cultural context, and close reading; it lies somewhere between the cultural explication of the cultural critic Greil Marcus and more traditionally academic studies. What I hope—not unlike my subject's aim—is that this book proves readable and engaging for a variety of audiences. In terms of academic study, it relies on reception study, media studies, biography, semiotics, close reading, and literary studies. In other words, it is all American studies, which puts the text at the center of its scholarship and tries to decode it through a workable lens or lenses by going to its toolbox of interpretive tools. In trying to understand Cash, I argue here, we need to put the whole tool set to work.

My work relies not only on my perspective but also on the good graces of many people and institutions. I have to thank the libraries of Virginia Commonwealth University, Pace University, and the University of Massachusetts Lowell for giving me access to both their own and other libraries' holdings. The librarians at the Library of Congress introduced me to a variety of collections (which itself shows the diversity of Cashanalia). The Faculty Resource Network and particularly its administrators, Anne Ward and Magda Amaya, gave me access to the wonderful library at New York University. And local libraries in Richmond, Virginia; Millbrook, New York; Salisbury, Westport, and Fairfield, Connecticut; Brooklyn and Manhattan, New York; and Santa Fe, New Mexico, were also useful. I spent time as well in the libraries at Dartmouth College, the University of New Mexico, St. John's College, the College of Santa Fe, and the University of Texas–Austin. Libraries big and small are, of course, the bedrock of any sort of research and writing. But in addition, I thank the Time Café, the Fall Café (my first morning there in Brooklyn was accompanied by a Cash song), Naidre's, and various other coffee shops that let me refill my cup and keep the MacBook charged.

I have to thank more thoroughly the staff at the Country Music Hall of Fame and Museum, particularly John Rumble, Michael Gray, and Dawn Oberg, all of whom helped me locate additional Johnny Cash material, made arrangements for me to look at it, and on one day even fed me!

I owe a debt of gratitude to all those who let me interview them, including the Fab Four of journalists I interviewed at the beginning of the project: Bill Friskics-Warren, Brian Mansfield, Barry Mazor, and Robert Oermann. I also interviewed Joel Baldwin, Louis Black, Jack Clement (who also bought me lunch), Robert Elfstrom, Rita Forrester, Jeff Goldstone, Susie Hopkins, Bob Johnston, Jonah Lehrer, James Mangold, Chance Martin, Jim Marshall, Guy Maxtone-Graham, Mark

Romanek, John Schorr, Ed Shane, John Sutton, Flo Wolfe, John Wolfe, and Christopher Wren.

I want to thank the people who helped give me institutional support at the University of Massachusetts Lowell and Pace University, including Charles Carroll, Katherine Conlon, Nina Coppens, Carol Dollison, Nira Hermann, Marlowe Miller, Melissa Pennell, Sid Ray, Michael Roberts, Walter Srebnick, and Adelia Williams. I also want to thank the Norwegian teachers and students who listened to me talk about Cash during my stint as a Fulbright Roving Scholar and Tove Lain Knudson, who provided technical and geographical support.

My gratitude goes as well to people who read drafts: Elizabeth Abele, Nancy Berke, Jeannie Chiu, Kristen di Gennaro, Amy Foerster, Linda Grasso, Matt Hedstrom, Jeff Melnick, Trisha Pender, Carol Quirke, Sid Ray, Nancy Reagin, Rachel Rubin, Catherine Zimmer, Krystyna Zamorska, and Karen Zukowski. Even more special thanks go to Greg Barnhisel, Karla Eoff, Catherine Ingrassia, Lauren Osen, Dean Rader, Joel Silverman, and Jason Silverman, who read multiple drafts and/or full drafts. My most special thanks go to Tom Henthorne, who read more of this work than anyone should have had to.

I also want to thank Tony Szczesiul for letting me look at his work on Southern hospitality.

My thanks as well to Jan Grenci and Paul Hogroian of the Library of Congress Prints and Photographs Division for their help locating and processing Joel Baldwin's photographs from *Look* magazine.

I would like to thank Patricia Sterling for copy editing the manuscript so well, and Carol Betsch of the press for in general making the book better in so many ways.

I have to thank most insistently Clark Dougan—who believed in the project before it was a project—and my parents, Beverly and Melvin Silverman, for giving me support in so many ways.

NINE CHOICES

INTRODUCTION

"Hello, I'm Johnny Cash." For twenty five years of his performing life, and even at the height of his fame, Johnny Cash greeted his fans with this phrase.[1] Given his popularity, one might think that his self-referential opening line was superfluous. But given a career that took so many turns and engaged so many audiences, perhaps he did need to reintroduce himself at every step.

Almost everyone knows him as the singer of "Folsom Prison Blues," "I Walk the Line," and "Ring of Fire." Most readers probably know the movie *Walk the Line* (2005), the engaging but problematic portrayal of Cash's early life and career. Yet fans who love him for his classic country may not know that he put out five well-received albums in the last two decades (and another four-CD set of outtakes and alternative versions) under the guidance of producer Rick Rubin, two of which received Grammys. His posthumous albums too, have been immensely successful: in January 2006 the compilation album *The Legend of Johnny Cash* reached the top 20 of the *Billboard* charts, and in the summer of 2006, his *A Hundred Highways,* the fifth installment of Rubin's *American Recordings* series, hit number 1. Fans who helped buoy Cash's success may not know that at the same time as his 1994 comeback album, *American Recordings*, he also released a sixteen-CD reading of the New Testament. His Christian artistic output was extensive: he made a movie about Jesus; wrote a novel about the Apostle Paul's conversion, *Man in White*; appeared regularly with Billy Graham at crusades; and even sold electronic Bibles at Christian trade shows. Neither group of fans may know that he spent seven single nights in jail but served no prison sentence, produced several collections of folk music in the early 1960s, and covered modern artists such as Elvis Costello and Bruce Springsteen long before his experiments with Rubin. For a man everyone seems to know, these divisions of knowledge are striking.

Indeed, Cash's biography reveals a wealth of curious tidbits. He was a highly religious liberal, a southerner whose family depended upon a socialistic government project; an ex-serviceman who received the high-est clearance in decoding Soviet communication (he claimed he was responsible for letting the West know that Joseph Stalin had died); an amateur photographer; a wrecker of hotel rooms; a drug abuser; a man who underwent codependency training with his second wife, June Carter; and a man who was unmarried for only three months in the last forty-odd years of his life. In addition to the above-mentioned work, he wrote two autobiographies and a science-fiction story, and he won a Grammy for his liner notes. At different points in the 1960s, he called himself both a cowboy and an Indian. He received an associate degree in Bible studies. He recorded his own songs in German. He and June Carter worked on revitalizing Asbury Park in New Jersey. He was attacked by an emu. He set fire to a national park. He taught his daugh-ters how to water-ski.

While these facts may demonstrate the trappings of an interesting life, Cash also mattered as a cultural figure in the turbulent period his career straddles. He first emerged in the 1950s at the same time as the national introduction of rock and roll, suffered because of decisions he made and how musical culture changed in the 1970s and 1980s, and reemerged in the 1990s as an icon of what might be the natural combi-nation of rock and roll and country—a subgenre called alt-country or Americana. In negotiating these cultural shifts, Cash often acted in ways that seemed at once bold and idiosyncratic—by leaving Sun Records for Columbia Records, recording live at prisons, hosting a tele-vision program, and choosing Rubin as a producer, for instance—and thus situated himself as a risk-taking performer. These fragments also mark a complex life, the narrative of which in itself only partially explains how Cash became famous, the heights and depths of his career, and why he had such a renaissance in later years. Getting answers to such questions requires something different from a biography, whose aims are directed more to knowing about the subject than to explaining the subject.

Rather, this work explores Cash's personal and artistic choices as a way of understanding his life, his impact on American culture, and its impact on him. Cash made decisions about where he lived, who would produce his albums, whether he would have a television show, and even if and when he would flip his famous "bird"—the image of him grimacing and giving the finger is plastered on posters and T-shirts—in the context of cultural forces both visible and less so. Although he made many of these choices because of his own agenda, he made others in consultation with a variety of people who were often concerned about how audiences would respond. Cash had the power to make choices, but he understood how they existed within a context of external, often uncontrollable forces. He made choices in this context that were unconventional and wise, foolish and shortsighted, but never uninteresting.

Nine Choices posits that Cash's choices (or anyone's, for that matter) are interpretive texts. While biographically oriented works such as Michael Streissguth's fine work, Cash's own autobiographies, and even James Mangold's problematic biopic *Walk the Line*, all effectively recount Cash's life, *Nine Choices* is more concerned with the complex interplay between artist, producer, and audience, an interplay made even more complicated by Cash's iconic status. As Streissguth correctly notes, "Cash's legends are legion, and they are stubborn." He points out too that such legends did not happen accidentally, that "the myriad aspects of Cash's legend were cultivated over the years by Cash himself and by the marketing machine around him."[2] Reading his choices as texts allows us to understand the various forces at work in making Cash the legend he was. As Leigh Edwards notes, "There was no single Cash. He was always multiple, changing, inconsistent." Edwards's fine academic work (which appeared as I was finishing this book) also regards Cash from a more theoretical and cultural perspective, engaging many of the same texts as I do but through different lenses—southern masculinity and the idea of contradiction the most prominent.[3]

What sets Cash's decision-making apart from ours is a matter of degree; his decisions were public and on a larger stage than most of ours, and I argue that they are a useful way of organizing his life and career. Our understanding of other public figures might benefit from such an interpretive frame, including Barack Obama, Hillary Clinton, and especially Bob Dylan, whose decision-making seems as determinant as Cash's. In this work, Cash's decisions serve as windows into both his experience and American culture. For example, I use his choice to go to Memphis in the 1950s to examine not only his desire to become a music star but also the further decisions it inspired, how place functions in the creation of musical genres, and why places matter to performers. Choices here function as windows, as texts, as umbrellas for discussion of issues related to Cash and American culture, and as threads of a life woven from a wide variety of experiences and ideas.

Finally, his choices reflect the idea that Cash was a man in search of an audience. I do not mean that he necessarily "sold out" or pandered to a particular audience, though he understood the factors that might make one thing more popular than another. He often made decisions, musical and otherwise, on the basis of how audiences might receive them, choosing his words carefully, becoming angry when other people got between him and his audiences, and downplaying or emphasizing genre depending on whom he was trying to reach. Of course, most artists think about reception, but most of them work in a particular genre or their production history is limited. That Cash had a variety of musical interests over an almost fifty-year period of production makes his decision-making even more important.

To analyze the man and the icon, I draw upon additional analytical and theoretical tools and lenses. One such lens is authenticity. Cash often deliberately sought to be authentic, and others often labeled him as authentic, but the term is problematic in many ways. Nonetheless, part of his appeal and many of his greatest successes came from perceived authenticities. Another part of his appeal came from the difficulty in categorizing him as a musician or as an individual. Daniel Menaker describes him as "the guy who wrote and recorded dozens of hits that weren't rock and roll, country, rockabilly, or pop but all those things at the same time."[4] Cash also fought against other forms of categorization, especially in politics and religion. At the end of *Winners Got Scars Too*, Christopher Wren's wonderful 1971 biography, Cash expressed frustration with the need to be consistent from one year to another: "I'm always changing. I intend to keep changing. I'm building. I'm expanding. I am still being born. You haven't seen the complete me yet. Don't ever tell anybody how John Cash feels about *anything* unless I've told you in the last five minutes."[5] Part of Cash's appeal came from his storytelling both in his songs and, more important, about his life. From the beginning, he sketched out a narrative, both complex and simple, that involved darkness, redemption, rebellion, and authenticity. Although his career had its ups and down, most of the elements of his story were established early on.

But the story is not only Cash's, and it is often others who are telling it. We know him through various forms of media, whose representatives often had his help but were not under his control. My arguments about storytelling, authenticity, and categorization are also about Cash's relationships with the media, relationships I relied on in putting this book together. His participation in the media (and June Carter's as well) was quite extensive and sophisticated, and he also teamed up with producers who shared his media savvy. Some parts of this work are devoted specifically to these media relationships, but others have this relationship as a subtext. Cash understood that information and music needed to be transmitted not only to his chroniclers but also to his fans, and that his own career was dependent on both his and his audiences' relationships to the media. In other words, one of the primary goals of *Nine Choices* is to trace the reception of Cash by a variety of audiences over time.

As Cash became in part a product of the media-entertainment industries, his audiences, his producers, and journalists added to, simplified, falsified, and exaggerated his story—and so did he. One of my goals is to untangle and explain that story and to show how others have helped write it as well. As Cash's choices often demonstrate, both his and the American obsession with authenticity reveal a paradox: his life as a performer and celebrity almost demanded inauthentic behavior. He had to perform as Johnny Cash whenever he was in public. His appeal nonetheless suggests a success in tapping into common desires that range across many different audiences. His relationship with authenticity was central to the story that his producers, the media, and his audiences all tell, one that resonates deeply in the American psyche.

To the extent that I engage with the notion of who listened to Johnny Cash, this is a book about reception. A combination of critical response, media attention, marketing efforts, anecdotal response, and record sales gives us some idea of who listened to him and, to some extent, why they did. Understanding this, even to a small degree, can help us understand some of his choices. But this audience tracing can be only partial, as Cash's career spanned so long a time and so many places that his audiences were and are probably more diffuse and varied than we can firmly establish. Capturing the nature of a particular audience in a fifty-year career with hundreds of album releases is more a snapshot than a movie. Audiences may have been diverse and various at the beginning of his career, but marketing efforts and the music business were smaller and less diffuse then. Today we have almost a hundred defined genres or subgenres, and a culture much more fragmented in terms of how we receive information.[6] More important, Cash and his recording companies often pushed him toward crossing over between genres but with little effect. And his audiences did not necessarily grow from direct participation by record companies—as my own experience in recognizing the depth of respect for Johnny Cash among younger fans *before* the Rubin reemergence suggests. Accordingly, Cash's genre ambitions and associations do not necessarily equate with or connect to his audiences; producers and record companies' efforts to define genre and audience is at best an imperfect effort. And both audience and media perceptions often ascribe to him qualities he did not necessarily have. So discussions of Cash's audiences is also about Cash's "implied listeners," as Marie-Laure Ryan calls them, the audiences he imagines he's reaching.[7] Cash's choices illuminate the tensions between his ambitions and his audiences' reception and the way forces between the two—producers, record companies, and the media—facilitated or hindered these relationships.

Finally, I also argue that a factor related to authenticity seems to tie many of Cash's audiences together and summarizes a core aspect of his artistic and personal vision: informed simplicity. People often saw the elemental in Cash—his size and stature, his voice, the choice to wear a single color, the simplicity of his most powerful works—and he often strove to provide that image and content. Informed simplicity frequently mimics what we consider to be authentic, but it differs because it focuses on the tangible, achievable, and observable rather than the abstract and arbitrary. Audiences of all stripes seem to appreciate the elemental, whether from a love of nostalgia, nonadornment, innovation, DIY (do-it-yourself), or modernity. In other words, audiences may have seen the simple in Cash but differed in their interpretations of him and his music.

In all of this, I try to keep two goals in mind: explaining the context of Cash's decisions and determining the motivations behind them. In doing so, I hope to offer the reader a nuanced perspective on Johnny Cash.

CHOICE

The idea of choice has become fascinating to us in recent years. We see a focus on choices—and the essential dilemmas associated with them—in such works as Peter Howitt's *Sliding Doors*, in which a single closing door changes the life of a young woman in Great Britain, and Robert Frost's "The Road Not Taken," which famously explores the path "that has made all the difference."[8] Even George W. Bush plans to write about his time in the White House through the decisions he made. There are also books such as Barry Schwartz's *The Paradox of Choice* (2004), James Surowiecki's *The Wisdom of Crowds* (2004), even Malcolm Gladwell's *Blink* (2005), all of which examine decision-making. Recent research compiled and synthesized by Jonah Lehrer in *How We Decide* (2009), suggests that the decision-making process, even after years of study, remains much of a mystery. As Lehrer observed in an interview, people tend to organize their lives through choices and to "magnify the idea of choices. We can't help but look at ourselves through our choices."[9] Still, discovering Cash's thought process is (and has to be) speculative because of how flawed that process of making a decision—and our subsequent understanding of it—can be.

And though Cash may have based his choices on his own judgment, many people made smaller decisions for him and kept counsel on larger ones: varying members of his band, his managers, his producers, record companies, television producers, his family, and his two wives, Vivian Liberto and June Carter. Though Cash's name goes on every album, television appearance, and video, it bears mentioning that many people participate in making such texts.

Though I did try to interview Cash before he died, and those close to him later, to find out why he made the choices he did, the details of decision-making, as Lehrer pointed out, are "lost with time," and subsequent discussion is "just narratives we tell ourselves"; in other words, "people are spectacularly bad at understanding their own motivations." As I discussed with Lehrer, my own long-standing attempts to find a more scientific and theoretical boost to the idea of choice were thwarted by the assumption made by game theory, choice theory, and other theoretical explanations of decision-making—that people are rational. Cash may have made his choices rationally, but it is difficult to say that his decisions were made through a rational and logical process. Indeed, I found books such as Lehrer's and Timothy Wilson's *Strangers to Ourselves* (2004), those that assert the difficulty of understanding personal motivations, to be more convincing than those that were more definitive. Cash himself understood that the past is fuzzy.

That is why this book focuses on choices as interpretive texts rather than as psychological examinations. It relies on the basic semiotic notion that almost everything is an interpretive text. Choices make compelling texts, because they not only encompass the motivations of the individual and those advising him but also occur at a moment in time; they encapsulate a combination of the personal, cultural, and temporal.

Of course, there are also the choices listeners make. Why we choose certain types of music is a mystery still being unraveled. Exposure to music plays a part, socioeconomic affiliations play a part, and so does allegiance to genre. But it is rare for people to base their love of music on emotional and demographic appeals. Though the following statement is true, I would never make it: "I like Johnny Cash because his songs about heartbreak and loss and his voice are compelling, plus I'm essentially the target audience—a forty four-year-old highly educated man who likes to think of himself as musically enlightened." Musical tastes are more mysterious than that, and we make the decision to listen to a song on the radio or to change the station emotionally, not logically. And yet we do choose, and sometimes we choose outside what demographers suggest we should be listening to.

And so why listeners choose Johnny Cash is a question I want to address as the book progresses, even though my interpretations can only be speculative, for the same reasons that Cash would have some difficulty unraveling his—we know ourselves only so well.

AUTHENTICITY

In the movie version of Nick Hornby's novel *High Fidelity* (2000), Rob, the lead character (played by John Cusack), calls *Cash* by Johnny Cash "his favorite book."[10] Given Cash's reputation and that *High Fidelity* is a paean to authenticity, such a revelation is not surprising. Perceived as truly authentic within a world largely defined by superficiality, Cash tried to remain "real" even as he became a superstar. In the movie, the characters try to keep those who are not worthy of listening outside the loop of the record store employees, a small subset of the tastemakers who rule rock criticism. The authenticity to which Rob refers focuses on originality in both music and persona, as well as independence from corporate pressures, all of which Cash seemed to have at various times in his career. Indeed, these perceived critical and personal authenticities are central parts of his enduring appeal. As Jody Rosen, writing critically about Cash's latest work, says, "Cash was an icon of authenticity."[11] But what does that mean? Is authenticity even a workable concept? I argue here that although audiences are seemingly united in their belief that Cash was authentic—when they like him—and that he sought approval from his audiences on those terms, such concepts are at best unstable—despite Cash's perceived stability—in a profession that focuses on performance. In addition, musical tastemakers often use authenticity as a tool to elevate some artists and even genres over others. More important, authenticity as a concept is hard to accept on a basic ontological and logical level. Still, because Cash worked in a world that values authenticity—and he was often a beneficiary of the perception that he was real in his art and life—it is crucial to understand how he, his audiences, and his producers used it in his career. Different audiences had individual notions of what authenticity meant, yet somehow Cash appealed to all of them during different parts of his career.

The idea of authenticity rests on a shifting foundation that reduces its value as a classifying term, especially over time. Richard Peterson explains that authenticity "in a living art form can have a number of meanings, but as we have seen, in popular culture, where experts and authorities do not control the particulars of the word's meaning, the definition centers on being *believable* relative to a more or less explicit model, and at the same time being *original*, that is, not being an imitation of the model." What was authentic at the beginning of Cash's career was not necessarily authentic at its end. As Peterson concludes, "Thus what is taken to be authentic does not remain static but is continually renewed over the years. The changing meaning of authenticity is not random but is renegotiated in a continual political struggle in which the goal of each contending interest is to naturalize a particular construction of authenticity."[12] Interested parties renegotiate what this means over time and often in print. In the early part of Cash's career, authenticity was a buzzword. Folk musicians employed the term; Camus and Sartre referred to it indirectly, and the Port Huron Statement—the founding document of the Students for a Democratic Society (SDS) in the 1960s—referenced it directly.[13] Now, the idea of authenticity is applied to anything from travel to behavior to music. Yet from an ontological standpoint, one's existence is one's reality, and one's reality is one's authenticity. As Marshall Berman writes, "There is something strange about such a concern. It seems to violate the most basic principle of logic, the law of identity, that A is A. After all, isn't everyone himself already? How can he help being himself? Who or what else could he be? To pursue authenticity as an ideal, as something that must be achieved, is to be self-consciously paradoxical."[14] And considering authenticity as a more artistic problem, we have additional difficulties; authenticity, like "cool," its sibling in the art family, retreats as one approaches it. In this paradox, authenticity becomes less tenable as it becomes more visible.

Another paradox comes from the very nature of performance. As Peterson notes, Buck Owens's "Act Naturally" contains within it the prescription for becoming a big star—"All I have to do is act naturally."[15] Performers do so as part of their livelihood. But acting naturally still means acting. Cash's perceived authenticity comes from the idea that one's ideas and personality should match one's art. Simon Frith considers all authenticity in pop music to be fake, because it rests on commercial and performance concerns: "All pop performance rests on a series of frauds: show-biz stars fake sincerity, rock poets fake intimacy, everyone fakes an image and a voice. The gap between the appearance and the reality of a performance is the source of pop lyricists' central tool—irony—and of their central verbal device—banality. It is in this gap that skilled song interpreters work, bringing a personal intensity to all-purpose phrases; and it is here as well that listeners work, applying the words to their own situations."[16] Frith crucially identifies the dilemma all performers face: being "real" in a medium that demands falsity, one that Cash increasingly encountered as the music business became more professionalized.

Cash seemed to know that authenticity was part of his appeal, which might have altered his own behavior. As Derek B. Scott notes:

> "Authenticity" can be seen to be constructed as just one more style. Values of truth and authenticity will be set up in the dress codes and styles of singing of performers (folk singers do not wear pin-stripe suits), perhaps in the instruments they play (for example, acoustic instruments tend to signify such values better than electronic instruments). A performer who can be pinned down to a particular image, such as Bruce Springsteen, will communicate a deeper impression of authenticity than a performer who plays multiple roles, such as David Bowie.[17]

Cash's multiple identities nonetheless were fused into one universal image—"The Man in Black." So even though he may have seemed like Bowie at times, he was much more like Springsteen. It is not just performers who might use authenticity as a marketing strategy. As Edwards notes, "Theorists have long argued that authenticity is a construct of ideas and values reflecting specific socio-historical contexts of production and reception; thus audiences and record companies might deem artists or their music authentic because they seem to convey honesty, truth, and an organic relationship to their roots of fan base."[18] Though Cash sought authenticity in various forms throughout his career, his best success occurred when authenticity seemed "natural" rather than deliberate. When Cash lived up to his reputation as the Man in Black, when there was something seemingly dark and wild about him, he achieved his best record sales.

I reference authenticity here primarily as a perceived quality of being true to artistic and personal principles, and I discuss the way critics and audiences engage Cash's authenticity by introducing two terms, *authentikos* and authenticant, as shorthand for the relationship between renowned artists and their fans, an outline of a limited reception theory.

The first is the Greek antecedent of the modern use of "authenticity," and it means in vague terms, "originator." To be an *authentikos*, one has to be present at the inception of some form of expression or development, and one has to have been praised for his or her success and the very fact of having been an originator. In the modern era, Picasso is an *authentikos*, and so are Gertrude Stein, Langston Hughes, and Stan Brakhage. Musicians in the modern era who fit the *authentikos* label include Elvis Presley, Bo Diddley, Muddy Waters, Carl Perkins, Jerry Lee Lewis, Bob Dylan, Leonard Cohen, Joan Baez, Lou Reed, Patti Smith, all of the Beatles and the Rolling Stones, the Ramones, and so on. This status often comes retrospectively (for example, Nick Drake, the English artist, found success only after his death). Cash's status as an *authentikos* drives at least some of his appeal; his movement through culture was facilitated by his presence at Sun Studio at the time that many perceive as the birth of the genre of rock and roll (a problematic notion, since many similar forms of music existed before Presley). More important, we give the *authentikos* license within culture. Being an *authentikos* means that one has a type of wisdom that comes with creation and endurance. Cash's own appeal, especially later in his career, often depended on this distinction.

His *authentikos* status earned the respect of authenticants (think Rob in *High Fidelity*), meaning those who worship authenticity, often in opposition to a text's popularity in popular culture. Modes of production may seem as important as the product itself to authenticants, who tend to claim they can tell what is "real" as opposed to what is "fake." Authenticants exist in every genre and era: sometimes they hold real power, as Alan Lomax and Harry Smith did in folk and blues; at other times they serve as *de facto* gatekeepers or curators in their roles as critics. My term is pejorative only in the sense that the concept of authenticity can hardly be applied consistently or usefully; I do want to note that authenticants' efforts and their application of taste standards is an essential part of how music arrives to audiences, and the music we love often comes from authenticants' taste and vision.[19] Still, the authenticants' conceptions of authenticity can turn an artist's musical success into a permanent Catch-22, since the more popular one gets, the more difficult it becomes to remain authentic. The irony, of course, is that it is quite hard to be a working artist without attaining some level of popularity. In Cash's case, his *authentikos* status among authenticants was enhanced by the legends and myths attached to his bad behavior, his southern upbringing, his prison performances, his music, and his longevity. Regardless of whether we think authenticity exists, Diane Pecknold notes that audiences are often savvy enough to understand the complicated relationships among themselves, artists, and commercial concerns and to recognize that there is no strict dichotomy between authenticity and commerce.[20]

Authenticity also means different things to different genre followers. Cash's audiences overlapped in some of their reasons for loving him, but each genre that Cash performed in essence demanded a different sort of authenticity. Country fans have built their own version based not only on the personal integrity of the artist but on an artist's origin and relationships with fans. Folk *aficionados* demand a commitment to the people, both personally and professionally. Rock fans often value rebellion. Those without a particular genre preference—the elusive general public—seem attached to a more generalized notion that the performer be real. But they also want a story, and they want that story to be true. As with the concept of authenticity *writ* large, these values change and vary both over time and within audiences—clearly, some parts of audiences, critics especially, value different aspects of a music star's work and character— but these broad strokes go some way in explaining Johnny Cash's appeal. At different times and in different genres, he at least tried to satisfy the authenticity desires of different audiences. For example, all three of his primary genre audiences found something to like in *At Folsom Prison*, his live album that signaled his first comeback, and the story of a man with a troubled past playing a concert in a prison satisfied a general audience. They liked the connection, even if inflated, between Cash and prison, for that too was a satisfaction of authenticity—even if parts of the story they believed were not true.

Cash and the whims of authenticants are all part of a larger history of authenticity and a critical tradition within music criticism and genres. For example, in Cash's folk music of the early 1960s, he mixed rerecorded standards and traditionals with original material, packaged to highlight its authenticity through either its rerecording or the spirit of production (see chapter 2). Before the advent of mass-produced music, as Richard Crawford notes, authenticity had to do with imitation; to perform authentically, one had to stay true to a composer's intent: "Performers who followed the ideal of authenticity believed that compositions were animated at the time of their creation with a certain original spirit and that players and singers were duty-bound to be guided by that spirit."[21] Miles Orvell argues that authenticity became a watchword for art only in the twentieth century: "A major shift occurred within the arts and material culture from the late nineteenth century to the twentieth century, a shift from a culture in which the arts of imitation and illusion were valorized to a culture in which the notion of authenticity became of primary value." Even considering movies and popular music as legitimate art forms represented a radical new concept. As Orvell indicates, the mass production of art was relatively recent, as was the impulse toward democratic consumption of such art: "the twentieth century culture of authenticity . . . sought to elevate the vernacular into the realm of high culture."[22]

Much of the work in the Great Depression, the era in which Cash was born, engaged the notion that real art was produced by the populace, not by highly trained artists; WPA mural painting, folk music, jazz, and country—then often called hillbilly music (including the music of Cash's future in-laws, the Carter Family)—moved toward this more democratic idea of art. The imitative idea of authenticity competed against others in the folk music heyday of the late 1950s and 1960s. Cash himself subscribed to it in trying to bring new versions of traditional songs to a listening public, and the debate over whether folk songs could be new rather than old, was part of an intense discussion over folk music in the 1960s.

Country music, as Edwards notes, "often nostalgically celebrates an 'authentic' folk culture as part of a premodern rural past."[23] Cash's understanding of country music culture grew during the 1960s and 1970s, and as time passed, he hewed closest to its idea of authenticity. He came from the farm, he lived a hard life, and he understood the personal relationship between himself and fans: "In fact," writes Alessandro Portelli, "the ideal country star must be born in a cabin and live in a mansion, like Loretta Lynn; and, as she does, must travel back and forth between them, at least in imagination. Most importantly, they are expected to live in a mansion as they would in a cabin. Stars must look dazzlingly glamorous on the stage, declaring distance; but must open their homes to visiting fans and tourists, stressing familiarity."[24] Cash famously lived that way, showing up regularly at Fan Fair, the yearly country music conference that gets fans and music stars together. He also thought about the South and its place in the world, and his obsession with rural America comes from his southern upbringing. Even after his new music failed to find country audiences, they seemed to count Cash among them—Aaron Fox recounts the notion that bar patrons in Lockhart, Texas, were sure Cash himself would not make the bar pay ASCAP fees for its jukebox if he knew their situation. In short, authenticity in country music depends deeply on origins, loyalty to the genre, and behavior—it does not necessarily have to be good behavior, just within the context of country music star behavior.[25]

Folk was the genre Cash tried hardest to enter; country was the one to which he most belonged; and rock and roll (or mainstream pop) brought him the most breakout rewards—his affiliation with Sun, his essentially rock-and-roll concert at Folsom Prison, and the reemergence through Rick Rubin and MTV all spurred him to superstar status. But of the three genres, achieving authenticity within rock and roll had the least sure path; three concepts with vague values—originality, personal integrity, and rebellion—make up part of this definition. And as Kelefa Sanneh notes, "rockists," which include most critics, tend to celebrate rock over all other genres, and Cash's status in rock was crucial to his mainstream critical success.[26] Cash's producers were well aware of this path to success. Note how both Rick Rubin and Bob Johnston, the two producers who shepherded him to his biggest post-Sun success, characterize him. Rubin says, "He was a country artist but not really a country artist, you know? I saw in him the essence of what rock n' roll is." In an interview after Cash died, Bob Johnston, the producer of the two prison albums, said, "Cash is going to be inscribed as the best dead rock and roller."[27] His ties to rock and roll are crucial for his reputation among authenticants. Where Cash was concerned, Barry Mazor says there is or perhaps was a perception that "rock music is the real music," and Simon Frith agrees: "Rock, in contrast to pop, carries intimations of sincerity, authenticity, art—noncommercial concerns."[28]

The case for Cash's rock authenticity comes from those three factors plus a style of music that seems unique in its formation, though it certainly had precedents. No one in Cash's band was a proficient musician when they first formed, so in retrospect their style had some of the earmarks of early punk music in its DIY quality. Cash's perceived rebellious personality, deriving from bad behavior, started with his Sun songs, aided by the prison concerts, and augmented by Rubin's marketing. Rubin, in fact, seemed to present Cash as a solution to the ever-present problem of rock authenticity, which continues to be a source of debate and controversy among music tastemakers, particularly regarding the question of whether commercial concerns should play any part in artistic production. Michael Coyle and Jon Dolan write that "authenticity is not a quality but a way of affirming quality that now figures in many of the ways in which audiences [and] performers use recordings in identity formation. . . . The discourse of authenticity encourages us to perceive our condition as being in the middle, caught between plain truth to ourselves and alluring sellout."[29] "Plain truth or sellout" remains the discourse of authenticants. It is not selling but *trying* to sell that to authenticants violates the guiding notion of "art for art's sake." And in fact, most arguments that dismiss mass culture, including corporate music or Hollywood movies, are authenticant arguments; they demand a strict definition of what constitutes "good" artistic expression, with criteria that are often external to the product itself. In other words, authenticity marks a particular work as "special" beyond its entertainment value. Indeed, authenticity has as its goal separating one's taste from that of the mainstream. Coyle and Dolan point out that authenticity is an unstable, subjective quality that some use to differentiate their taste from others'.

More important, authenticity arguments often focus on raising one form of production or even just one idea of taste over another. David Sanjek finds that "debates about authenticity really come down to distinctions about repertoire": "It's almost as if each of us were programming a jukebox and endeavoring to prove our personal list superior to another's." He finds this phenomenon to be particularly acute "whenever the mainstream taste of the wider public descends into a pattern that the cognoscenti consider debased": "Dismissing the Top Ten out of hand and replacing it with cultish preferences bears an unappetizing similarity to the educated classes barricading themselves against the barbarians at the gates"[30]—which brings us back to Rob of *High Fidelity*, who undertakes this form of musical snobbery but elevates Cash.

Indeed, audience perception that Cash is authentic was only partially based on music; much of his perceived authenticity resulted from a persona he seemed to consciously project. According to Anthony DeCurtis, "While creating his music, Cash also crafted a larger-than-life persona. His 1971 song 'Man in Black' codified an image that the singer had assumed naturally for more than 15 years at that point. Part rural preacher, part outlaw Robin Hood, part patriot, part populist, he was a blue-collar prophet who, dressed in stark contrast to the glinting rhinestones and shimmering psychedelia of the times, spoke truth to power."[31] This personal authenticity is much harder to pin down, though DeCurtis's description is a start. What is most important about this imprecise, or perhaps diffuse, nature of Cash's authenticity, is that it allowed the audience to participate in its construction.[32]

Clearly, rebellion and authenticity are connected; those who confront authority in any context and assert their independence from conformity often have a claim on authenticity. And separating musical authenticity from personal authenticity is difficult, as they seem predicated on each other. But authenticity as it exists today comes as much from those who perceive it as from a performer. Audiences, with assistance from Cash's managers and producers, participated in constructing his perceived authenticity. Different audiences may find different ideas of authenticity in Cash; all of them recognize a performer whose inner life seems to match his artistic output. But some see, alternatively, "American values," darkness, and genre confusion as authenticizing factors. Other elements contributing to the perception that Cash was real include the "Man in Black" nickname, his early criminal posing in "Folsom Prison Blues" and recorded prison concerts, and his friendship with the über-real Bob Dylan in the 1960s. Even his arrests and drug use serve to remind us of how real Cash was or seemed to be.

We see such multiple levels of authenticity at work in Cash's comeback in the 1990s, when he reclaimed traditional notions of authenticity by incorporating newly traditional forms. He became a singer-songwriter in *American Recordings*; the name of the album highlighting the emphasis on authenticity sounds as much like the name of a collection of

American songs as it does an album by an individual artist. In *Unchained*, performance becomes the crucial element as he is backed by a rock band, Tom Petty and the Heartbreakers. The last album released while he was alive, *The Man Comes Around*, plays with the conflation of Cash as the Man and Cash's own perception of who is really the man—namely, God. The levels of ambiguity are a fitting sendoff for a performer who had always projected indeterminateness. And the marketing of such work suggested Cash's realness, even as it acknowledged his long career.

In the 1990s, Cash's age also began to substitute for authenticity. In one of the last defining moments of his career, the montage video of "Hurt," we see the aging Cash at his old museum, the House of Cash, along with multiple images of him in various stages of life. But we are also confused—does the montage draw a straight line to the man, seemingly upset, who is sitting at the table? Why is he spilling all that wine? Why does June Carter Cash look so sad? Collectively, all this suggests that the real Cash, is sad and on the verge of a regretful death. But Mark Romanek, the director of the video, notes that Cash was cracking jokes during the filming and that his faith made him unafraid of death.[33] So it is just a song, and not even his, but one playing actively with our conceptions of Cash and age, where additional knowledge ultimately undercuts those conceptions. Still, we tend to believe that Cash is authentic. Rob certainly thinks so—and so do the Jonas Brothers. In their *Rolling Stone* interview in 2008, they hope one of their future projects will be a record of Johnny Cash covers, a sure sign that Cash still carries the sign of authenticity: Nick Jonas says the album could be called "*Jonas Brothers Pay Tribute to the Man in Black*." Knowing they are not (and perhaps cannot) be taken seriously as musical artists for a variety of reasons (age, Disney affiliation, home schooling/religiosity), the Jonas Brothers turn to an artist whose bonafides are now beyond reproach in hopes of increasing their own.[34]

"DON'T PUT ME IN A BAG":
THE DETERMINED INDETERMINATE JOHNNY CASH

In a *Penthouse* interview in the 1970s, Johnny Cash listed children, church people, and convicts as members of his audience: "I try to remember that the airwaves belong to everybody—*anybody* can turn on a radio—so I try not to put my music in a bag. The same is true of myself, 'cause I never wanted to be put in a bag either."[35] The metaphor of a bag is instructive; a bag separates and categorizes (if nothing else by separating its contents into the categories of "bagged" and "not bagged"). A bag is useful because it carries something. A musical genre is in essence a musical bag—a place where music of a similar kind is placed. Like bags, genres are useful because they allow listeners to choose music in a general way, rather than having to make individual distinctions between artists. But Cash and some other artists, notably Bob Dylan, Ray Charles, and Willie Nelson, did not like these bags, because while including some audiences, they excluded others. As Cash notes, genres include artists as well as their music. Edwards notes that "musical genres serve as organizing principles—they hail audience segments, imagined communities, subcultural affiliations, marketing categories, radio play, industry labels and awards—and they also signify musical and lyrical forms that artists choose to respond to in some way, even if their response is to reject the conventions." She observes that "Cash is an important model of cultural mixing and ambivalence because he stages the pleasure that audiences take in both transgressing and reasserting categories like musical genres, styles, and traditions."[36] Indeed, Cash's ability to remain both uncategorized and familiar helps account for his continued relevance as a musical artist and his status as a musical—and American—legend.

Edwards identifies Cash's contradictions as a large part of his appeal, using as a jumping-off point Kris Kristofferson's labeling of him as "walking contradiction / partly truth and partly fiction," a description that "fetishizes Cash for being a paradox."[37] I argue, as she does, that contradictions are part of a larger narrative of ambiguity. Identifying himself as a cowboy and an Indian on consecutive folk albums (*Sings the Ballads of the True West* and *Bitter Tears*) suggests a more complex identity. Even the narrator of his earlier album *Ride This Train* takes on multiple identities that Edwards argues (and I agree) enhance his reputation. Still, Cash managed to seem consistent while experimenting with music, behavior, and even identities. So although he often sought authenticity, that was genre based, he also sought authenticity through lack of genre boundaries—contradiction indeed.

And people liked Johnny Cash, thought he was authentic, and perhaps even fetishized him *because* he moved fluidly between country music and other forms. Edwards notes "a large part of what counts as his projected 'authenticity' is the image that he was a walking contraction with respect to the different components of his performance."[38] The way he appealed to readers of the *New York Times* in the 1960s and '70s and listeners to National Public Radio (NPR) more recently suggest that Cash benefited from media efforts to broaden their coverage of performers outside the traditional audience affiliations. And it is no coincidence that each of the producers most responsible for ensuring Cash's legacy was a genre-busting *authentikos*. Sam Phillips, Don Law, Bob Johnston, and Rick Rubin all produced artists in multiple genres or helped define genres. Perhaps they recognized in Cash an appealing universality that allowed freedom to explore a range of musical forms, an approach to which Cash subscribed. As he told DeCurtis in an interview late in life, "From the time I was a kid, I didn't know that you're not supposed to like some kinds of music. I remember loving everything that came over the radio, even the pop songs of the '40s. . . . They played them all on the same program; the music was all mixed up. . . . What is this separation business? Why separate them? But I started selling a few records and they had to have a category to put me in, I guess, so they called me country." Jack Clement confirmed that Cash would sing almost anything in everyday life.[39] Even though his physical home was in Nashville, the issue of where Cash belongs in terms of music genre remains complicated, for very good reason that he is considered an important figure in so many: country, rock, rockabilly, folk, folk-rock, and Americana. Accordingly, he was inducted into both the Country Music Hall of Fame and Rock and the Roll Hall of Fame. We rightly see this as an honor, but it is also a sign of the genre confusion surrounding him.

Still, as evidenced by Cash's interviews over the years, he largely considered himself a country music artist, living near Nashville most of his life, though he seemed to have an uneasy relationship with Nashville because "even in the fifties, people in the country music business in Nashville considered me some kind of unorthodox left fielder mostly because I came down from Memphis, where Elvis and Carl Perkins and Jerry Lee Lewis and I had been putting out all that strange stuff on Sun Records." To him it did not matter; he didn't mind being regarded as out of the mainstream: "I thought a lot about being considered weird—and it was all right with me."[40]

Even in the 1990s, when he finally turned away from Nashville after decades of rejection there, he talked about how his rock career had been dwarfed by his country career:

> You know, you mentioned all these young people in the rock 'n roll connection that I have. If you look at the overall picture you'll see that 99% of my work has been in the country [music genre] with country people. Over the years since I started on network television in 1968, I've done approximately 100 specials. 68 of them were from the stage of the Grand Ole Opry house in Nashville. And at that time I sang with practically every country star in the business, plus everybody else from every other field of music. So this late connection here with the rock 'n roll world is just really, if you look at the overall picture, it's a very small thing.

Yet, in the next breath, Cash insisted that his connection to rock and roll was real: "But for me it's a very big thing because I really feel energized by it."[41] What he meant was that his country music audience was long-standing and consistent but his rock-and-roll audience was not. Because his career was attached to darkness—witness "Folsom Prison Blues"—and experimentation, including the concept and prison albums of the 1960s, Cash's genre confusion never became much of an issue. And with hits such as "I Walk the Line" and "Ring of Fire" and a willingness to tour, record companies did not much care what he was; he sold product.

Still, he never lost the desire to be understood outside the country music genre. In the 1970s, Robert Hilburn wrote that Cash was "pleased" when asked by *Rolling Stone* to be part of its interview series: "I've often read those interviews and wondered if they'd be in interested in someone like me."[42] This showed a man concerned with larger audiences. Indeed, Cash himself was aware of the his genre, tensions, particularly the process of promotion that comes with genre—"demographics! They were always ramming that stuff down my throat."[43] Tom Petty recalls Johnny Cash's antipathy toward the country music establishment, particularly its mainstream radio, after years of being ignored. After playing Soundgarten's "Rusty Cage" at a concert, Cash said, "That ought to piss off every country music fan! Country radio is made for people who hate country."[44]

Country music fans *are* different from people who listen to country music radio, or perhaps the latter are a subset of the former. But a listener to modern country might indeed not like Cash. More likely, as Cash knew, the quotation would be heard by his new college radio listeners, who would set themselves off from a country audience. Still, by most people's traditional definitions—and his chart history at Sun and Columbia before his live recordings at prison concerts—Cash was country.

His indeterminateness went beyond music, as his comment to Wren about his feelings changing every five minutes suggests. Even in talking about history, Cash seemed to understand that there is an essential greyness to it. In his 1997 autobiography, he made a more subtle point about the arbitrary nature of history, as he was writing his own:

> It makes you wonder about the whole idea of "historical fact." I mean, I just finished *Undaunted Courage*, Stephen Ambrose's wonderful account of the Lewis and Clark expedition, and I really enjoyed it. But I was aware of how the other works I've read on that subject, some of them very authoritative and most of them based on Clark's journals, differed not just in detail and interpretation, but in matters of basic chronology and geography: what happened where, when, in what order, to whom. And once you get into the writings of other Lewis and Clark expedition members, events start slipping and sliding even more energetically—but everybody, every journal writer out there on the plains in 1820 or back in Washington or talking out his memories in his parlor, is quite certain of his facts. Which of course is only human. Sitting down with pen and paper (or tape recorder and Microsoft Word), the words "I don't remember" and "I'm not sure one way or the other" don't seem adequate, even if they do reflect reality more accurately than whatever you're about to write.[45]

Here Cash not only recognizes that everyone's perspective, including his own, is subjective and flawed, which on one hand undermines the storytelling of his autobiography, but also confirms his wisdom in bespeaking a complex, existential, and perhaps even postmodern relationship to the world.

The tantalizing mix of knowability and unknowability—and his awareness of his own role in creating it—may account for the many different audiences who found and find commonality in Cash. "Johnny Cash" is a text created both by Cash himself and by his audiences. As such, he was like many other artists and celebrities who construct their identities and also have them constructed. Carrie Brownstein of the band Sleater-Kinney bemoans the fact that the artist loses control of the product once it goes out.[46] Cash seemed to understand this, continually undertaking a dialogue with his fans about his work and life, itself not atypical for country musicians, but he extended it to a greater degree than most. More important, his own cultural production—two autobiographies, thematic albums, a movie and a book about Jesus, open letters and ads directed to the music industry—inviting engagement and interpretation, implied that his work was part of a conversation. Indeed, his desire to remain uncategorized, with the meta-process and self-referentiality this effort often takes, may have been his chief marker of authenticity (if such a thing exists). Cash was who he was, not who cultural forces would have had him be, but that identity was continually shifting. In *Man in Black,* his 1975 autobiography, Cash explained his writing of it as a reaction to the media: "Many times the secular press has reenacted on center stage the low and high points, and the changes which have come about, both in my personal and professional life. Likewise, the religious press has rushed to print things which happened to me and quote comments I have made in interviews, comments I often wished I had taken more time to explain—and even to understand—myself."[47] This passage reveals Cash's awareness of his place in two different forms of media and acknowledges that one's identity as a cultural figure is difficult to control. It's telling that the words that seem to swirl around Cash, particularly words like "authenticity" and even "black," are themselves ambiguous and multidimensional in their meanings. But Cash also presented his public identity as in part his own construction. If he was indeed ultimately unknowable through his public persona, that unknowability was anything but accidental. In Edwards's words, "Cash insists on irreducible complexity."[48]

AUDIENCES

This paradox of knowability and unknowability led directly to one facet of Cash's success—his ability to gather multiple audiences, several of whom were at odds in politics and musical tastes. When he died in 2003, he received tributes from Al Gore, Billy Graham, Snoop Dogg, Bono, and many others; at the 2004 presidential conventions, both parties used to him to celebrate their own ideologies (Cash was probably a Democrat, despite famously expressing his support for Nixon in the 1970s). And as Edwards notes, his posthumous video for "God's Going to Cut You Down" essentially shows a veritable cornucopia of celebrity attached to him.[49] The diversity of Cash's audience—and of those who want to attach themselves to him—concerns genre, authenticity, and indeterminateness. This sets him apart from other artists in that these audiences seem to create their own versions of Cash which seem at once discordant and cohesive.

I argue here that although genre and authenticity, and indeterminacy and contradiction are crucial means of understanding the music contexts that Cash confronted, it is also true that his audiences do not neatly coincide with supposed genre audiences. For one thing, his audiences were as defined by time as they were by sound. Although he played music that sounded similar over a fifty-year career, genres changed and expanded tremendously over that span of time. I'm talking here more about the fans he actually engaged than about the various genres and their audiences to which he tried to appeal. The distinction lies in his reception rather than his intention, the choices he made versus the consequences of his choices, the actual audiences versus the implied ones. Indeed, one might argue that when Cash tried to appeal to an audience, he was less successful then when he let audiences find him. Authenticity sought does not mean audience gained.

And yet Cash seemed to make most of his choices *because* of his audiences. He was an artist who wanted not just any audience but one that understood what he was singing and why. In the end, he felt lucky to have found Rick Rubin, who helped him choose his audiences. Sometimes this search for audience manifested itself in the genre in which he recorded, but often that genre choice was a means to an end: it was not only in decisions that this search manifested itself but in the way Cash fashioned himself. Edwards's idea of contradiction was one way, but so were a larger desire for indeterminateness, his relationship to the media, and his sharp perception of how his music, both recorded and performed, might have been perceived.

Cash's work currently has at least four distinct audiences, some of whom have emerged more recently than others. In marketing materials Columbia Records explicitly names two: classic country and college radio listeners. Classic country fans generally listen to country music recorded before 1980, tend to be conservative in taste, and often view music as an unchanging canon. The college radio listeners—who were crucial in Cash's comeback in the 1990s, as they most quickly responded to Rubin's marketing—generally listen to whatever is cool or "cool."

Of the two other audiences, the well-educated listeners of National Public Radio, who find Johnny Cash appealing for a variety of reasons, are important because they include many cultural decision-makers. They want to stay current not just on hard news but on popular culture. They may also may like classic rock or its related genres but want to broaden their musical horizons—a desire to which NPR programs such as *All Things Considered* regularly caters. A search on Lexis-Nexis shows that Cash's work or Cash-related material was cited on *All Things Considered* fifty times between 1995 and early 2009, compared to thirty times for Willie Nelson. Other comparable figures include Bob Dylan (113), the Rolling Stones (51), Bruce Springsteen (93), and Elvis Presley (73).[50] This audience corresponds closely to the *New York Times* audience of the 1960s, in both demographics and the way Johnny Cash appealed to them.

And fourth, there is the large audience that found Cash again after "Hurt" and *Walk the Line*, a rather ill-defined group that had existed in various forms since he first started recording. This large audience likes not only Johnny Cash's music but also his *story*. A country audience follows the music and the story, the cultural location for Cash; the NPR and college audiences engage the complex elements of Cash's genre and his music; and the larger, more diffuse audience simply connects Cash's iconic and mythic life with the music he sings. And among some Cash fans, this last group is not seen as authentic—witness the *Facebook* group, "I Liked Johnny Cash BEFORE the Movie."[51] The fact that Cash's primary two audiences in the early 2000s were college radio and classic country listeners—the ends of the spectrum in terms of political affiliations—suggests that he had found a way to break though boundaries of genre and audience.

Then there is the matter of class. I do not address class to the extent that Edwards does, but as she, Bill Malone, Richard Peterson, and Aaron Fox among others note, country music itself is inextricably linked with working-class expression. Edwards observes that although "audiences for country music have always been broader than a Southern working class," there is reason to believe that "there remains a large working-class component" to country music audiences.[52] The question to be addressed is whether Cash is indeed country. His classic country, college radio, and NPR audiences clearly differ in class identification, and their class perceptions must also influence their reception. But other factors, such as age and gender in particular, also influence reception. And class is further complicated by Cash's own fluidity as a performer who made it big, and by any tendency among audiences from both working and middle classes to view cross-class relationships romantically. And to what degree is Cash responsible for his ability to cross over in a world where artists and artistic output have become commodities, where notions of authorship are undermined by the music industry, when many hands always have a part in any career? Cash, like other artists, was dependent on cultural forces beyond his control but managed to make many good choices through his own personal will and vision.

INFORMED SIMPLICITY

Though the notions of authenticity, genre, and indeterminacy are in their very nature muddled, a few ideas or methods seem to have aided Cash's success. One is his storytelling; another is a particular kind of simplicity: informed simplicity.

In his work, Cash often focused on a type of elementality or simplicity. Simplicity, which here does *not* connote "simple," represents a focus on a single idea or concept, a lack of adornment, a search for the essence of the subject. Though his late Sun and early Columbia work, his Mercury work, and some of his mid–American Recordings work featured instrumental ornamentation typical of country music, Cash's music is best known for its simplicity, which, Edwards notes, "also contributes to a sense of sincerity, his ability to deliver emotional rawness and 'truth.'" As a late arriver to the pop stage—few make it at the age of twenty-four— and a musician with only tentative musical homes in both genre and geography, Cash recognized the music world in complex terms and yet saw the power of the simple. He focused on the elemental in his folk albums of the early 1960s, the live prison albums, and the Rubin comeback records, which all share a lack of adornment. But this goes beyond music; he expressed his religious faith in simple terms, and his political causes such as prison reform often had a focus on the essence. Mistaking simplicity for the shallow would be wrong; indeed, much of his music is conceptual, and his worldview was complicated and often contradictory. Cash himself was not simple, and there is a tendency to mistake simplicity for the simple. As Edwards says of his music, "the idea of musical simplicity in Cash is misleading, because his rudimentary sound is distinctive."[53] Still, he favored his early music over the later; he practiced his Christianity in its essence; and he wanted the prison concerts to include his band, the prisoners, and little else.

Cash's attitude was consistent with the third of three states of knowing that Matthew Frederick describes: simplicity, complexity, and informed simplicity, which means "an enlightened view of reality. It is founded upon an ability to discern or create clarifying patterns within complex mixtures."[54] Cash applied his flexible, evolving conception of simplicity to many elements of his career over a long period of time, discovering how his chosen form of simplicity is favored by certain audiences both inside *and* outside country music. Country music audiences appreciated his focus on direct expression and Christian values—being a man or woman of few words has its value in country discourse. Critics and urban audiences might appreciate his unadorned aesthetics. And the aesthetically simple, borne out by magazines such as *Real Simple* and retailers like IKEA, which emphasizes the elemental in design, has become popular for young, urban professionals, who likewise often appreciate Cash.

Cash's informed simplicity is tied to the idea of concept as well as personal vision. In the 1960s and '70s he was virtually a conceptual album machine, putting out more than a half-dozen albums, including *Bitter Tears*, *Johnny Cash Sings the Ballads of the True West*, and *Ride This Train*. And one can certainly count the live prison recordings as concept albums too. Even his *Live at Madison Square Garden* has conceptual elements—he tells his New York audience what it means to be from Arkansas (part

of the process of explaining the distance between the first and second
photos in the preface). Working with concepts requires a guiding vision
plus a way of executing that vision through details. Frederick's term,
though it had appeared in different forms in previous scholarship, comes
from architectural practice, which seems appropriate given the way that
Cash builds his albums around a concept. If one thinks of Henry David
Thoreau's *Walden* as the elaboration of a particular idea—to live in the
woods for a year—we can see how the complex grows from the simple.[55]

The idea of informed simplicity also explains one of the reasons
Johnny Cash and other musical performers, especially country artists,
have been misunderstood. Not understanding that simple things often
represent more complex ideas is a fault often made by authenticants and
dedicated audiences when evaluating other genres and their audiences,
not only in music but in art generally. Whether it is abstract art, modernist architecture, or country music, audiences often ridicule a text
when they cannot understand its complexity (or popularity). At the
same time, they do honor and value simplicity (but often misread that
too). Indeed, those who dislike country music often reflexively dismissed
Johnny Cash during his career. Only in last phase, when he was reex-
plained by a producer outside of country to a larger audience, did Cash's
status become more firmly established in American culture. Throughout his career, but especially in the down times of the 1970s and 1980s,
he kept trying to return to Sun Studio, because it had been a beginning,
the music was unadorned, and it was much less complicated than his
later existence. Rick Rubin, with a complex and sometimes controversial career as a producer well under way, recorded him with the understanding that Cash was not simple but that finding the simple in the
complex suited his talents.

THE JOHNNY CASH STORY

Audiences can relate to the stories that Cash told about his life, which
were then replayed, and sometimes changed, by the media and audiences.
The narrative Cash created includes several defining elements: life in the
country, a darkness born of experience, a resistance to categorization,
and a continual effort to remain, or appear to remain, authentic. These

elements appear repeatedly throughout Cash's life, allowing audiences to create their own concrete and recognizable concepts of the man. But a more complete narrative also includes Cash's emphasis on religion, his desire to be taken seriously as an artist, his struggles with addiction, and a savvy engagement with the entertainment and media industries. One note here: as I tell this story, there is necessarily some repetition—some parts need reinterpretation within separate contexts.

The story begins on the farm in Dyess, but its ending is still being written. Cash and his producers reinforced this narrative whenever possible, revising it but keeping it fairly intact for the length of his career. His life on the farm established his country bonafides and working-class background. "Folsom Prison Blues" reinforced Cash's embrace of his own dark side; the famous line "I shot a man in Reno" seemingly leads to "Hurt." "I Walk the Line" was about the literal temptation he faced on the road, but others have seen it as a metaphor for a man who seemed to travel between a number of opposites—drug addiction and sobriety, the South and the North (Arkansas and New York), rock and country, and so on.[56]

Cash had some control over the story, making changes that he thought would benefit him. For example, in his autobiography he discusses how he changed his name from John to Johnny at the behest of Sam Phillips. His purpose was to talk about the corrupting influence of the marketplace: though he wanted to be referred to as John and was originally known as J.R., the story he tells about becoming Johnny signals to authenticants that he was sometimes an unwilling participant in the commercial mode of production; resistance to commodity culture is an important element of being authentic. Yet in letters to his future wife in the early fifties, he regularly referred to himself as Johnny.

His early life shaped a great deal of his career. Cash grew up on a farm in Arkansas—giving him authenticity as a country star—graduated from high school, went to Michigan to work for Fisher Body, came back and enlisted in the air force. While training in San Antonio, he met his first wife, Vivian Liberto, and then soon shipped off to Germany, where he served for three years. When he returned, he chose to move to Memphis, where he worked as a salesman while enrolling in radio school under the GI Bill. He also began jamming with a few bandmates whom he met through his brother. After a short time, he auditioned for Sam

Phillips at Sun Records and, with a little persuading, recorded "Cry, Cry, Cry." He soon became a star, with "I Walk the Line," his breakthrough hit. His Memphis career too became a part of the story; he was linked with Elvis in some manner for the rest of this career. By the time he left Sun Studio and Memphis, he and his producers and his audience had developed a Cash narrative that included an emphasis on darkness, an authenticity based on regional and class concerns, and a geographic tie to another artistic center that would become increasingly important.

Irked by lack of attention, not being allowed to record religious music, or the desire for more money, he left Sun, choosing to sign with the Columbia studio in Nashville, where he recorded both religious and pop country and soon moved into folk music. He tried to become a folk singer, releasing half a dozen albums that could reasonably be called folk, but they did not take among the folk community (though Bob Dylan was a fan). His move to Columbia roughly coincided with a move to California, in part to try his hand at acting. The move to Columbia (detailed in chapter 2) led to some less well-known threads in his story—an emphasis on religion, a turn to politics, and the search for authenticity—as well the love affair with June Carter. After recording a gospel album, Cash's choice to turn to folk music represented an effort to become a serious artist and also began a phase when he became more explicitly political. It was here too that he first began to choose his audiences. The release of *Bitter Tears*, a Native American–themed album, alienated him from some in the country music establishment. This period also revealed the beginnings of his explicitly religious bent, which generally problematized him for all his audiences save for classic country fans. "Ring of Fire" (another nod to originality as authenticity) and his permanent connection to June Carter came out of this period as well and are thus intertwined.

Cash also began taking drugs in this period (a common practice for many touring musicians, who needed to stay awake to drive to the next location). He was arrested in El Paso in 1965 for trying to smuggle amphetamines into the country, one of the seven arrests (though without a conviction) that cemented his bad-boy reputation. Cash used both his musical reputation—as the author of "Folsom Prison Blues"—and his personal reputation as having been arrested seven times as ways of appearing authentic in front of a hardened prison crowd. (His decision to record at

Folsom Prison is detailed in chapter 3.) Cash married Carter in 1968, after infidelity, lack of attention, and drug use helped end his first marriage. This performance was echoed in an unlikely way in his relationship with Carter, with whom he embarked on a very public marriage punctuated by two autobiographies each (see chapter 4).

In chapter 5, my focus turns to a non-choice: his difficulty finding a stable position on the Vietnam War, one that would seem real and satisfy his multiple audiences. I also discuss the relationship between the North and the South, and especially the way a northern institution such as the *New York Times* tried to make sense of the southerner Johnny Cash. The newspaper marked him as a symbol of real America and, in doing so, tried to mark itself as an institution that understood America beyond the East Coast. At the same time, Cash began to realize that his decisions were having an impact on keeping audiences: his previous choices may have failed to garner the audiences he wanted, but they were not losing audiences either.

Cash's recordings at Folsom and then San Quentin—which led to his first number 2 hit, the Shel Silverstein–penned, "A Boy Named Sue"—had landed him on a national television show, where he carried an undeniably potent visual presence. But this presence did not always translate into success in other artistic forms: he was no better than a below-average actor and a sometimes-awkward television host. Yet in front of live audiences, he seemed at home. I argue that his problems as an actor came because he could not fake authenticity—he always seemed aware that he was acting in a way that he did not while performing his music. Chapter 6 goes beyond television in discussing how Cash's career in the visual arts and as a visual presence played off audience perception of his authenticity. As a visual icon, Cash has a distinct place in American culture as a masculine, almost universal star, and his producers from Phillips to Rubin used this visual presence as a way of marketing his music. The chapter also explores the role of audience in constructing meaning from an unstable symbol: Cash's famous "bird" (a flashed middle finger) became a marker of authenticity. At the same time, his audiences used the bird as a potent symbol of *their* authenticity. In other words, they saw ownership of various forms of the bird as a way of showing their rebellion. Indeed, Cash's presence was increasingly self-referential after the

1960s, and his visual chroniclers and employers made use of his image as a way of selling his authenticity.

He lasted a few years as the host of *The Johnny Cash Show*, probably hastening his exit with a national declaration of faith. Becoming more religious in this period led to his producing a movie, *The Gospel Road*, as well as writing a novel about the Apostle Paul, *Man in White*. (Cash's first autobiography, *Man in Black*, was a largely religious and confessionary tale.) Cash lost his hold on his two crossover audiences—the large audience that had found him through the prison albums and the eastern elite that had found him in part through the *New York Times*—for a variety of reasons; his religious views, and playing at the Nixon White House probably served to alienate him from both. Cash's religious devotion was authentic; the question is to what extent he and his audiences collaborated on downplaying an element in his life that did not fit with his public perception of him as a rebel. In the 1970s, his religious devotion along with changing tastes in Nashville seemed to derail a career that had seen a new high.

A fallow period followed for Cash, who probably did not really kick the drugs until he died—he ended up in the Betty Ford Center in 1983. Cash continued to record with Columbia until he was dropped in 1986, and then signed with Polygram/Mercury which also soon dropped him. After struggling through the 1980s and early 1990s, he found a new champion who seemed not only to understand the source of Cash's appeal but also the audiences that might be willing to take a chance an aging star. His big comeback came when Rick Rubin, erstwhile producer of the Beastie Boys, produced at least eleven CDs with him—six single albums and a five-volume set of outtakes. I argue that Rubin used his audiences' previous perceptions of Cash to relaunch Cash's career as a recording artist, basing his appeal on the performer's authenticity. At the same time, Rubin used previous musical notions of authenticity to market him. Cash participated in this process by referring to his genre confusion and to Sun Records (where he became an *authentikos*), and by writing another autobiography, this one emphasizing the postmodernity of his status as rock star in the consonant period. Cash did not make it past the alternative audiences that Rubin arranged until the fourth CD, *The Man Comes Around*, which broke "Hurt," the Nine Inch Nails cover that hit wide airplay, and the accompanying video, by Mark Romanek, which seemed to break even bigger. Cash died not long thereafter, at the age of seventy-one, about four months after June Carter's death. As has been true for many performers, Cash's sales arched even further after his death, mostly because of the biopic *Walk the Line*, which starred Joaquin Phoenix as a brooding, awkward Cash and garnered an Oscar for Reese Witherspoon's portrayal of June Carter.

Cash's career reinforced the story of a working-class man tempted by evil, who was politically involved, and played music ambiguous in genre. This narrative was shaped by his explicit choices, as well as the contexts in which he made them. Although there are other ways of making narratives, the author of a career can make his narrative only through choices, and clearly Cash knew he was making decisions that would have an impact on his career. In other words, he and his producers were authors of the narrative attached to his career, a narrative—like others in a postmodern world—that his audiences, depending on who they are, read differently.

Though authenticants would not approve of Cash's deliberate self-fashioning, he retained their respect, in part because of their limited lenses but also because his art and life seemed unified. Like Bob Dylan, he seemed to be aware that performers live a hyperreal existence and, like Dylan, engaged his status as an actor directly within this context. Cash's search for and embrace of tradition and the universal also resonated with audiences and, combined with this hyperreal touring life, made for an intriguing paradox—a man living an exceedingly modern life who was inexorably linked with the mythical past.

My own interpretation is that when Cash hit it big on the country charts so quickly, he turned to find more fulfillment within and without the music business. Achieving the success he wanted meant negotiating the matrix of continued popularity (and financial success), artistic integrity (authenticity), and personal belief. What made Cash different from many other performers was the consciousness of the turns needed to fulfill this idea and the energy with which he pursued them.

Cash's decisions provide a window into the life of a remarkable performer and the changing culture he navigated. When in 1994 Cash sang, "I've been everywhere," he spoke literally and metaphorically. And the song's revival as a corporate pitch only heightens the layered place that Cash has in American culture (it is only coincidental with this work that the pitch is for Choice Hotels and that Days Inn is playing the Carter Family standard "Keep on the Sunny Side"). Although studying Cash's choices cannot resolve the contradictions I have detailed throughout, it can bring a greater understanding of how performers generally and Cash specifically have navigated the complicated roads of American culture.

1
CASH CHOOSES MEMPHIS

After years of touring, Johnny Cash claimed to know the country so well that he could "wake up anywhere in the United States, glance out the bus window, and pinpoint my position to within five miles. . . . I don't think talent has anything to do with it. I think it's just lots and lots of experience. Like the song says, I've been everywhere, man. Twice."[1] Though one must acknowledge the playful tone in which Cash described this feat, it nonetheless was a claim for authenticity: such ability, gained through experience, gave him legitimacy as a chronicler of American life. Life on the road was only part of his complicated relationships with place. He spent a great deal of time in many places, including Port Richey, Florida; Landsberg, Germany; the Carter compound in southwestern Virginia; and Jamaica. But he lived primarily in four locations—Dyess, Arkansas, where he grew up; Memphis, where he settled after leaving the air force (1954–1958); Southern California, where he went to become a movie star (1958–1967); and the Nashville area (1967–2003), where he lived for more than thirty years. This chapter takes as its beginning Cash's choice to move to Memphis to make a living but also focuses more broadly on the way place functioned both in his music and in musical culture generally.

Cash had a twofold relationship with authenticity and place. His associations with symbol-laden locales like the farm, the country, Memphis, Nashville, and California contributed to his audiences' perception that he was real. At the same time, through his own writing and singing, he tried to create his own authentic world, that of the small town. Both relationships rely on the general idea that some places are more authentic than others. Cash benefited from Memphis's associations with Elvis Presley, Sam Phillips, Sun Records, and the "birth" of rock and roll. His recording and performing history in Nashville gave him credibility with country audiences, as did his formative years on the farm. Even his California associations, fraught as the Golden State is with a reputation for fakeness, led to an enhanced reputation for realness through his recorded concerts at two California state prisons, Folsom and San Quentin. His time on the road led to both his claim that he became geographically savvy and a sense that musicians lived a romantic if itinerant life.

Despite (or perhaps because of) his peripatetic ways, he returned to the small town over and over again in his music, creating a world of sorts, one I call Cashville, after the reconstructed train station he built in Hendersonville, Tennessee, his home near Nashville. This vision was his version of informed simplicity—he saw the small town and farm as a base for complex moral dramas, as witnessed by his covers of "Long Black Veil" (about a narrator who would die rather than reveal his affair with his best friend's wife) and "Dark as a Dungeon" (the musings of a coal miner), not to mention "Ballad of a Teenage Queen" (about an actress who marries "the boy next door" after rejecting Hollywood), and his own compositions such as "Five Feet High and Rising," (his account of the 1937 flood on the family farm), "Drive On," and "Mean Eyed Cat." His compositions and covers display for multiple audiences a version of their ideal America. As Jennifer Senior wrote recently, "In American lore, the small town is the archetypal community, a state of grace from which city dwellers have fallen (thus capitulating to all sorts of political ills like, say, socialism). Even among die-hard New Yorkers, those who could hardly imagine a life anywhere else, you'll find people who secretly harbor nostalgia for the small village they've never known."[2] Cash used this nostalgia as a staging ground for human drama and dilemmas, sometimes with a romantic tinge but often with what Leigh Edwards notes as country music's loss and desire associated with nostalgia, "the metanarratives of a perceived opposition between market pressure and a nostalgic idea of purity."[3] By focusing on small towns and the farm, by linking the past to the present, and by writing about his life as a traveler, Cash painted a picture of a nation where people know each other, an idealized working-class world that takes as its starting point his own—the farm—but also celebrates the many other places he has lived and visited. Benedict Anderson writes about nations as "imagined communities": communities because we think of a country's inhabitants as part of a larger whole; imagined because they cannot be a real community, given their geographic scope. A nation, Anderson argues, is as much idea as reality. In a sense, the way Cash infused the small town with meaning created a type of imagined community writ small, with a sense that these places represent the "real America," a stance theoretically legitimized by Cash's lived knowledge of American geography.[4]

There is also a rough parallel between Cash's career and the reputations of the places with which he was involved: Memphis was a place historically associated with innovation; Nashville represented a more conservative city whose goal was often consolidation. Cash's biggest disputes with Nashville came when he ventured outside its norm, both personally and professionally; his biggest successes there came when he settled down and worked within the system. California's reputation has much to do with performance, in Hollywood in particular, and Cash's two prison performances made him a star. On the road one gathers experience; similarly, one reaps what one sows in small towns and on the farm, and Cash harvested his experience in rural and Interstate America as a bumper crop.

Cash made choices about these places based on living space, subject matter, and professional affiliation. Landscapes generally and towns specifically become what they are because of both geographical characteristics and choices that planners and inhabitants make. And the choices we make or are made for us likely resonate with us for the rest of our lives, as they did with Cash. Whether we live in the North or the South, the suburbs or downtown, in a demographically diverse place or one more homogeneous, places shape not only our everyday lives but probably our own ideas of ourselves, and others' ideas about us as well. In short, places, like musical compositions, are texts, and our complex relationships to them can be examined.

Places served as more than backdrops for Cash's musical travels; his affiliations with multiple locales and the road were also consonant with his genre fluidity or instability. His partial home in country music and his associations with other genres, including folk and rock, mirror his lack of a single permanent residence. I would argue, however, that the multiple place affiliations *mark* this instability rather than *cause* it. In his career, musical boundaries began in flux but became more defined.

The broad range of music Cash played also fits within an American musical tradition that, like place, suggests a broad sameness in structure and difference in perception. Rock, country, rhythm and blues, folk, and soul fit under an umbrella of popular music that contains many of the same elements—three- or four-chord progressions, structured lyrics and choruses, repetition, bridges, and instrumental solos. Yet people feel passionate about the differences. Regionalism and geographical rivalries small and large parallel the passion people display when trying to determine whether music is rock, folk, country, or pop. For example, every small town has a post office, city hall, school, and church. In small-town west Texas, almost every town has an Allsup's (a convenience store); many northeastern towns have prominent steepled churches. We understand that these signal regional difference, as different instruments signal different genres. More important, it often matters to people *what* they listen to just as much as *where* they live.[5]

Many people care about both, and those people often value Cash. Accordingly, his various associations with place can add up to perceived authenticities.[6] Although finding a philosophical or logical basis for saying that one place is more authentic than another is difficult, so is saying that any one place is not authentic. Doreen Massey writes in her discussion of authenticity and place, "There is, in that sense of a timeless truth of an area, built on somehow internally contained character traits, no authenticity of place."[7] Authenticants might disagree: in a hierarchy of places, they consider cities and rural places to be more real than suburbs; the old highway system more real than the interstates; family-owned businesses more real than chains; small clubs more real than arenas; dirty run-down studios more real than sleek high-priced ones; where culture is born more authentic than where culture is refined. Robert Sullivan calls this conception of "the real America" "calculatingly heartwarming," a "kind of antique-shop America" and an "America that appears in magazines alongside recipes; it's the America where presidential candidates are televised." He believes that "the real America is also the America that Americans generally think they are *not* seeing on the roads they use to cross the country"—the interstates.[8] As the quotation that opens this chapter suggests, Cash not only understood such authenticity concerns but also seemed to use them in telling his own story.

All Cash's choices relate to audiences in some way. He chose to go to Memphis for his original desire to be a recording artist; chose the road to find his audiences and then turned around and used it as a sign of authenticity; chose Nashville to consolidate his country audiences; and chose the small town as a subject matter that he knew would resonate with his audiences' nostalgia and ideas of authenticity. Places were more than locations: they were settings for his own desires and those of his audiences.

THE FARM AND AUTHENTICITY: COUNTRY, PART I

Living on the farm indelibly shaped Cash's career. Although he was born in Kingsland, Arkansas, the Cashes moved in 1935 to Dyess Colony, an experimental agricultural community in the northeast corner of Arkansas, started by the federal government during the Great Depression.[9] In this community, families received a house, twenty acres of farmland, and a mule, all of which eventually became theirs. Cash drew from his experience on the farm often quite directly, such as his account of the 1937 Mississippi Flood in "Five Feet High and Rising": "We can make it to the road in a homemade boat / That's the only thing we got left that'll float/It's already over all the wheat and the oats."[10] Cash's farm affiliations also tied into a larger American narrative. The Jeffersonian idea that farmers should form the bedrock of American society has resonated in American culture in a much more general form for centuries: the farmer gets up early, works hard, and has something tangible to show for his troubles. But leaving the farm, or a rural setting generally, was also an essential experience for country musicians, for whom it seems, as Bruce Feiler notes, that psychic dislocation is part of their oeuvre.[11]

Indeed, growing up on the farm, in the country, gave Cash legitimacy in country music circles and beyond. Aaron Fox notes in his study of Lockhart, Texas, a rural community whose identity is buffeted by its proximity to the technological and cultural hotbed of Austin, that country offers up a host of meanings that encompass both the genre and the place: "'Country' simultaneously named the real and imagined place in which they lived *and* their most highly valued genre of artistic expression, a genre that celebrates both intense sociability and intense abject depression, often in a tense and mutually constitutive dialectic." Fox names the complicated nature of country which belies the simplicity of its concept—an informed simplicity that is a concept and a code, with performers and audiences understanding the deeper meanings many country songs allude to. Country music serves as the soundtrack to their existence, and as Fox notes, only a particular type of country, "real country," the country music of Cash, Merle Haggard, George Jones, and Patsy Cline, plays on the radio and, more important, in the honky-tonks, social centers of the community. Fox writes that in Lockhart, "'country' as music is inseparable from 'country' as an identity and a description of social experience, a linkage that is reflexively embedded in a matrix of verbal art, ordinary language, aesthetic, ideological and moral discourse, and distinctive forms of sociality, and that emerges explicitly in the rituals of country music performance."[12]

To be "country," in other words, means not only listening to the genre but in effect living it. After leaving Dyess for Memphis, Cash tried to keep these ties alive, sometimes literally in his home in Bon Aqua, Tennessee (and at the Carter Compound in Virginia), but also in his music. Everett J. Corbin, in his 1980 jeremiad against modern country music, *Storm over Nashville*, defines country music very specifically as being of and from the country: "Country music is music of the people; songs of the soil; the heartbeat of America—is an expression of life as it is lived by the simple people of this great nation." To Corbin, it is a music "of simplicity; a music of the banjo, guitar, and fiddle; a music which speaks of simple things in a simple, understandable, singable way. . . . Country music is the music of country people."[13]

Dyess was and remains country. It lies at the dead end of State Route 14 in Arkansas, cut off from everything but deliberate traffic, in the middle of flat Delta land that to the beholder still looks to be active farmland. Dyess's prime was at its inception; a steady decline after the Depression paralleled the decline of farming nationwide. The town today, decades after Cash left, has not prospered. There is not much in the town itself, a process of decline that was clearly under way long before the present day. In the documentary film *Cash: The Man, His World, His Music*, Robert Elfstrom shows Cash visiting his old town and house, which lay in disrepair even in the late 1960s. Cash pointed out how things had changed—

there was no library, no cannery, no "nice restaurant" as there had been when he lived there.[14] In 2004 and 2007, when I drove through Dyess, not much marked it as a living town save for a water tower, a school, a sign, and a worn-out circle that served as the town center. The land was beautiful, with farmland as far as you could see. The "Hurt" video, includes numerous shots of Cash visiting the farm, holding a cotton stalk (some of those scenes are taken right from Elfstrom's documentary).

Both the documentary and the video show Cash looking at his home with a seeming nostalgia, reflecting an idea about the farm that many Americans share, even those whose experience with farms is more distant. Farms remind us of our country's origin and of the eras when rural populations outnumbered urban ones—a point passed almost at the same time as the invention of radio. Radio shortened the distances between Americans of all groups, but particularly those in rural areas whose previous access to national culture had been limited.[15] Like many other Americans, Cash saw his hometown as a jumping-off point for a life that was destined to be lived elsewhere. The irony attached to his early life was the overwhelming sense that his time in Arkansas was a prelude, and Cash acknowledged that the farm, so often a site of stability in the American ethos, was impermanent: "When we grew up, it was second nature that we wouldn't live in Dyess when we were grown. It was the aim of every person to get a better job. But if I hadn't grown up there, I wouldn't be what I am now. It was the foundation for what I became."[16] When he returned after his stint in the air force, however, staying there was not an option: "There was nothing at home. Our land was exhausted, producing barely half a bale of cotton to the acre."[17] Still, the farm continued to produce—if not crops, then memories and notions about place.

His leaving for Memphis is part of the narrative that made Cash a success, and it's a story with which many of his country audience members identify. As Feiler points out, the story of country music is "country comes to town"—the only place musicians can make a living, and country musicians make their living selling back memories of the country to displaced country residents: "Country music, with its themes of religion, family, and home, became a link to the places these people had left."[18] In this context, Cash was indeed country: coming from a rural area, he often wrote about the themes Feiler discusses. Indeed, when fans and critics place him in the country genre, they cite his voice, his distinctly southern accent, and his courtly manner as identifying characteristics of his genre. Columbia president Clive Davis describes meeting Cash at Country Music Week in 1971: "He finally saw me and came over to shake hands, calling me 'Mr. Davis' as usual. Country artists have a tendency to be courtly and formal. I asked him repeatedly to call me Clive, for there was no lack of warmth between us; but I remained 'Mr. Davis.' So it was Johnny and 'Mr. Davis' again."[19] This conversation reveals a sense of formality that is country in origin, but not just southern—it's important to note that country music is not only regional.

Edwards adds that class is also a marker for both Cash and country music. Historically, country music relied on the self-perception of its listeners as working class (though that has expanded over time), an association that farmers generally share. Nicholas Dawidoff writes that "country music was a way to express frustration at the social exclusion experienced by people they knew, and also a means of solidarity for people who felt marginalized by American society."[20] Cash's appeal goes beyond the working class, but the places he celebrated most distinctly in his music were the working-class-dominated small towns, the environment in which he grew up.

After Dyess, Cash lived in three other locales before making his move to Memphis. Soon after finishing high school, he worked for the Fisher Body plant in Pontiac, Michigan, before deciding to enlist in the U. S. Air Force, where he became a specialist in breaking codes.[21] His next stop, Landsberg, Germany, where he was stationed, seems to have registered lightly, though it is where he wrote "Cry, Cry, Cry" and "Folsom Prison Blues" and cemented his childhood dreams of becoming a musician; he had performed a little growing up in Dyess and had a band in Landsberg.[22] (His experience as a code breaker of Soviet transmissions—for which he says he received the highest security clearance—may have inspired him to write a science fiction story, "Holografik Danser," in which he recounts a man's life in a country ruled by communist authorities.)

In his autobiographies, Cash described his life in the armed forces as both rewarding and difficult. He bristled under the demands of authority but found camaraderie with fellow soldiers. After his first tour of duty, he cited the air force's poor treatment of him—granting him limited leave to see his family—as one of the reasons he did not reenlist. He returned to America, and married Vivian Liberto, a San Antonian he had met while stationed in Texas before going overseas. With his prospects in Arkansas limited, and his desire to continue his musical career in one form or another, he headed to Memphis. But he never forgot Arkansas. Stephen Greenblatt observes that Shakespeare "used his boyhood experiences . . . as an inexhaustible source of metaphor," and so did Cash.[23] But leaving Dyess made a break with his rural past, despite attempts to bridge it later by purchasing Bon Aqua and spending time in Hiltons, Virginia, at the Carter Compound (known as the Carter Family Fold). His relationship with his past became a commodity as well as a performance.

MEMPHIS, ROCK AND ROLL, AND AUTHENTICITY

Dyess gave Cash his country bonafides, but it was Memphis that gave him his long-term, mainstream perception of authenticity among authenticants. Despite what happened with Elvis's career in the 1960s, Cash never lost his reputation as an *authentikos*, and whatever reputation he did lose, Sam Phillips, Sun Studio's legendary proprietor and producer, gained. So Cash's farm background and his Memphis affiliation, provide a good start for understanding Cash's positive relationships between place and authenticity.

Memphis is some forty miles north-northeast, as the radio signal travels, from the Dyess Colony. In the 1950s the city was a capital of the Mississippi Delta region, a role diminished today but still intact. "What the writers have always said about Memphis is true," Cash said. "Musically speaking, it was the capital city of the whole Mississippi Delta, not just a river town in western Tennessee." A veteran with a wife and a baby on the way, Cash needed to leave Arkansas, where it would be difficult to make a living: "I took myself there as soon as I could after parting company with the air force. In a way, I had to. Or at least I had to take myself somewhere. Quite apart from getting on the radio, I needed to be someplace I could find a job to support myself, my new wife, and the family we wanted to have."[24] Cash was part of a larger trend both regionally and nationally, when millions moved from the rural South to cities. According to Pete Daniel, "the fabric of rural life was torn apart as millions of dispossessed farmers spilled out of the countryside and settled in towns and cities across the country."[25]

These newcomers provided energy that went beyond the music. "Memphis has been a place for innovation," writes Robert Gordon. "Among its contributions are such ubiquitous concepts as the supermarket (Piggly Wiggly, 1916), drive-in restaurants (Fortune's, 1906), motel chains (Holiday Inn, 1952), and efficient overnight package delivery (Federal Express, 1972)." Still, as Gordon says, "though no city has had more of a lasting impact on modern culture, Memphis has never been a company town. The forces have all been independent, renegade. . . . [It's] a place where cultures came together to have a wreck: black and white, rural and urban, poor and rich."[26] Because of its reputation as a hustling, open location as well as its placement in the mid-South, Memphis in the 1940s and 1950s became a destination for many arts-minded individuals. Its physical location on the Mississippi contributed to its reputation as a place that encouraged migrants of all sorts. Its power arose from the diversity of the people who sought it out, fulfilling, as described by Lewis Mumford, the classic function of a city: "to convert power into form, energy into culture, dead matter into the living symbols of art, biological reproduction into social creativity."[27] Cash was attracted to this energy: "There was no question it was where I needed to be. Ever since that Sears Roebuck radio came into our house, Memphis had been the center of the world in my head, the one place where people didn't have to spend their lives sweating bare survival out of a few acres of dirt, where you sing on the radio."[28]

In this period, Memphis intensified its reputation as a boomtown and a place where musical worlds collided.[29] Not only Sun served to symbolize this reputation; other record companies such as Stax and especially the growth of radio helped transform music in Memphis and eventually nationwide. Peter Guralnick writes that Memphis radio was "an Aladdin's lamp of musical vistas and styles."[30] Cash characterized Memphis radio, and Dewey Phillips (no relation to Sam) in particular, in much the same way: " I loved Dewey Phillips's radio show on WHBQ, 'Red, Hot, and Blue,' which mixed everything up together—hillbilly, pop, blues, gospel—without regard to what anyone but Dewey had to say about it. Of course, he knew the big secret: that there were a lot of white people listening to 'race music' behind closed doors. Of course, some of them (some of us) were quite open about it, most famously Elvis." Sam Phillips took advantage of Dewey Phillips's genre-busting by producing Elvis, in whom he had found the perfect performer to mix black and white musical styles. Memphis enabled Cash, as it did Presley, to experiment with his own mix of country, blues, and folk (as opposed to Presley's mix of country with rhythm and blues).[31] Cash introduced the world to this mix—spare, voice-dominated, southern-inflected, innovative in its freshness. Like Cash and Presley, artists such as Robert Johnson, Woody Guthrie, Billie Holliday, Ray Charles, Jerry Lee Lewis, Little Richard, Hank Williams, and Bob Dylan all put fingerprints on the legacy of American music but have few successful imitators. Memphis aided musical innovators through its commercial sanction of musical mixing and experimentation.

Elvis and Sam Phillips are a crucial part of Cash's Memphis story and together a big reason why Cash became who he was. Cash's first mention in *The Billboard* (as *Billboard* was originally called) was a small reference to his touring with Elvis in 1955, but there are also metaphorical connections between rock, Elvis, Phillips, and Cash (despite the fact that *The Billboard* labeled Presley as country in 1955, rather than as popular). Memphis bestowed the title of rocker on Cash, and despite steadfastly identifying as country, he never lost the label. Rock was not a choice but a circumstance.

Cash's struggle when he first moved to Memphis did not last long enough to find its way into his musical work. John Schorr, the president of Sun, notes that the garage where Cash met his bandmates, Marshall Grant and Luther Perkins, was located "equidistant" from Sun and the Greyhound station—on one side lay on success and the other a trip back to Arkansas.[32] While working as an appliance salesman, Cash trained, on the GI Bill, to be a disc jockey and persisted in requesting an audition with Sam Phillips at Sun until the producer gave him a chance. His first songs were successes, first "Cry, Cry, Cry," then "Hey Porter," and "Folsom Prison Blues" (which hit the top five on the country charts). In 1956, "I Walk the Line" became a number 1 country song that also hit the pop charts. At that point, Cash was able to move to a bigger house; he lived at some four addresses in Memphis, each move reflecting an increase in stature. Ironically, as he became more popular, he spent less time in these multiple places. A reflection of his growing status and success was that the road became his home.[33]

Cash's decision to leave Sun for Columbia and California was hardly isolated (see the next chapter). Presley and most rockabilly stars also left Memphis which began a steady decline as a musical center in the 1960s. Martin Luther King Jr.'s assassination there effectively closed down Memphis as a culture maker; as Schorr notes, Sun had become a much smaller a factor in music making in the early 1960s, in fact moving its operations to Nashville. Now Memphis exists as a bizarre tribute to authenticity and fakery at the same time, the site of Sun Studio (still open for tours and even some recording) and Elvis Presley's Graceland. For Cash, though, Memphis became a symbol of his first and, in his mind, most authentic success, before stardom and genre confusion, marketing surveys, and Nashville. He and his last producer, Rick Rubin, often evoked Memphis and Sam Phillips as a sort of Camelot of creativity, innovation, and fun, a place where he wanted to return but could not. And according to Schorr, Cash's renewed popularity at Sun Studio came not with Mangold's *Walk the Line* but with the release of *American Recordings*—evidently the strategy of Rubin to tie Cash to Memphis worked.[34]

THE ROAD

As songs like Bob Seger's "Turn the Page" and Willie Nelson's "On the Road Again" demonstrate, the road is an unstable symbol in the hands of musicians, reflecting freedom and delight on the one hand, alienation and unrest on the other, and perhaps a restlessness that many Americans feel. "Turn the Page" speaks of the drudgery of road life, whereas "On the Road" celebrates it. In *Lost Highway*, Peter Guralnick describes the road for traveling musicians as a "journey, arrival, process, definition, virtually replacing in almost every instance the very impetus that set them out on the road in the first place." For whatever reasons performers go on the road—to play the music they love, to make a living, to fulfill unspoken desires, to feel the roar of the crowd—Guralnick argues that the road becomes a defining force in their lives. For some performers, he writes, "the road has become a kind of metaphor for all the psychic dislocations that a career in show business naturally entails." There is another kind of metaphor—one more in line for "seeking success in the conventional sense, for doing business in the everyday meaning of the term."[35] For Cash, travel replaced a normal home life in the 1950s and 1960s. It contributed mightily to his deteriorating marriage and his drug use, yet it also became a place where he did his work and where he became comfortable. And it was the place (or places) that allowed him to see the country in a way that influenced his folk music and ultimately became part of his perceived authenticity. He chose the road because he chose the life of a performer.

The road itself is crucial as a place in American culture. The road took on new meaning in the 1950s in the United States with the rise of the interstate highway system and publication of Jack Kerouac's *On the Road*, which related Sal Paradise and Dean Moriarty's journeying around the country. *On the Road* became a cult classic because of its juxtaposition with the growth of the interstate, a symbol of authenticity in a traveling world that began to be dominated by sameness. As Guralnick suggests, one could say that because Cash lived and visited so many places, place was merely an accident of what in many ways was a typical rock star life. As Wren writes in *Winners Got Scars Too*, Cash's touring embodied many of the same behaviors and principles as those of such later hotel-wrecking stalwarts as The Who and Led Zeppelin—drinking, drug taking, room destroying, and, more philosophically, freedom mixed with obligation. Wren relates a number of hijinks that Cash and his bandmates Marshall Grant and Luther Perkins undertook in hotels: repainting rooms a variety of colors; bringing hay and manure into a hotel hallway and pretending there was a loose horse; taking a stray dog off the street, cleaning it, and putting it in Perkins's bed (at the same time shooting a gun into a bucket of cole slaw so it spattered across the walls); and breaking through adjoining walls of hotel rooms. It also included filling bathtubs with Jell-O, putting sardines and Limburger cheese in the indirect lighting in elevators, and pouring water and breaking raw eggs on guests entering the hotel.[36] In a sense, this behavior became as routine as taking out the garbage. Each hotel presented a familiar scene, ready to be exploited. Those who travel frequently may not destroy hotel rooms but are nonetheless well aware of the tendency to establish routines that make unfamiliar places more like home.

Some of Cash's songs exemplified the tensions of the road, as Mangold makes explicit in *Walk the Line* (and as admitted). Early in his career he covered a standard "Frankie and Johnny," shifting the name to "Frankie's Man, Johnny." The song details a country singer's aborted attempts at straying with his wife's sister, vowing "I'm your man, I wouldn't do you wrong."[37] (Note here his shifting into the self-naming even in 1958.) "I Walk the Line" bespeaks the necessary watchfulness that the narrator must undertake to stay out of trouble on the road, trouble Cash apparently did not avoid. When he sang, "I keep a close eye on this heart of mine / Because you're mine, I walk the line," he was making a statement about temptation and fidelity—those who are not tempted do not need to keep a close watch on their hearts. The deliberate watchfulness as well as the metaphor of walking a line, an image that speaks not comfort but peril, deepens our understanding of Cash's potential pitfalls. Even in "Wide Open Road," in which the narrator tells his wife, to his later regret, that she can travel the "wide open road" if she does not want to be with him. In "Mean Eyed Cat" another wayward lover uses the train to escape.

Edwards observes that although "Cash's protagonists are devoted to home and family, they are also drawn to the rambling life."[38] She also identifies a larger tension in travel generally. Because the places are often common in type and style, the patterns of the road lend themselves to a sense of dislocation and, accordingly, mythologizing. Anyone who travels a lot knows the familiarity of the hotels and the people who work and stay there, yet the feeling that something unexpected will happen, either bad or good, lingers or looms. Travel for some feels transcendent because of this controlled adventure and the sense that one can exist anonymously inside it, an idea on which *On the Road* relies. The well-worn phrase "the comforts of home" describes accurately why being home feels good—it provides familiarity, insularity against the uncertainty of the world beyond it. As John Jakle, Keith Sculle, and Jefferson Rogers note, "*Home* symbolizes security; *road*, the underlying uncertainty of travel."[39] For most of us, the two ideas of the uncertain road and comfortable home form only a minor amount of tension, as we know where our identities and loyalties lie; we live at home and often use travel as an escape. For musicians, the relationships between home and the road are much more ambiguous.

For many musicians the road itself comes to serve as a home of sorts, as seen in Adam Gopnik's description of Willie Nelson's relationship to his tour bus:

> It takes only a few minutes for an outsider to grasp that waiting on the bus is not just what they do; waiting on the bus is who they are. Though Willie is officially staying at the Carlyle Hotel, which he has favored for thirty years, he seemed uneasy there—earlier that day, leaving the hotel, he had sought out and gravely shaken hands with the room-service waiters, the doormen, the bellboy, and two elevator men before he felt he could decently depart—and was eager to get a limo back to the bus. That the bus has this kind of hold on Willie and his family has led people who are not often on the bus to believe that this is because of what goes on on the bus, but once you are on the bus you come to understand that the hold of the bus lies in what does not go on there.[40]

Curtis Ellison explains that touring was an essential part of country music—there were even buses constructed so musicians could wear their cowboy hats.[41] Then there was "Tour One," Cash's tour bus, of which he wrote fondly: "I have a home that takes me anywhere I need to go, that cradles and comforts me, that lets me nod off in the mountains and wake up on the plains: my bus, of course."[42] The bus is a sanctuary, a closed environment that helps take the road out of the road. Both the Clinton-Gore campaign bus and John McCain's "Straight Talk Express" were rhetorically and symbolically successful because they were on the ground, traveling in the same sort of vehicle that those without means use. They were also romantically tied to the road's power and history.

Now, of course, buses travel on the interstate and make touring different from what it was when Cash first started. The American highway system, with its long stretches between towns, has rewritten much of what we experience in American life, replacing with interstates and chain hotels the system Cash was a part of in the 1950s. Still, some roads remain symbolically significant. As Feiler recounts, 1-40 has become a crucial road in country music: it links Memphis and Nashville with the middle of the country and some of country music's largest stars: "Even in the age of airplanes, most of those artists drove an old family vehicle, a borrowed truck, or a dented van into Nashville not along a dusty dirt road, as they might have us believe, but along the six-lane comfort of Interstate 40, which, when approaching Nashville from the east, passes within honking distance of the Grand Ole Opry."[43]

Despite authenticants' adoration of Cash and the ties of the current metaphor to the old "Blue Highways," as William Least Heat-Moon calls them (Cash's last label was "Lost Highway"), Cash himself embraced the interstate. He had to, given his constant travel. The difference between "I've Been Everywhere," recorded in the 1990s, and the earlier "Ride This Train," a more focused sociohistorical travelogue, is that the sort of aimless place accumulation of the former seems to focus on travel for travel's sake, whereas the latter has more to do with teaching his audience. The narrator in "Everywhere" simply lists places he has been as a way of trumping his companion's offhand remark, "Have you ever seen a road with so much dust and sand?"

Perhaps Cash had already come to the conclusion that the road had become merely a commercial space. In a 1972 commercial for Amoco, the opening shot features a car on a highway in, presumably, the Southwest as Cash intones, "There are millions of miles of roads in this great country and you can drive down every one of them and never find a gasoline like Amoco super premium." Even posthumously, he pitches for Choice Hotels using "I've Been Everywhere." One scene in *Cash* relates how he and June Carter described various towns: "June and I rate places that way—'This is a Wal-Mart town, I bet. It's easily big enough,' or 'Hang on, honey. Don't stop here. Tomorrow's a two-Wal-Marter.'"[44] This was far different from pouring Jell-O or ice water on hotel guests. Choosing Choice Hotels and Amoco gasoline to pitch was just a more overt way of acknowledging that while being on the road was romantic, it was always about business.

CALIFORNIA

Cash went west between two Tennessee addresses, moving to California to take advantage of a favorable touring schedule there and with the hope of becoming a movie star. Later, he did much of the American Recordings work with Rick Rubin in the Los Angeles area. Though Southern

California is too large and diverse to categorize as a single region, its stereotypes focus on the unreality of the weather and the culture that surrounds the movie industry (which relocated there because of the weather). People often believe California is fake. For Cash, the move meant trying to become an even larger star, more like Elvis, who parlayed his music career into a film one (though as it turns out, another icon, Bob Dylan, became Cash's role model). That goal could be counted at best a mixed success; although he made films and appeared on television, he never reached Presley's status as an actor. His two recorded prison concerts did bring him the kind of success he wanted—national exposure with the added benefit of doing something that made him seem authentic—but he never became an acting star, though he did appear in minor feature films such as *Door-to-Door Maniac* (1961) before becoming a regular in television movies (see chapter 6).

Despite his established stardom, Cash's West Coast experience had distinct working-class ties. As John Steinbeck's *Grapes of Wrath* so dramatically shows, California lured a number of migrants from Cash's neck of the woods, and like many of those migrants, he found California less than utopian. After moving there California in 1958, he lived in three places: an apartment in North Hollywood, Johnny Carson's old home in Encino, and Casitas Springs in Ventura County, where he felt more comfortable; Wren says the area at the time had "an oil field and agriculture economy" that attracted "a great number of blue-collar Midwesterners and Southerners since Dust Bowl Days."[45] Yet although moving to California had been intended to allow Cash a more stable home life, he stumbled instead into the apocalyptic world that Joan Didion described in the 1960s. In "Some Dreamers of the Golden Dream," she calls the San Bernardino Valley, not far from Cash's residence and not long after he left, "ominous country": "Here is the last stop for all those who come from somewhere else, for all those who drifted away from the cold and the past and the old ways. Here is where they are trying to find a new life style, in the only places they know to look: the movies and the newspaper."[46] One could say that Cash's ambitions resembled these, as the Golden State took him far away from the farm and Memphis, which was still home to family and close by his childhood home. In California, his addiction to methamphetamines ramped up, leading to numerous near-death and destructive experiences.

In his biographies, Cash himself relayed many incidents involving death-defying luck. He talked about fighting with his wife and being "so stoned every time I'd leave home to go to the desert or the mountains that I'd wreck whatever I was driving. I totaled a lot of vehicles, and I guess I must've broken twenty bones in my body—my toes, my jawbone, my nose, my fingers, my elbow, my foot, my kneecap. I don't know why I didn't kill myself then."[47]

Although Cash's situation differed from that of the people Didion was characterizing, her descriptions of hippies, divorcees, murder suspects, and celebrities carry a sense of forthcoming destruction. Both Didion and Cash recognize the divide between Hollywood and the Oklahomans and other mid-South migrants who packed his Town Hall appearances in 1959 near Compton, where the oil industry was based. California has a reputation as a dreammaker, but it's this image that allows its flip side, the *noir* that's inevitably set there. Cash's true artistic constituency comprised not his Hollywood neighbors but the sons and daughters of the Oklahomans who had ventured west during the Dust Bowl era and some of whom became inmates at the sites of Cash's greatest California triumphs—the San Quentin and Folsom prison concerts. Like the experience of these inmates, Cash's time in California had not gone well, as he acknowledged at San Quentin: "June said she knew there would be some people from the South here tonight. Because some of you guys get out here in California, the damn place is so crazy you just gotta get something to eat some way."[48] His reference to class here brought him full circle from "Folsom Prison Blues" and the "rich folks smokin' big cigars." The inmate who had shot a man in nearby Reno just to watch him die had undoubtedly become unmoored from a more stable life somewhere else.

Given the growth of television and Elvis Presley's successful transition to movies, one can hardly fault the logic behind Cash's move to California. With Memphis losing its importance as a music center, and, as we will see, Nashville becoming less receptive to his music, California seemed a sensible choice. Indeed, it was his triumphant California concerts that made him for a time the number 1 recording artist in the country and gave him a reputation for authenticity that his folk music experiments had not. But departure from California was just as smart. For example, when ABC offered him a TV show, it was based in Nashville, not Los Angeles. Though the darkness of California prisons was at least partially responsible for his success, Cash preferred and ultimately chose Nashville, even though Nashville did not always prefer—or choose—him.

NASHVILLE: COUNTRY, PART II

Defined by his record-buying public, his producers, and even his residence, Cash called Nashville (both as place and as metonym for the country music industry) home. But such a relationship was fraught with discord: "I have never been, and never will be, part of the record-making machine of Nashville. I love the people here and this is my home—I hope for life, here in Hendersonville, Tenn. But I refused to conform before, and I refuse now, because I think it greatly hampers and restricts artistic expression to have to be tied to that machine. How can you expand your horizons if you're going to be restricted to riding that same train on that same straight track all that time?"[49] Cash did not always consider himself country, and Nashville did not always like his musical—and political—choices.

As a commercial enterprise, Nashville eventually moved on to younger performers who were considered more marketable, a process that was (and is) a point of contention among country music fans. Such a division ultimately meant that Nashville cut Cash loose but made him popular among classic country fans, who hew to a more traditional definition of country, adding new stars to their pantheon slowly and reluctantly. At the core of Cash's relationship with Nashville was authenticity—in terms of what he wanted to play and what was considered country music. Nashville itself values authenticity, but what that means is unstable. It often means tradition in musical styles, but the real business of Nashville is making and marketing country music. What country music people listen to at any moment in time in some ways constitutes real country, just as one could argue that the interstate is where people really travel. Nashville's values overlap: in popular institutions like the Country Music Hall of Fame and the Grand Ole Opry, they value tradition and history, but in more commercial enterprises, they value the new. (Of course, commercial enterprises often underwrite the traditional ones.) Musical artists can easily get lost in such a configuration, and even at the height of Cash's popularity there was little to suggest that it was permanent.

Country music fans expect what Nashville produces to be country music. As Richard Peterson notes, country music as a genre demands authenticity—the focus on the real is paramount both in the statements of its practitioners and in the very ethos of the establishment: the Country Music Hall of Fame and Museum itself. Still, there is disagreement among country music fans about what constitutes real country. Everett Corbin's jeremiad against modern country and the bifurcating of country music subgenres—hot country, classic country, and alt-country among them— suggest that despite mainstream country radio's dominance, Nashville is not the only judge of what real country music is. Indeed, as Aaron Fox notes, what the longest-listening fans consider to be country—duration of time being a prime determining factor of authenticity—is not always played on the radio.

For much of his career, Cash had a stable though sometimes strained relationship with Nashville's recording industry. Cash's story and his subject matter fit easily into Nashville's own narratives—he was the son of a farmer who sang about small towns. The industry also accepted, though less easily, his rebellious streak (read: drug use); many others, including George "No Show" Jones and the authentic beacon of country music, Hank Williams, lived similar stories. Cash's religious redemption and remarriage also fit neatly within the mores of the country music world.

But Cash eventually became disgusted with Nashville, which tolerated his musical idiosyncrasies only as long as he sold records. In other words, his efforts to maintain what he considered to be an artistic authenticity met up with an industry that like all industries was concerned with catering to its audience's desires. Still, Cash continued to think of Nashville as a validating force, long after his music was being played on country hit radio. Without another obvious audience, Cash was stuck with Nashville's listeners.

Cash and Nashville grew up at the same time—Nashville's first recording studio was built less than ten years before Cash started recording, and hillbilly, country, and country and western were still evolving genres when he began. Nashville had become a prominent music-making center only in the 1940s and 1950s.[50] Bill Malone cites the growth of the recording studios, evolving from WSM, the host of the Grand Ole Opry, into Castle Studios and then studios for individual record companies later in the 1950s.[51] As the 1950s ended and the 1960s progressed more and more record companies established studios in Nashville; by the time Cash returned from California, it had become the entrenched establishment of country music, home not only to record companies but other arbiters, including the Country Music Association. By the time Cash died, Nashville had more than 180 recording studios, and the economic impact of country music exceeded $6 billion a year.[52]

Nashville thus permanently established itself as the creative center of the country music world, fueled by the bedrock establishment of the industry's back offices and recording studios and the legacy of the Grand Ole Opry, whose radio presence allowed it to thrive as a musical tastemaker in a way that few if any other institutions could match. The Opry's combination of radio and physical presence became a symbol of country music in both space and place (though it now seems like an appendage to the Opry Mills mall on Nashville's outskirts). Almost as old as radio itself, the Opry began as a show in November 1925. Challenged and surpassed at first by country music programs in Fort Worth and Chicago, it cemented its dominant position as country music's main broadcast venue first with a willingness to play up "its hillbilly characteristics." Although the Grand Ole Opry often serves as a symbol of Nashville, the associations are much more complicated. Daley points out that "Nashville has been for nearly fifty years a magnet that attracts those who would be part of country music."[53] But Nashville's own self-image, built over more than two centuries, obviously predates country music and interferes with such simple associations. As Peter Taylor notes in his much of his work, Nashville has a conservative image that stands in contrast to Memphis. Taylor's narrator in *A Summons to Memphis* recounts Nashville's changes over the years: "Nowadays it seems strange to have once lived in a Nashville where phrases like 'well bred' and 'well born' were always ringing in one's ears and where distinctions between 'genteel people' and 'plain people' were made and where there was rather constant talk about who was a gentleman and who wasn't a gentleman."[54]

Until the 1970s, Nashville did not celebrate its legacy as a site of musical importance. When doing research for this book, I tried to find consistent coverage of country music generally and Johnny Cash specifically in Nashville's daily paper, *The Tennessean*, both on microfilm and in the archives at the Country Music Hall of Fame, but little appears before 1975. (Interestingly, the *New York Times* coverage of Cash alone surpassed the coverage of country music generally—see chapter 7.) Robert Oermann told me that a lack of information was symbolic of the whole attitude of Nashville toward country music in that period, that of polite disdain; he became *The Tennessean's* first reporter to cover country music full time in 1976.[55]

The relationship between Nashville and Cash was complicated by the way he used the city as a backdrop and sometimes a straw man for the establishment of a series of overlapping and sometimes contradictory authenticizing maneuvers. (All but a few of his recording sessions took place there in the 1960s despite his living in California.) As a way of showing his rebellion, he once kicked out the lights at the Opry—the preeminent symbol of Nashville and country music—and got himself booted from the regular lineup. At the height of his folk career, a country music magazine demanded that Cash resign from the Country Music Association because his "crowd are just too intelligent to associate with plain country folks, country artists and country DJs."[56]

In the mid-1960s his drug use and self-destruction reached a peak. (At one point, he shared a Nashville apartment with Waylon Jennings, who shared Cash's drug habits). Still, his move to Nashville preceded several positive turns: his initial giving-up of drugs, his marriage to June Carter, and the release of his most successful album, *At Folsom Prison* (though certainly one could note that his success came at Folsom, not in Nashville). He bought a house in Hendersonville, a community just outside of Nashville proper, and then a farm in Bon Aqua. Bob Dylan recorded in Nashville, suggesting that it was more real than Dylan's previous recording homes in New York. For a brief moment, even in the middle of the Vietnam War, Cash made Nashville seem more real than Los Angeles and perhaps even New York. He hosted his television show from Ryman Auditorium, home of the Grand Ole Opry. Dylan's appearance on the show coincided with his recording sessions in Nashville, which arguably changed the way the world thought of Nashville—and perhaps what Nashville thought of itself. This television show made Nashville more accessible to the country's psyche and allowed it to participate more willingly in the production of its greatest cultural asset—country music. Cash became an ambassador for country music, hosting the Country Music Association awards for many years (ironic, given his previous status). In all these cases, Nashville made rebellion *easier* through its own conservative ethos. Without that, Cash's gestures would not have had the same impact.

Cash also helped bridge the gap between Nashville society and country music. As Bruce Feiler notes, "From its inception, this struggle for Nashville has always, to one degree or another, come down to class." Nashville scions wanted nothing to do with the rural immigrants trying to make it big in their town. Ironically, as Feiler notes, Cash himself was a crucial link between the upper class of Belle Meade, an upscale area of Nashville, and the working class country audience. In 1971, "under twinkling white lights and flowing canapés, Johnny Cash, the man in black, a relentless yokel from Kingsland, Arkansas, made his first-ever trip to Belle Meade. . . . As comical as it must have been, the Belle Meade debut of Johnny Cash, deep-voiced, darkly sexual, and by his own account high on drugs for most of that decade, was only the most symbolic of gestures that were begrudgingly uniting Nashville."[57]

To Johnny Cash, Nashville was the system, and depending on what he was doing, he was in or out of it, as he had been with Hollywood's definitive rules and tastes. He had little patience with rules that interfered with his artistic intentions, rules that dictated both sound and content. Nashville served as the source both of Cash's redemption—as Nashville reembraced him after his prison concert success—and, eventually, of his distress. As Brian Mansfield says, "He was never an establishment guy—whatever the prevailing winds were, Johnny was never there." And the writer Robert Oermann noted in an interview that Cash did fine in Nashville the place but did not do so well in Nashville the metonym.[58] When he left his television show, Nashville and its establishment eventually dropped him, taking up musicians who were younger and more marketable to a younger demographic.

Anyone who reads Cash's unflinching description of how record companies treated him in the 1970s and 1980s can't help but think how close he came to being a novelty act in the 1990s. He said that in the early 1980s his record company, CBS, had essentially identified him as a "long shot": "They, and all the other major record companies in Nashville, were betting on the younger generation and starting to play by the rules of 'youth appeal.' If you were a little too old and your anatomy not quite 'hot,' it didn't matter how good your songs or your records were or how many fans you'd had for how long: you weren't going to get played on the radio."[59] By the time Cash moved there, his music did not fit into the emerging Nashville sound, and ultimately he gave Nashville the finger— openly so, when *Billboard* printed his ad sarcastically thanking "Nashville and country radio for its support."[60] It was a simple gesture, and the music establishment, bent on profits as any industry is, made an easy and convenient target. But he never moved away, and he is buried in a Hendersonville cemetery

Nashville today remains concerned with authenticity. The epigrams outside the Country Music Hall of Fame suggest that being real is important, and the stores that sell cowboy wear and "authentic" southern artifacts on Broadway, the main tourist area downtown, show that Nashville merchants traffic in many southern symbols. The many shades of brown inside the museum is to signify the land from which country music is supposed to spring. And despite his tumultuous relationship with the city, Cash is still beloved. There is more Cashanalia here than in Memphis, supposedly his musical home. He was both a resident and, more important, a commercial draw. After all, what is most real for many in the Nashville country establishment is the bottom line. Today, the storied Grand Ole Opry is no longer in Ryman Auditorium but in an appendage to the large Opry Mills mall, itself marked with wooden paths that lead to national and regional chain establishments.

SMALL TOWNS: CASHVILLE

In 1980 a note appeared in *Our Kinda Cash*, the organ of the Johnny Cash and June Carter Cash International Fan Club, announcing that "the train station at the House of Cash is now open to the public, at no charge to go thru it. It is furnished with authentic furnishings of the oldtime stations."[61] The item featured a small photo of a sign reading "Cashville."

It is no surprise that the House of Cash (which was also the name of his song-publishing company) hosted a train station or that it was called Cashville—or that the release labeled the furnishing "authentic." Trains run throughout Cash's songs, and Cashville seems the ideal title for the mythical small towns that these trains run through. And although the reference to "furnishings" suggests one definition of authenticity, there are others related to small towns. For one, small towns for many people—especially country music artists—are at the top of a hierarchy of "real." Even those who have moved away consider small towns authentic launching places.

Some of this attitude is rooted in nostalgia. Small towns populate our imagined American past, and as Simon Frith observes, country music depends on looking back: "Contemporary country records symbolize the past, exude nostalgia, describe a way of life that city dwellers value more now that they don't have to live that way again. . . . Country music reacted to social change by reemphasizing rural values and patterns; it entered the mainstream of American mass music as a *sub*-urban means of expression."[62] In the era when Cash came into prominence, people were already reminiscing about America's agricultural past. A volume produced by the *Farm Quarterly* in the early 1960s and simply titled *The Good Old Days* is devoted to a rapturous recounting of farming days. The introduction says of "the old-time farmer" who "gloried in the battle with nature" that: "when he won, the victory was sweet; when he lost he kept his dignity, for he had lost to a respected foe." This special issue was in response to the "moments when the realities are too stern, the business of life too demanding, the daily battle for survival too frustrating. In these moments he looks beyond the horizons, or goes back in memory to a better day when man seemed more free, when the pursuit of food and shelter was uncomplicated and direct, and all had peace and security."[63]

Cash embodied these battles between a simpler time and technological advances. For many cosmopolitan city dwellers, the past and the country seem like a release rather than a lifestyle in themselves, and Cash and his audiences were not immune to nostalgia. Edwards suggests that they may have used "mass media forms to contemplate the loss that commodity culture is furthering (in this case, the loss of an agrarian past and way of life), yet also generating complex collective expression and recreated senses of identity through mass music listening and making."[64] Though he did not specifically yearn for the past, he loved trains and the Old West, which feature prominently in the kitsch sold up and down Broadway in Nashville's tourist district, and even his newer songs sounded old—partly because of their references to trains, the West, and God. But some of it has to do with Cash's Old Testament voice, which itself seems to resonate from the past. (He is not the only one—Gordon Lightfoot, Nick Cave, and Loretta Lynn, just to name a few, seem to have voices that emerge from the past.) If we entered a world based on Johnny Cash's voice, Cashville, we would find a small town surrounded by fields as far as the eye could see. There would be a sheriff, a preacher, and a train that stopped right on the edge of town.

Cash is often perceived in much the way small towns are, as signs of a different time: finite, contained, and ordered at least in their structure. Small towns are authentic because people there know each other for better or worse; there is a community. But they were authentic to Cash because he grew up there; they represented *his* past, a past that yet became more imagined as he aged. And because they existed before he became a celebrity, they were tied to a time much less complicated. His experience with small towns led to a larger relationship between small towns and country music. They have to exist in relationship to cities and towns as the place one returns to metaphorically but never completely.

Accordingly, many of Cash's songs were about small towns and farm life. He seemed to construct worlds that bore less resemblance to the current state of farm or country than to a time and place that seemed authentic by its connections to history and memory. Much of Cash's own writing was set in fictional places—the Old West figures prominently in his work—and he rarely wrote or sang about modern issues. As he told Dave Hoekstra, "After I got in the business and life got to be on such a fast pace, I wrote songs about the farm life as I knew it. Songs like 'Pickin Time,' 'Flesh and Blood,' and 'Five Feet High and Rising' were my way of reflecting on the quieter and more peaceful times. I was thinking about the country, the creeks and the hills and I think the country and farm influences come out pretty good in a lot of my songs."[65] But even songs not directly about small towns, like "Mean Eyed Cat," "Long Black Veil," and "Sam Hall," have the small town as a backdrop, as does some music he recorded but did not write: "Jackson," his duet with June Carter, depends on the contrast between their hemmed-in lives in a small town and a narrator wanting to "steamroll Jackson." Carter suggests that such an approach will be mocked by Jackson's women, and Cash will come home "with his tail between his legs."

If Hendersonville hadn't become half home to the stars and half miracle mile, it might well have stayed a small town (and certain elements of Hendersonville—where the House of Cash lies fallow, for example—breathe Cashville). Cash's sojourns in southwestern Virginia at the Carter Compound, in Port Richey, Florida (where the Carter family had a house), and in Bon Aqua all provided echoes of the life he knew growing up. But he also rode around on a luxury bus, stayed in hotels, and for part of the year lived on an old Jamaican plantation. No one would begrudge this transformation—indeed, we expect our celebrities to live well.

His embracing of small-town life indeed was as much about his audiences as it was about reliving his own past. The Jeffersonian ideal of the farmer lives on in our nostalgic notion of the small town. Cash's oeuvre is a testament to these ideals and other American myths. Karen Schoemer finds that, "his songs take their imagery from American mythos: train wheels, state lines, prison walls, barroom brawls, cotton fields, rivers and floods as great as those that swept the Bible. His characters—the boy named Sue, the Folsom prison inmate, the rider on the Orange Blossom Special—live by a rigid code of ethics that harks back to the Old West, yet Mr. Cash gives them all a resonance that speaks to the rebellious spirit rock cherishes so dearly." Schoemer locates this impulse in Cash's desire to bring the past into the present: "By living these songs as he sings them, Mr. Cash is able to revive moments from a bygone time and place. His music inhabits an era before air traffic and interstate highways, when the whistle of a train still signaled promise and escape."[66] Perhaps Cash never wanted to neglect so rich a source of material—the gaps between how people should behave and how they do behave, where people came from and where they wound up.

CONCLUSION: CASH AND PLACE

Cash chose Memphis for many of the same reasons that forty-niners chose California, immigrants chose New York City, African Americans chose Chicago, potential stars chose Hollywood, geeks and nerds chose

Silicon Valley, and hipsters chose Austin. These places became boom-towns for the cultures they contained and encouraged, and for the oppor-tunity they offered. Memphis combined the lure of work with the possi-bility of stardom, both because of one man, Elvis Presley, but as numerous commentators have stated, also because of its complicated network and intersection of black and white culture, open-minded white producers (Sam Phillips) and culture brokers (Dewey Phillips and the DJ Sleepy John, who was the first to play Cash), and ambitious culture makers such as Cash and Jerry Lee Lewis. Cash chose Memphis because it was a cul-tural boomtown and because he needed work. It takes a particular type of person to move to Memphis seeking his fortune, but Cash lived in a place and time where such dreams were not uncommon.

What was uncommon was his complicated relationship to place dur-ing his lifetime—a particularly dislocated existence, with residence in at least five locations, and significant time spent on the road. When Cash started in the era of Kerouac's *On the Road*, it was a different world, where the interstate culture had not yet begun (where, in fact, there would have been no point in using "I've Been Everywhere" in a hotel commercial). By the time he ended his touring career, the road had become a safe, pod-driven, culture-absent concern. Not all interstate travel is negative, but there are reasons why people sometimes like to avoid the interstate. The experiences related in *On the Road* may no longer be possible, though generations of college students have certainly tried to recreate them.

Cash's experiences with the road, with place and with a shifting sense of "home" are increasingly common. Witness for example, President Barack Obama, whose nominal home is Chicago but who has strong ties to Hawaii, Kansas, Indonesia, Cambridge (Massachusetts), New York City, California, and now Washington, D.C. (Even Sarah Palin's Alaska journey begins in Idaho.) The proliferation of miracle miles and high-way pods ensures a sameness in living and travel, as does the growth of Netflix, digital cable, and satellite radio. Yet there is a way of viewing sameness as a means of making people across the country less isolated. What if one had never heard of Johnny Cash's *new* music; what if there had been no MTV to promote it? As Robert Sullivan suggested, in his musings about the interstate, common culture can serve as a way of demo-cratizing taste.

Cash's experiences mirror those of many people who grow up in more than one place and move around the country. The general cosmopolitan view of place as something more generic, nonthreatening, and welcoming—as opposed to a provincialism rooted in tradition—represents America's future. Our search for authenticity on the road becomes more confused. We honor places where music making has passed for the most part (Memphis) and have an ambiguous relationship to those places where music making is vibrant (Nashville and Los Angeles). We go to fast food joints, feeling bad about neglecting the small businesses. This raises questions: What makes a place real? Is it popularity or single ownership? Is it quantity or quality? Is it the Midwest Miracle Mile or the kitsch shops in the East Village? While undoubtedly nostalgic, Cash understood the democracy of place. The listing of cities in "I've Been Everywhere" and in the beginning of *Ride This Train*, and the universal temptation in "I Walk the Line," all suggest an expansiveness and even cosmopolitan attitude about place. When we think of Cash, we think of the Wanderer (as U2 has Cash guest sing on the song of the same name) as well as the farmer. We think of someone who ended up in Nashville after moving from Arkansas to Memphis, and three very different places: Nashville is a rival to Memphis; Arkansas farm boys might have to put up with the insult from Memphis inhabitants to "go back to your cotton sack" (to which Cash's narrator in "I Never Picked Cotton" responds by leaving his tormentor "in the dirt").

What ultimately ties these places together are audiences, both real and implied. At Folsom and San Quentin, Cash played for convicts (and producers and recording engineers) and for millions of people around the world. Recording at Sun Studio, Owen Bradley in Nashville or Hollywood, in Rick Rubin's living room or his Tennessee cabin was front of a few people, but it led to millions listening. More important were the 10,000-odd performances that cash gave in every continent but Antarctica, playing placed big and small. In each place he gave a concert, Cash forged a tie. And in each place he gave a concert, the concertgoers forged a tie to Cash. When I was in Norway, one teacher proudly told me that Cash had played only a few kilometers away from his suburban high school. Because the teacher had seen Cash where he, the teacher, lived, Cash still resonated with him. Multiply that by the thousands of places

Cash visited, and one can see how traveling bolstered Cash's hold on his audiences.

Cash's visits to small towns also suggest that renewing his ties was a key part of his identity. The *Look* photographer Joel Baldwin said that when he was with Cash for an extended period of time, Cash would frequently play at small shows: "He would stop at Grange Halls with a few dozen people." Baldwin believed that this impulse came from a desire to be "in touch with the audience": "It says more about country music performers," Baldwin said.[67] Though Baldwin and Robert Elfstrom successfully lured Cash back to Dyess to photograph and film him during his comeback, the truth is that Cash had willingly and necessarily left his hometown as soon as he could. The photographs and film show Cash comfortable there, but that comfort can be read as nostalgia, the same emotion he might inspire in his country audiences and perhaps even his larger ones.

We can also place Cash in a number of other locales, just as he makes music in a number of different genres. The similarities between genres an places are made more apparent by looking at Cash. As much as we see Cash as a representative of the Old South and yes a welcome vision of such, he himself saw the overriding beauty of an America of great commonalities. He would surely have agreed with the landscape scholar J. B. Jackson, born in the same year as Cash: "The beauty we see in the vernacular landscape is the image of our common humanity: hard work, stubborn hope, and mutual forbearance striving to be love. I believe that landscape which makes these qualities manifest is one that can be called beautiful."[68]

CASH CHOOSES COLUMBIA

During a tour out West in the 1950s, Johnny Cash was asked by fellow Sun Records musician Bill Justis, author of the instrumental hit "Raunchy," to help distribute his records. Cash says the band "stopped at a beautiful scenic overlook on Mt. Hood and distributed those big, brittle old 78s by hand, one by one. They flew really well," he said. "That record became a hit, too; we were always proud of being the first to distribute it."[1]

Such was the state of music organization in the 1950s, when independents in the country, rock, and rhythm and blues genres were trying to get a toehold in the music business, while larger pop-oriented companies focused on churning out the same type of music, more or less, that they had produced for decades. Only in the 1960s would genre music like rock and roll become big business without crossing over into pop.

But it was not only Sun's small size that prompted Cash to leave for Columbia Records in 1958. Seeking more artistic control of his work—not to mention higher royalty rates—he left a struggling record producer (for all intents and purposes, it did not survive the 1960s) for one of the most storied recording companies; Columbia and its antecedents had been around for decades. Cash's signing with Columbia was surely both practical and symbolic, an indication that he had made it to another level, despite the enormous success he had at Sun.

Cash used his freedom at Columbia to record religious music and then folk music. In the early 1960s he released multiple folk albums, including several prominent theme-oriented ones: *Ride This Train,* a musical journey around the country; *Bitter Tears,* songs about the plight of Native Americans; and *Johnny Cash Sings the Ballads of the True West,* a collection of new songs and old standards, in addition to albums about working-class concerns and the Grand Canyon.[2] If at any time

Cash himself sought authenticity, it was expressed here in his desire to reclaim, rediscover, and at times relive American culture in order to be taken seriously as an artist.

This chapter discusses Cash's recording history generally and his move to Columbia specifically, but focuses on his folk career at Columbia as a crucial moment in his efforts to move from a country audience to a wider one. For Columbia, mixing Cash's popularity with the possibility of producing folk music with Don Law (who discovered and recorded the bluesman Robert Johnson) must have seemed like a good bet. Working with Law matched well with the idea of himself that Cash had seemed to settle upon—a wandering, peripatetic, broken hero who found his refuge in reclaiming culture.

Recording folk music meant drawing on a form of authenticity in the genre most associated with artistic integrity and reclaiming the voices of the people. Within the folk genre, however, that concept was further complicated. Some thought authenticity meant imitation or reproduction, the standard definition in the early part of the twentieth century, whereas others thought it meant originality, which was becoming the definition in this new musical era. But it was not a simple divide. Bob Dylan, for example, although he acted like a folk singer in his nods to Woody Guthrie and traditional country music, turned to singing about society as it stood (and could become) in songs that were often oblique and funny rather than direct and easily interpreted.

Even though Cash often chose to reproduce traditional songs rather than write new folk music, the originality of his concepts was beyond debate. The idea that there is a music of the people, advanced by collectors such as John and Alan Lomax and performers like Guthrie, suggests in its very conception that folk music is *the* authentic American music, not only because it comes from the people but also because it eschews commercial motivations. In *I'm Not There* (2007), Todd Haynes's fragmented motion picture about Bob Dylan, one actor says she likes folk music "because it's honest. Commercial songs, pop music, can't be honest. It's controlled, it's censored by the people who run society and make the rules." In making his Americana albums in the early 1960s, during a time of intense folk revival, Cash was guided by the idea that traditional songs (such as those on *Ride This Train* and *Johnny Cash*

Sings the Ballads of the True West) and songs about marginalized groups (such as those on *Bitter Tears*), were more real than his pop/country work. It also fit his idea of informed simplicity: as the concepts of a musical travelogue, recording Native American protest songs and old western ballads were simple on their surface, but required a complex research and recording process to bring them to a listening public. And they stood in for the complexities of both Native American lives and the historical record of the West.

Though Cash received only limited plaudits for his folk music, it was a genre that seemed to fit his ambitions and one he returned to at various points of his career. (For example, he did a short radio series called *Johnny Cash's American Folklore* in the 1980s.)[3] And Cash won the Grammy for best contemporary folk album in 1994 for *American Recordings* (a fact that is somehow missing from the Country Music Television (CMT) time line of Cash's life).[4] Though one of his most prominent producers, Jack Clement, declined to define Cash's genre, he did say when pressed that Cash was "broadly folk."[5] And until later in the 1950s, *The Billboard* placed country under its folk umbrella. But such a conception was a harder sell to some folk enthusiasts in the 1960s who saw in Cash an artist still tied to his more conservative country base. They also saw him as a commercial star, which disqualified him among folk authenticants in the 1960s, who were strict about enforcing their ideals. (Just ask Bob Dylan, whom Pete Seeger tried to unplug when he went electric at the Newport Folk Festival in 1965.)[6]

As to why Cash chose Columbia, like Elvis Presley or anyone else he sought more money and artistic control. But until he made another decision—to record at prisons—he never had the success for which he hoped. And it was only the beginning of his concerted effort to seek authenticity. Though working with bigger music companies usually signifies "selling out," Columbia was the home of Don Law and Bob Dylan, each an *authentikos*, and Bob Dylan and Cash used each other to become more authentic.

Choosing Columbia involved Cash's choice of genre, the time he thought most prominently about musical genre (later decisions to move back into the country fold were as much or more about lifestyle and affiliation as they were about music). As someone who disliked metaphoric bags and boxes, Cash's choice of folk was even more remarkable.

As in choosing various places to live and work, his decision to sign with Columbia was about audience—finding a larger one, yes, but also finding one that would listen to his ambitious and personal agenda about the country and God. Discussing both Cash's recording history specifically and recording history generally allows me to place this crucial choice of genre in context with the tensions in the recording industry then and now.

In terms of audience, Cash's chart history is only part of the story. But this chapter on his recording history documents what his charts tell us: that he was largely a country music phenomenon save for two relatively brief periods in his fifty-year history—his prison-concert-fueled comeback in the late 1960s and the latter part of his Rubin-aided comeback in the 1990s and 2000s. That his current audiences are so diverse and taken with his independent spirit makes it even more remarkable that his success is so rooted in country music.

SOME THOUGHTS ABOUT THE RECORDING INDUSTRY

Cash's folk music period serves as a microcosm of one of the central tensions in the recording industry. Recording companies embody the dilemmas involved in seeking authenticity within a commercial venture. Like all businesses, they must make money to survive, but for their products to succeed, they also must appear to care about art. These concerns are transferred to the artists themselves. As Patrick Parsons notes, "Most groups . . . do not start out intending to become simply commodities, but unless they eventually perform like successful commodities, no group will last in the *business*. The word is emphasized because [the] popular music industry is, and always has been, first and foremost, a business enterprise."[7] It's a tension built on the conflict between authenticity and commerce. And audiences complicate the matter further—finding the audience that will buy what record companies produce requires not only skillful selling and marketing but luck and vision.

Authenticity in recording also has to do with a romantic conception of how art is produced, within which, economies of scale to some degree diminish the value of any particular record. According to authenticants, the more something sells, the less value it must have. Some of this attitude is irrational, but there is a logic there, even if it is flawed. Often in a musician's or musical group's early work there is a rawness that later production lacks, and rawness, in all its forms, almost always equals authenticity. Cash's later recordings with Rubin are, in fact, a testament to this equation—his aging and sometimes failing voice makes listeners believe in its realness.

Those responsible for producing stars must look for the authentic (unless they begin with the idea of the band, as the creators of the Monkees and Spice Girls did) and then sign artists, which inevitably propels them into a world where music becomes a product and, presumably, less artistic.[8] In addition, the music industry has to market an artist's personality as well as the music. Cash himself was part of concerted marketing plans that included interviews, tours, and print advertising. But so many aspects complicate reception that whatever marketing has to be done to get music into the ears of a listener—photo shoots, interviews, tours, videos—is all part of a process that Geoffrey Stokes's book *Star-Making Machinery* (an allusion to a Joni Mitchell quote) describes. Stokes compares the music process in the 1970s to Hollywood: "The record we hear on the radio or on our equipment is the end product of a long chain of events that shapes the nature of the music as surely as the commercial imperatives of the thirties' Hollywood dream factories changed their films—which in turn changed their audiences." Stokes addresses not only the popular image of authentic music's beginning but also its seedier side: "The rock chain may begin with a musician strumming his guitar in a tenement walk-up, but it includes a bewildering array of technology, armies of lawyers and accountants, and considerable wheeling and dealing in money and in drugs."[9]

Popular music itself has had a rough road to acceptance. Although the idea of popular recorded music as a form of serious art gained ground in the twentieth century, its acceptance by cultural arbiters has hardly been absolute: there have been levels of acceptance for different genres by these arbiters, and such acceptance has varied over time. In 1950s and 1960s, folk music was the closest thing to an accepted popular art form, given its increasing codification by such figures as Harry Smith and Alan Lomax, who began collecting folk music to archive it. Cash may have recorded folk music to strengthen his credentials as an artist, but he also did it to avoid being categorized as country, a genre that has historically been denigrated. "In 1953," Nolan Porterfield writes, "nobody paid much attention to country music, at least not publicly. If you had any pretensions at all to culture and sophistication—if you just wanted to be 'normal' and have nice people like you—you ignored country music whenever possible. If you could not ignore it, you made fun of it." Porterfield addresses one of the central tensions of the genre—that its early place in culture was much more unstable than its rescuers tend to remember. Cash's search for folk music—his rock-and-roll affiliation came only in retrospect—makes more sense in this context. As Porterfield notes, "Historians of country music like to think of the 1940s and 1950s as 'The Golden Age,' but in those days everybody called it 'hillbilly music,' and practically no one took it seriously."[10]

Cash's folk venturings also offer insights into the ongoing struggle between artists' desires (both to have their work heard and to make money) and the corporate mandate (to sell product both to current audiences and, hopefully, new ones). The history of corporate music in America begins in the early twentieth century. The Victor Talking Machine Company and the Columbia Gramophone Company (an "amalgamation" of smaller companies) dominated the early twentieth century until the birth of radio. After a series of mergers and purchases, three record companies controlled the scene until the end of World War II: CBS, RCA, and Decca.[11] Through his second marriage and his subject matter, Cash had early ties to the recording industry. June Carter was the daughter of Maybelle Carter; she and A. P. and Sara Carter were first recorded in Bristol, Tennessee, in 1927 by Ralph Peer, only a few short decades after records were born. (That period also marked the first country hit, Vernon Dalhart's "The Prisoner's Song," released in 1924.)

At this time, singers rarely had anything to do with writing the music. It was the assembly-line aspect of Tin Pan Alley, most prominent in the 1920s and 1930s, which got the attention of cultural critics. Even early country and folk singers focused on performing traditionals, and the idea of authenticity in the early twentieth century was still imitation. Of course, there was a great deal of variation in popular music; jazz and the blues came to national attention in the first half of the twentieth century, and no forms have more authentic cachet. They were often produced by smaller companies that found a niche in recording and selling to jukebox operators records that were not often played on the radio.[12]

By the 1950s, the recording field had expanded to include six major corporations, the three listed above plus Capitol, MGM, and Mercury. All six produced records and distributed them nationally, though RCA and CBS had an advantage because of their affiliation with the radio networks owned by their parent companies. The explosion of rhythm and blues, country music, and especially rock and roll in the 1940s and 1950s, however, put independents in the forefront, because of what Parsons terms the labels' hesitancy "to get into rock 'n' roll."[13] But without national distribution, many of the smaller record companies struggled. This era both made and unmade small labels, which at first held the reins of genre change and power and commanded a surprising shift of musical importance to the middle of the country: Detroit, Memphis, and Nashville arguably became as important as Los Angeles or New York. Cash's jokey flinging of records off a cliff may be funny to read about in retrospect, but it symbolized the failure of small companies to compete nationally, despite their innovations. To keep afloat, Sam Phillips famously released Elvis Presley to RCA for $35,000. Such deals were not uncommon, nor was it rare for small companies to break in the new artists and larger companies to sign them afterward, as happened with Cash and Ray Charles.

Columbia/CBS and RCA eventually discovered country music and rock and roll, which had been disdained by the older generation of executives associated with more traditional conceptions of pop music. Columbia's head, the former big band leader Mitch Miller, called rock and roll "the comic books of music."[14] Such disdain persisted deep into the 1960s. Even in 1967, writes Clive Davis, "the company's creative makeup was predominantly, stubbornly middle-of-the-road," which meant that Columbia focused on anything but the wild genre of rock and roll.[15] Steve Perry observes that, in the 1950s "the industry conceived of three distinct and exclusive pop music audiences. The white middle-class urban audience went mostly for Tin Pan Alley standards, the black audience consumed R&B, and rural southern and midwestern audiences bought country records."[16] But the conception of audiences did not always match reception of material, as smaller companies fed an increasing appetite for genre busting and forming music by Presley, Cash, Jerry Lee Lewis, and Little Richard. The retrospective romanticizing of Sun and other small houses is not unwarranted in its focus on the way the artist's production was so directly and quickly put into the marketplace. But for artists like Cash, who had larger dreams, such a system had its limitations, even though before his prison albums, he was more successful on the charts at Sun than at Columbia.

In trying to assimilate new musical trends, the majors responded not only by searching for consonant artists but also by cannibalizing the new product. In the 1950s, the majors responded to the birth of rock and roll and the evolution of country not solely by hiring major artists such as Presley and Cash but also by rerecording country and then rock-and-roll songs. Prime examples include Tony Bennett covering Hank Williams's "Cold, Cold Heart" and Pat Boone covering Little Richard's "Tutti Frutti." Of course, this process has some modern counterparts that Cash has become a part of—Boone made an album covering heavy metal songs, most famously "Enter Sandman" by Metallica; Paul Anka made rock songs into a swing/lounge act. These are different from the 1950s efforts to dilute the power of rock and roll for a mainstream audience, a motivation that often had bias, if not straight-out racism, behind it. Now, covering artists from one genre in another is kitschier and oddly innovative; there's something about artists recording songs in other genres that actually comments positively on the nature of popular music. Eventually, music companies did take the new genres seriously. Columbia and others soon built studios and back offices in Nashville to take advantage of the burgeoning country music industry. Cash's first recordings in Nashville were at the Owen Bradley studio; later he recorded at Columbia's Nashville studio.

His move from Memphis was symbolic on several levels. It signaled, for example, that the city would have difficulty holding its status as a music center. As Robert Gordon notes, Memphis was still an active place for music making for some time after Cash's departure, with a number of influential bands emerging from there, and Stax Records remaining a vital force in rhythm and blues. But the departure of Cash and Elvis made its vibrancy diminish. The big studios' discovery of rock and roll and country helped dim the stars of smaller studios, which were sometimes purchased by competitors and sometimes went out of business.[17]

After the 1960s, bigger companies themselves became the targets of takeover. Consolidation occurred on a large scale. Columbia was purchased by Sony, and every small label seemed to be swallowed up by a larger company, either directly or with large stakes that focused on distribution deals. But because of the lower cost of production and distribution, it's easy to begin an independent, small label, and in the era of digital recording, the focus is turning to songs rather than albums—individuals can buy what they want at iTunes (or take what they want on Limewire or BitTorrent). So it was when Cash started at Sun; he never produced an album there—only a series of singles.

CASH AND RECORDING

Cash had moved to Memphis to get on the radio, and getting on the radio meant being recorded. His story about how he came to record, which he tells in both autobiographies, is that after turning him down a few times, Sam Phillips, gave him his chance, asking him, however, to focus on secular rather than religious music. Cash writes in his second autobiography: "When I made my first move on Sun, I told Sam Phillips on the telephone that I was a gospel singer. That didn't work. The market for gospel records, he told me, wasn't big enough for him to make a living producing them. My next try didn't work, either—that time I told him I was a country singer."[18] In *Man in Black* he recounts the dialogue more specifically:

> When I finally got Sam Phillips, the owner of Sun, on the phone he was very kind, but very firm in his rejection.
> I told him about *Belshazzar* [a religious song] and asked for an audition.
> "I love those hymns and gospel songs, too, John, but we have to sell records to stay in business. We're a small company and can't afford to speculate on a new artist singing gospel."
> "I'm going to record them, Mr. Phillips. I don't know when, but I know I'm going to," I said.[19]

The religious issue was related to the larger one of genre that Cash faced during this period. In 1955, genre confusion was rampant, with categories previously separated by race and region merging and forming new genres—most prominently, of course, rock and roll. In that sense, Cash was lucky he had chosen Memphis and smart to have chosen Phillips, who, sensing the instability of genre, was deliberately looking for idiosyncratic music. Later, in moving to Columbia, Cash chose money and autonomy over Phillips's instincts. But he grew increasingly nostalgic for his Sun days after musical success became more fleeting.

Colin Escott asserts that Sam Phillips changed the form of Cash's name for commercial reasons, but Vivian Liberto, his first wife, recalls his introducing himself as "Johnny," and when she asked if she could call him J.R., he wrote: "I don't think it would sound right for you to call me J.R. honey. I've been called John and Johnny for 3 years."[20] The renaming issue may seem minor, but it speaks to an authenticant argument: because Cash resisted the commercial impulse but knuckled under, any success that derived from the renaming is not his fault, but the fault of the producer who made him more commercial.

In 1958, when Cash signed with Columbia, country music was in the process of concentrating its industry in Nashville, and rock and roll had no real recording home, though it had certainly become its own genre. Cash's gospel dreams, as persistent as they were, never made much impact in the music world. As he says, even doing the *Hymns* album (1959) did not "bring the joy and fulfillment" it would have earlier: "The importance of a hymn album was minimized by so many in the record business that it had lost some of its importance to me."[21] Popular culture shaped Cash's own opinion about his music.

In his autobiographies, Cash lingered on the year or so it took him to become successful in Memphis, but once he got his chance, he quickly became a success. Indeed, Cash's story with Sun reads as a boilerplate music triumph: artist hangs around hoping to get recorded, fails, records, and then zooms up the charts. Success came so quickly that it left very little time for drama. Director James Mangold's biopic *Walk the Line* shows one climactic singing scene and then quickly moves to the road story with June Carter—unlike musical movies such as *The Buddy Holly Story* and *La Bamba*, which focus on the American Dream aspect of becoming a music star.

Cash's Sun oeuvre reveals a variety of music, some of it fitting comfortably into Hank Williams territory and some less so. Cash was known for a few large hits: "I Walk the Line," "Cry, Cry, Cry," and "Folsom Prison Blues." Other memorable singles included "Hey Porter," "Get Rhythm," and Jack Clement's "Ballad of a Teenage Queen" and "Guess Things Happen That Way." Cash quickly hit it big on the country charts. He had six songs in the top ten in 1956. The peak was "I Walk the Line," which hit number 2 on August 18 and 25, having begun its run in the top ten in June and not leaving it until March 1957. He had seven songs in the top ten country in 1957, with "I Walk the Line," "There You Go," and Train of Love" achieving the highest charting. His first number 1 country song for Sun was "Ballad of a Teenage Queen" in February 1958, followed by "Big River" in March and "Come In Stranger" and "Guess Things Happen That Way" in June.[22]

Obviously, Cash's Memphis success was important to him—he went from a struggling appliance salesman to a wealthy star in a matter of a few years. But it was not enough. Cash tells two stories about leaving Sun: one in *Man in Black*, his religious autobiography, plays up his not recording religious music; the other, in his more straightforward autobiography, is more ambiguous. Clement, an old friend of Cash's, believes his departure had more to do with the attention he was or was not getting from Phillips compared with new artists.[23] And there was, of course, the fact that Columbia was not only going to give him control of what he recorded but also pay him a higher royalty rate. Cash may have needed to mitigate the "inauthentic" move of leaving a small shop for a larger one for the money, so his departure story focused on authenticity. He told Anthony DeCurtis about leaving Sun to choose the music he wanted to record, including religious music: "But I wanted to do it. It was one of the reasons I did go to Columbia, because I didn't want to be restrained. I didn't want to be held back from doing anything I felt was important for me to do. I didn't want to be held back as a writer. If I wrote these kinds of songs, I wanted to put them on record, and I didn't want anything to stop me."[24]

Cash almost immediately recorded two albums for Columbia: *Hymns by Johnny Cash* and *The Fabulous Johnny Cash*. According to Don Law's recording logs at Columbia, he first received a 5 percent royalty for a series of four one-year contracts, with $10,000 per year as a guaranteed advance against royalties. The contract was signed on November 1, 1957, and though it was to take effect on August 1, 1958, recording actually started on July 24. "Oh, What a Dream" was the first song listed in the log. "What Do I Care" and "It Was Jesus"—a Cash original slated for his hymn album—were among those recorded in the first session.[25]

Cash's move to Columbia and his increasingly folk- and gospel-oriented sound meant less though fairly consistent chart success. He had no top ten country or pop songs in 1960 and 1961, and only "In the Jailhouse Now" hit the top ten in 1962. "Ring of Fire" was a number 1 hit on the country chart from July 27 to September 7 in 1963 with "Matador" also rising into the top ten. The next year brought the top ten hits "Understand Your Man" and "Ballad of Ira Hayes"; "Orange Blossom Special" and "It Ain't Me, Babe" were top ten hits in 1965. The year 1966 brought the novelty hit "The One on the Right Is on the Left" and 1967 brought "Jackson," his duet with June Carter, which charted at number 2. Then came the success of "Folsom Prison Blues," a number 1 charting hit in country, followed by "A Boy Named Sue," his only top ten cross-over hit, which was number 2 in 1969 (his previous best had been "Guess Things Happen That Way" at number 11 in 1958). "I Walk the Line" and "Ring of Fire" initially had only modest success. Still, Columbia must have been happy with Cash: he signed a half-million-dollar contract on July 1, 1964, guaranteeing twenty semiannual payments of $25,000. And despite publicity about his drug use, he was busy with some seventy recording sessions between 1958 and 1967, about nine sessions a year, all while undertaking an extensive touring schedule.[26]

Although the Johnny Cash story suggests an artist who did a lot of crossing over, we can see by the chart history that this simply was not true until he recorded at the prisons. And he remained primarily a country music artist who had limited crossover success not only early in his career but also until Rubin took over. That when it did come, the success was astounding—*At San Quentin* went number 1 (*At Folsom* peaked at 13) and "A Boy Named Sue" went number 2—is probably the basis for much of the belief that Cash was a crossover artist.

His limited crossover achievement was not for a lack of effort. Cash, Columbia, and even the press tried their best. *Billboard* wrote this about Cash's album *I Walk the Line*: "Johnny is thought of first as a country artist. However, he consistently makes the pop charts with singles. Cash is more than just a singer of songs[;] . . . he is a first-rate balladeer and music interpreter of the saga of the West. One certainly doesn't have to be a C&W music fan to dig the deep baritone of Johnny Cash."[27]

The crossover train did take Cash to a cover of Dylan's "It Ain't Me, Babe." *Billboard* made it was a country and western spotlight pick. Columbia took out a full-page ad with portrait-size photographs: "Cash swings on the harmonica on the first side and duets with mystery girl. Watch this for pop action, too."[28] Again, though, it charted in the top ten in country but not in pop.

Part of the reason may have been the sheer competitiveness of the pop chart: the country chart had fewer artists vying for inclusion. Nonetheless, he remained successful as a country musician throughout this period. The country charts did not list albums until 1964, and despite a downward dip in his prospects in the mid-1960s, Cash had seven number 1 albums from 1964 to 1970 (including the two prison concerts) and a number 2 with *Bitter Tears* in 1965. He did not hit number 1 again, however, until his work with the Highwaymen—Waylon Jennings, Kris Kristofferson, and Willie Nelson—in 1985. His pop album charting shows only minor hits, first his first Columbia album *The Fabulous Johnny Cash,* but nothing really significant until *At San Quentin,* which hit number 1 August 23, 1969, and then little until his Rubin hits.[29] This history shows why Cash considered himself country: that was where he charted if not always where he aimed.

The 1970s and 1980s show a performer trying to regain his popularity without losing his artistic footing. *Rockabilly Blues,* released in 1980, remains the highlight of this effort, though it's not the equal of either his 1950s or his 1990s work. *Class of '55* and his recordings with the Highwaymen self-consciously tried to pull rockabilly and classic country into the 1980s and 1990s. In *Johnny Cash: The Biography,* Streissguth documents how many pieces of Cash's past and future rumble through his recordings in the period of 1974–1994, which he labels "a cold, wild wind." He notes that Cash's songwriting was affected by his rise in celebrity; he remained "the face of country music but had slipped from the creative vanguard where the innovators remolded and propelled the genre."[30]

The 1980s were also the period that Columbia failed to renew him after more than a decade of a mutually unsatisfying relationship. The symbolism of being dropped by Columbia was undeniable; not many fifty-five-year-old artists are able to come back after losing a record deal. The fact that Cash was able to find not only one company, Mercury, but after losing his record deal there a second one, Rubin's American Recordings, showed an unusual staying power. And despite his difficulty with Columbia, he continued to sell records in the 1980s; his greatest-hits albums consistently charted. One could argue that Cash's steady reputation did not take much of a dip during this period—it just did not change for the better.

Because Cash changed recording companies only three times in fifty years after first hooking up with Sun Records, each change was significant and symbolic. But as the first significant artistic and personal choice he made after becoming a star, the selection of Columbia stands out in importance. Columbia offered Cash the chance to be personally authentic, to do what he wanted to do, and his output in the early 1960s shows an artist acutely aware of the reigning genre of authenticity—folk music. But it also competed with Cash's other authenticity: the gospel music in service to God, whom he claimed as his true master. So the Columbia years highlight this ongoing battle between different forms of authenticity: Cash's desire to keep what was dear to him in his life—namely, religion—and to become a more serious artist by turning to folk music, whose ethic bespoke authenticity.

WHO ARE THE FOLK?

Though Cash's desire for folk success may have come at the expense of success on the pop charts, it represents something deeper in his career: the quest to become a more serious, less commercially oriented artist. Folk music, with its ties to the civil rights movement, had a notable place in both popular and political culture at the time. However, his application for folk inclusion was viewed skeptically by authenticant judges because of his past as a country star. Cash's status was part of a larger debate: who can be a folk musician?

The debate was at its most heated during the folk music revival of the early 1960s, led by Bob Dylan and Joan Baez. Writing in the period, Agnes de Mille believed that folk music comes from the everyday expression of a group, not necessarily its "art" songs, but is also a function of a romantic and democratic impulse: "Here we come face to face with Anon. And he turns out to be quite a person; he turns out to be us."[31] De Mille's romantic trope seems a staple of 1960s folk, a corollary to the early Camelot romanticism of the Kennedy administration, which introduced folksy programs like the Peace Corps. And the civil rights movement's good-versus-evil, the people–versus–The Man thematics lent themselves to folk expression. Folk music was steeped in idealism and linked to a purity of spirit. Authenticity, however, did not always equate with originality. Folk music emerged from a specific tradition, the old British ballad, and was then transformed in America, particularly in Appalachia, reintroduced in the Great Depression, and revived in the 1960s. The purity and history of the form was not lost on its neopractioners. When asked by a journalist if she would call herself a folk singer, Joan Baez once replied that if she were, "she would live on an old farm in the Appalachians, wear dated clothes, and sing with a nasal whine."[32] Along the same lines, Jacques Vassal calls the Carter Family, "the most famous authentic hillbilly group" because of their recording history.[33]

Some critics wondered if a song's singer contributed to its status as a folk song. As Bruno Nettl writes, "If we assume . . . that a song may be folk music under some circumstances and cultivated music under other circumstances, it is possible that songs sung by the professionals are not, and cannot be, genuine folk songs."[34] Note the careful parsing that Nettl uses to determine whether something belongs to a genre! Only punk music seems to be as particular about its boundaries. One can see that authenticity, though not named directly, is a major concern; Nettl uses "genuine" instead. Simon Frith notes that folk authenticity goes even further—this ideal tries to measure one's sincerity and authenticity: "As Alan Lomax had written in Sing Out!, the 'authentic' folksinger had to 'experience the feelings that lie behind his art,' and it was this concept of authenticity—truth to self rather than truth to a movement or an audience—that the folkies retained as they became successful singer/songwriters, as they made the move from communal to commercial ways of music-making."[35] Folk music had to come from folk, and those folk had to mean what they sang. But as Nettl says, "folklorists have had considerable difficulty deciding who the 'folk' are."[36] When it came to being folk, Cash seemingly had no parallel. What Bob Dylan had to invent—a Woody Guthrie-esque life of rambling—Cash lived. His father had been an authentic hobo before settling on the farm, and Cash was a farmer's son. But the complications of his southern roots and his history as a country and commercial performer made it more difficult for him to assimilate into the folk scene.

CASH AS FOLK

Cash began his quest to play folk music at the beginning of the genre's revival, which Robert Cantwall locates between 1958, when the Kingston Trio sold 4 million records with "Tom Dooley," and 1965, when Bob Dylan went electric at the Newport Folk Festival.[37] In 1959, Cash told *Time* that he was trying to sell authentic folk music."[38] That same year, he appeared on the CBS-sponsored show *Playback*, in an interview with CBS Records president Goddard Lieberson, which seemed designed to authenticate him as a folk artist. Lieberson, dressed in a suit and tie, and Cash, in Western wear, sit in an office. Cash plays "Streets of Laredo," which Lieberson identifies and asks where Cash heard it. "Well, sir," he begins, he heard it from his mother, but "she must have heard those songs from somebody else." Lieberson responds, "The you do have a direct line to folk music because that's the way our folk music traveled." After the next song, Lieberson asks Cash where he is from. Cash replies that he came from Ireland and then his ancestors gradually made it down South. (He also claims Native American ancestry.) Lieberson, straining even more at authentication, says that that is also a "direct" link to folk music, because that's how the music traveled. When Cash says he is going to play "Lumberjack," Lieberson asks him if he has been a lumber jack. Cash says no, but he grew up carrying water for his brother and father when they were clearing the cotton fields in Dyess, braving the "bobcats" and "cottonmouths"—revealing that even then he understood the power of authenticity in cementing his appeal.[39] Later Cash appeared in *Hootenany Hoot*, a movie devoted to folk music (1963) and played at the Newport Folk Festival in 1964. He seemed obsessed with authenticity, as represented by the content of *Ride This Train, Ballads of the True West,* and *Bitter Tears.*

There was enough of an overlap between country and folk, however, that moving from one genre to another did not seem so threatening to his primary country audience. At least for a time in the 1950s, *The Billboard* considered country music a subset of folk music. In his column titled "Folk Talent and Tunes," Bill Sachs refers to the *Town Hall Ranch Party, Louisiana Hayride*, and *Grand Ole Opry*, all country music shows, and includes country stars such as Tex Ritter, Lefty Frizzell, Merle Travis, and Johnny Horton.[40] Switching to a folk focus did not require Cash to move to another recording company or producer. It required changing his content emphasis, a stated goal that seemed to pay dividends down the line.

Over the next three decades, Cash produced many albums that he wanted to be thought of as folk and others that could ostensibly be classified as folk. Beginning with *Songs of Our Soil* (1959) and culminating with his 1994 Grammy-winning *American Recordings*. Here I focus on three early mid-1960s albums, notable because they were produced at the height of the folk revival and they represent his most sturdy efforts to produce folk music: *Ride This Train* (1960), *Bitter Tears* (1964), and *Ballads of the True West* (1965). *Ride this Train* heartily played up its authenticity; in the liner notes to its rerelease in 2002, Cash wrote that *Ride This Train*'s travelogue details were his "own, fairly well researched for accuracy."[41] The original liner notes (not written by Cash) celebrated the "uncommon artistry and sympathy" in his "provocative tour of the country through narration and song" and in his reclaiming of the voice of "those who have left their mark on America."[42] Next to these words were thee photographs of Cash—one with his eyes closed, the second in which he appears to be singing, and the third in which he poses in philosophical, boilerplate folk stance. The cover features him in Western wear, unshaven, fiddling with a gun, on a desert landscape that could represent either an authentic cowboy or a tourist dressed for kicks. There was a train in the background, and the suggestion that Cash was going to rob it. Even in his folksiest moments, he (or his marketers) could not quite forget the dark side of the Cash story engendered by "Folsom Prison Blues."

Some of the dialogue that frames the album was deliberately folky. Cash began the first song, "Ride this train [presumably the one making the piped-in sound effects] up and down and across this strange wonderful land. It's almost like a fairy land, when you think about it. You go through places with names like Tuscaloosa, Kokomo, Muskogee, Oshkosh, Saginaw, Eureka, Bandera, Battle Creek, Sioux City, Chattanooga,

Hattiesburg, Lynchburg, and Bald Knob, Arkansas." Dominated by angli-
cized Native American and southern names, this list resembles the list
from "I've Been Everywhere." With its geographical diversity and emphasis on Native American place names, it nods to authenticity and seriousness; by acknowledging the presence of Native Americans before white
settlers, Cash showed both his knowledge and understanding *and* his
political savvy. He continued with his theme of universality: "You see I'm
a million different people from all over the world, and I've been coming
to this country for hundreds of years. This was the promised land for me.
But let's not forget when I came here, there were already millions of people living in teepees along the rivers and hunting deer and buffalo for
food and shelter." Of course, Cash drew on traditional, even stereotypical
ideas of Native Americans, but in doing so, he maintained his political
stance about the plight of natives while appealing to his listeners' immi-
grant pasts. It was a difficult task to appeal to everybody, but Cash's narrator seemed determined. He continued to tell his listeners about the
Native past in America: "And it's with a little regret that I think about how
I pushed them back and crowded them out and claimed this land for
myself or for another country. But the Indians' hearts must have been
full of music when they left names with me that seemed to sing. Names
like . . ."—he sing-talks a list of tribes that goes on for almost thirty seconds. This performance showed that Cash was serious about his role as a
reinterpreter of American culture through music and, in particular, stories about those disadvantaged or forgotten. His own working-class
background and sometimes self-described Native American background
(though settling on a non-Native background in his autobiography) made
him a natural for the task.

A third voice on the album's notes was Arthur Levy, who wanted to
"acknowledge Johnny's role in the 'folk process'" and ended by quoting
Cash's own words: "Some of us still wake up and find ourselves listenin'
for that long lonesome whistle in the night. That's the sound America's
dreams are made of. Close your eyes and make believe just a little bit
and I bet you can hear that whistle blow."[43] Cash was celebrating his
vision of the past through his use of the word "listenin'" and his desire
for us to imagine a train whistling (or "whistlin'"). The tone is decidedly
pedagogical, though nonetheless imaginative.

Cash's next folk album, *Bitter Tears (Ballads of the American Indian)* of 1964, had the most cultural impact and caused the most controversy among country music audiences.[44] The cover featured Cash in a sleeveless shirt in front of a Western landscape wearing what looks like a leather headband. The liner notes, written by Hugh Cherry, began with a series of debatable notions: "Individuality is a prerequisite for an artist! Johnny Cash is singular in his individuality. There is no artist on the American scene quite like this ex-farm boy from Arkansas." Cherry used "farm" as a signifier of authenticity, which he burnished through praising Cash's "perceptiveness": "His insight into the deep feelings of his fellows is startling. His few years rule out his having 'lived' all he sings of and writes about so well." Cherry suggested that "Johnny is gifted with a perception that allows him to express, so that others can understand, that which we did not see before. His quite unorthodox broach to the literature of song has brought home, with great impact, many things we have not taken the time to consider. This album contains an abundance of such literature." Like Whiteside, Cherry suggested, that Cash was bringing us information or insight we did not previously have, and in making this claim, he was also confirming Cash's authenticity.

The use of the phrase "great impact" suggests that Cash was seeking an audience that would learn, not only listen, an audience likely different from the one he had sung to throughout his career. Cherry told us why we need to listen: "The contents of this album is the Indian's side of the story. The songs, written by Peter LaFarge and Johnny Cash, view some of the problems cited here from the Indian's viewpoint." His advice: "Listen well to these words. They are the thoughts and feelings of a people who deem Custer's Last Stand not a massacre but an Indian victory over a foe who had broken a promise. Hear the words well and you will discern that simply because we are white, that does not make us pure." The reason Cash could sing them was that he comes from their perspective: "Johnny Cash sings well these tales of the Indian's woe. His facility for perception and insight lends validity to these tales of anguish. Johnny is justified in the stand he takes. Johnny Cash is proud of his Cherokee blood." Cherry used Cash's background for authenticity's sake—except that Cash did not have any Cherokee background, as far as he knew.[45]

Billboard noted the album in its Country Spotlight! column: "Cash, in narrative and song, documents the tragic history of the American Indian."[46] But more interesting was the advertisement in letter form that followed soon after. Cash indicted the entire recording industry because "Ballad of Ira Hayes" was, in his estimation, being underplayed. He was proud of the song and hoped it would spur an interest in Native American politics. It did in fact reach number 2 on the country charts but never made a mainstream splash. Cash suspected that its subject matter had turned off program directors and disc jockeys, and so he—and Columbia—took out an ad in *Billboard*."

It began with a description of the Iwo Jima memorial at Arlington National Cemetery, explained why he wanted to record the song, then issued the challenge: "D.J.'s—station managers—owners, etc., where are your *guts*?" It moved to "I think you do have *guts*—that you believe in something deep down. (And pardon the dialect—mine is one of 500 or more in this land.)" The lines together suggested that the reason radio professionals were not playing the music was something unseemly, and Cash, with his suggestion that he himself was Native American, pushed such an interpretation even further. His somewhat odd discussion of music industry demographic trends was designed to reach his insider audience: "Still . . . actual sales on Ballad of Ira Hayes are more than double the 'Big Country Hit' sales average. Classify me, categorize me—STIFLE me, but it won't work." Cash's perceived market and political independence, displayed here, belie the notion that he was some raw country singer who did not understand the music business (a necessary construct to help some audiences view him as authentic). He continued in the same way, moving to a more specific demographic discussion: "You're right! Teenage girls and Beatle-record buyers don't want to hear this sad story of Ira Hayes—but who cries more easily, and who always go to sad movies to cry???? Teenage girls." The logic might not have been airtight about the preferences of the teenage market, but the rant suggested an artist hyper-aware of his position in the market. He recognized this market as such: "Yes, I cut records to try for 'sales.' Another word we could use is 'success,'" he added. "Regardless of the trade charts—the categorizing, classifying and restrictions of air play, this is not a country song, not as it is being sold. It is a fine reason though for the *gutless* to give it thumbs down." Then he went back to being political: "Ballad of Ira Hayes *is* strong medicine. So is Rochester—Harlem—Birmingham and VietNam." Notice that he hit many of the subjects that other folk artists were covering, a complicated maneuver when he was trying to paint himself as at once as a mainstream artist and a folk artist. He then moved back to his own heritage: "But as an American who is almost a half-breed Cherokee-Mohawk (and who knows what else?)—I had to fight back when I realized that so many stations are afraid of 'Ira Hayes.'" In the end, he was appealing to the better instincts of his audience. Interestingly, the ad contains the Columbia logo—and this tagline: "NOBODY BUT NOBODY MORE ORIGINAL THAN JOHNNY CASH."[47] So in the end, the letter, printed in *Billboard*, an insider's magazine, was a bizarre marketing scheme that attempted to build on Cash's "originality."

It was an ad full of demographic frustration, geared toward an inside crowd, since *Billboard* is and was read mostly by music professionals. The point was both that Cash was angry that his music was not being played *and* that he knew why. Indeed, the inside nature of the ad—referring to formats, markets, relationships between program directors and DJs—was probably an attempt to address his audience of professionals on an equal level. More important, it showed that Cash was angry at music middlemen who were getting between him and his audiences. Cash expressed this tension throughout his career but rarely in the public sphere in real-time protest. Though one has to acknowledge the performative nature of anything Cash did, it seems clear that in this case he imagined listeners who were not going to be reached.

Cash probably thought of the ad himself, but the fact that Columbia put its name on it—as Rubin did later with the Bird—suggested that the rebellion was contained within the culture of the music industry. Still, "Ira Hayes" was one of the few songs that charted in that period for Cash; it was a top ten hit, and the album raced up the new country album chart to number 2. But it did not cross over.

Cash's next folk album was less controversial. He wrote the liner notes to *Johnny Cash Sings the Ballads of the True West* (1965), whose cover features him in a torn photograph on top of what is supposed to be a wood inlay. He is dressed in black wearing a cowboy hat, sporting an odd mustache, and holding a gun. The notes themselves are full of authenticizing moments, like the adjective "True" in the title. The first text page features a long explanation of how he came to choose these songs, including sitting down with books—"by John Lomax, Carl Sandburg, [Daniel] Botkin, [J. Frank] Dobie, and all the rest," which Cash found "confusing." Lomax, Botkin, and Dobie were famous folklorists of the West, and Sandburg collected folk music in *The American Songbag.* Eschewing books, probably because the process was not real enough (though later, Peter Guralnick cited the fact of Cash's playing pool with Dobie as a measure of his prowess as a folklorist), he called up the country music star Tex Ritter, who "sat with me three hours with a tape recorder running and we went over the possibilities of the album. We became so involved in going over some three hundred Western songs that we developed an intense 'true West' attitude toward it all."[48]

Cash throws three hours in there to show how much attention he paid to the project. The quote marks around "true West," however, are confusing; they undercut the authenticizing moment described earlier in the paragraph, as if to acknowledge there *was* no true West. But in a way, such a strategy did show Cash's knowledge of the West, as Johnny Whiteside writes in the 2002 rerelease notes: "The attempt to rectify myth with reality and genuine folk music with commercial Western song was a daunting one. 19th century historic fact, 1930s-era Hollywood fantasy and contemporary folkloric ideology, only recently codified by an Eastern elite who spearheaded the late 1950s folk revival, had collided in the popular mind as a mass of themes and images from which the notion of a true West seemed inextricable."[49]

Cash went further in this vein, acknowledging but not apologizing for "the modern sounds and modern arrangements on classics like 'I Ride an Old Paint' or 'The Streets of Laredo'; after all, they were meant to be heard on twentieth-century record players and transistor radios!" In this way he headed off complaints that the songs on the album did not sound as they did when first sung or recorded. "Cash's insistence on the appropriateness of using modern media to deliver his incarnation of the Old West's structure of feeling is telling," writes Edwards. "The cowboy becomes a flexible symbol reflecting the concerns of different socio-historical contexts." It was a fair contention given the nature of folk music's mutability. But in the liner notes Cash ended that thought with a grim nostalgia: "For today that same

West wind is blowing, although buckboards and saddles are lying out there turning to dust or crumbling from dry rot."[50] His ultimate authenticity came in describing his preparation for recording the album, which has Streissguth wondering whether it was a "a bad drug trip in his backyard or a lonely sojourn in the Arizona desert" that Cash was on: "How did I get ready for this album? I followed trails in my Jeep and on foot, and I slept under mesquite bushes and in gullies. I heard the timber wolves, looked for golden nuggets in old creek beds, sat for hours beneath a manzanita bush in an ancient Indian burial ground, breathed the West wind and heard the tales it tells only those who listen. . . . I learned to throw a bowie knife and kill a jack rabbit at forty yards, not for the sport but because I was hungry. I learned of the true West the hard way—a la 1965."[51]

Cash tried to live the old West in order to record it, but such a task was obviously symbolic and clearly meant to give him the authenticity he needed to create an album based on a quite unstable past; most historians count the cowboy era as lasting about twenty five years or so, and yet it's one of the most replayed eras in American culture. Cash replayed it because it linked with his assumed ethos of individuality and self-reliance. It also remained a trope of modern country music, whose stars often sport cowboy hats. Whiteside's take was that *Ballads* is "as focused and convincing an assemblage of the subject as anyone could put together" and that "Cash should be proud of what he achieved . . . because he brings us closer to the harsh reality and sublime romance of the untamed frontier than perhaps any other artist or historian has managed."[52] One has to note here that perhaps Cash was motivated by something more than exploration of the cowboy theme. Perhaps after his disappointment with Native American folk music, he turned to a more marketable and universal theme in order to reach a larger audience.

All three albums discussed shared a focus on common themes of universality and authenticity. The message behind all three: the United States is a beautiful and diverse country with as many stories as people, yet Americans do not know their common ancestry and humanity. Cash's ambition is not reflected in the movie *Walk the Line*, a one-sided tale of stardom and woe. In this period, he was clearly determined to educate and edify his audience. But because he had risen through the country music and pop worlds, such ambitions perhaps were not taken seriously.

One contemporary commentator on folk music, Jacques Vassal, suggests that Cash's stardom essentially disqualified him as a folk musician: "Johnny Cash, the recognized big daddy of country and western, has shown a most equivocal attitude. On the one hand, his sympathies for the Indians (it's rumored that he has Indian blood in his veins) and his belief in the rights of prisoners (he has in fact been imprisoned several times himself) are well known, and perhaps he is sincere." Interestingly, Vassal here cites two falsehoods, (both part of the Cash legend) as reasons for thinking Cash was sincere. Before we even reach his conclusion, we know what it will be—the "big daddy of country western" is dismissive in tone, suggesting that a "big daddy" in one field could not exist in another. And the emphasis on sincerity, in this context, made it a synonym for authenticity.[53]

Next the authenticant argument raised its head—anyone who was materially successful as an artist in turn could not be a serious artist: "On the other hand, he is a man perfectly integrated into the hideous American show-biz syndrome: his guitar (a splendid Martin decorated with his initials in mother-of-pearl) cost him more than two thousand dollars, and his annual income is tremendous." We know that Cash's income, though guaranteed, took a big hit in the early 1960s, but Vassal is writing at the height of Cash's comeback. "And then there's the tour in company with Billy Graham, the right-wing WASP Christian, whose principal claim to fame might be his practical suggestion that the punishment for rape ought to be castration." Vassal thus decried Cash's efforts to go mainstream—his Christian affiliations hurt him too in folk authenticity—the coup de grace came with Cash's political affiliations: "And to finish it all off in style, at the beginning of 1970 Cash went to the White House, accompanied by his wife, to give a performance with his musicians in response to a personal and official invitation from President Richard M. Nixon to sing for his friends and himself. We know a number of singers who would have refused, but the vast majority would never been invited."[54]

While Vassal at least included Cash in a discussion of folk music, he captured an attitude about Cash specifically and country music generally. Even after a decade of devoting himself to making himself a folk musician (it's hard not to count his prison albums as at least partially protest music), Cash was still considered by most a country and western star.

JOHNNY CASH, BOB DYLAN, AND AUTHENTIC PIGGYBACKING

In 1963 a simple full-page ad appeared in *Billboard* announcing Johnny Cash's recording of Bob Dylan's "It Ain't Me, Babe." Cash was in the middle of his folk phase, and Dylan had yet to go electric. Both were working in the same genre, though record companies and audiences considered Dylan folk, while Cash was trying to be.

Dylan and Cash appropriated different models of authenticity while traveling the same folk circuits. Cash rerecorded American staples; Dylan, the seeker, wrote about his rapidly changing world. Each left the folk world as it was narrowly defined—Cash with his two groundbreaking prison concerts and then his television show, and Dylan with his electric performance at the 1965 Newport Folk Festival. Both departures reflected the changing zeitgeist of American music: folk increasingly sat in the shadow of the British Invasion and protest rock and roll.

In general, the two performers were a mutual admiration society from which both benefited. Cash wrote to Dylan early in his career, and Dylan wrote back. Cash supported Dylan when Dylan went electric. Cash helped bring Dylan to Nashville, and Dylan was the first guest on Cash's television show. Dylan claimed he had followed Cash since "I Walk the Line," and Cash claimed the same about Dylan's work earlier in the 1960s. Both simultaneously fought and courted fame. Both were born again and persevered through devastating situations—Cash with his drug use and Dylan with a near-fatal motorcycle accident. As Peter Doggett notes, "both Dylan and Cash had walked the line, peered into the abyss, and been hauled back from the edge. Paired in the public imagination as champions of the oppressed, they stumbled through the mid-sixties as slaves to amphetamine addiction."[55] Both made a reputation based on inscrutability, and both pushed the boundaries of the folk tradition.

Their differences had to do with genre and origin. They did come from different places and made different music. Dylan began his career as a Woody Guthrie wannabe who ended up in Greenwich Village, looking for truth (and getting exposed by *Newsweek* as not the *authentikos* he claimed to be).[56] Cash came from the farm and ended up into the big city.

At times, they seemed to envy each other's beginnings. Cash was not fully taken seriously as a folk artist because of his beginnings as a country music star, and Dylan struggled to relieve himself of his reputation as the voice of a generation, as he indicates in his memoir, *Chronicles.*

Their admiration helped them both. Though Cash fought hard to burnish his folk credentials, those connections and his ties to authentic music in the 1960s were never fully realized. Dylan's own dreams of authenticity, driven by his early imitation of and homage to Guthrie and then by his status as a folk prophet, were not realized in the manner he would have liked. Part of it had to do with folk music's strict boundaries. He complained to Cameron Crowe in a way that might have explained Cash's difficulties too catching on as a folk musician: "Folk music was a strict and rigid establishment. If you sang Southern blues, you didn't sing Southern mountain ballads and you didn't sing city blues. If you sang Texas cowboy songs, you didn't play English ballads. It was really pathetic." Dylan had been criticized heavily at Newport; his drummer, Mickey Jones, said according to folkies, Dylan "was a traitor to folk music." Cash took on Dylan's critics after he went electric in Newport: "Came a Poet Troubadour, Singing fine familiar things. Sang a hundred thousand lyrics, Right as Rain, Sweet as Sleep, Words to thrill you . . . And to kill you. Don't bad-mouth him, till you hear him, Let him start by continuing, He's almost brand new, SHUT UP! . . . AND LET HIM SING!"[57] At Newport in 1963, Cash had given Dylan a guitar, and decades later, Dylan commented in *No Direction Home*, "Johnny Cash was more like a religious figure to me, and there he was at Newport. Meeting him was the high thrill of a lifetime."

So when Dylan came to Nashville to record what turned out to be *Nashville Skyline*, produced by Bob Johnston, he was doing double duty: he moved himself away from the folk spotlight and Cash toward it. Johnston produced both of Cash's prison albums and many of Dylan's greatest works—including *Highway 61 Revisited, Blonde on Blonde,* and *John Wesley Harding.* As Tom Smucker noted at the time: "This has neither made Johnny Cash a hippie nor Bob Dylan a country and western artist, but I think it has lent new respectability to both."[58] Streissguth notes that "the flirtation with Dylan and company never remolded Cash as a folk revivalist, but it did encourage and redirect his pursuit of music associated with the pleasant and the pitiful of the American legacy."[59]

Cash's nods toward folk and his embrace of Dylan did not move all mainstream opinion about his generic home. Robert Christgau, a fan of *At Folsom Prison*, believed that Cash's politics doomed his musical connection with Dylan: "I am not putting down Johnny Cash's music because he likes Nixon, or Dylan's because he likes Cash, nor I am suggesting that Dylan endorses Cash's politics by participating in his music. I'm not even dismissing Cash's politics. There are good reasons for conservatism, and I suspect he is sensitive to most of them; Dylan certainly is. That does not mean, however, that either is right."[60] Christgau's comments, like Vassal's, effectively dismissed Cash as an artistic force—an authentic force—because of his conservatism. Thirty years later, what other people thought of Cash and Dylan is overshadowed by their iconic stature, but in 1969 these affiliations still mattered. The story as told now seems to benefit both artists and complicates the Johnny Cash story, but it is unclear whether minds that could have been opened by such an odd pairing actually were.

When Cash chose folk he could not have been thinking about Dylan, but as the decade progressed, he could not help but see how Dylan mattered in American culture. Though his later folk albums may not have sprung from a desire to imitate Dylan, certainly his rant against the sparse play accorded "The Ballad of Ira Hayes" seemed to spring more from the desire to be recognized than from the wish to make money by being recognized. But the seemingly eternal problem was that, very little distinguishes commercial pursuits and exposure of one's message.

Though one could argue that Cash's turn toward folk was as dramatic as Dylan's toward rock, his persona did not alter as significantly. It's no coincidence that Todd Haynes had six actors playing Dylan in *I'm Not There*, whereas a few years earlier Cash got a brooding one-expression actor in Joaquin Phoenix. The distinction is part of a larger narrative about Cash's unchangingness and Dylan's multifaceted and multiple personalities.

3

CASH CHOOSES PRISON

Johnny Cash's connections to prison began with a bit of larceny, one that
was not uncovered until some years later. His "Folsom Prison Blues" is a
rewrite of "Crescent City Blues" by Gordon Jenkins, the tune itself borrowed liberally from a 1930s instrumental "Crescent City Blues" recorded
by Little Brother Montgomery.[1] Though "Folsom Prison Blues" takes its
melody and the lyrical framework from "Crescent City Blues," Cash was
inspired by a movie and not a particularly good one. *Inside the Walls of
Folsom Prison* (1951) was written and directed by Crane Wilbur, a Hollywood studio presence who also directed some thirty other movies,
including *The Patient in Room 18, A Day at Santa Anita,* and *The Story of
Molly X.*[2] An anonymous film reviewer from the *New York Times* said of
Inside that "most of the footage is standard and unimaginative" and that
the movie was "another prison picture indistinguishable from those
uninspired melodramas that have come regularly from the West."[3]

More powerful was the source of Cash's composition on which he
built to make his masterpiece. In Jenkins's "Crescent City Blues," singer
Beverly Mahr laments the narrator's being "stuck in Crescent City / just
watching life mosey by," a statement about the stultifying nature of
small towns.[4] Cash's song about prison is much starker, highlighted by
the famous line "I shot a man in Reno just to watch him die," a line that
has resonated in the public mind for fifty years.

Writing "Folsom Prison Blues" led to Cash's first invitation to play
prisons, which in turn led to the albums recorded at two prison concerts
in the late 1960s, *At Folsom Prison* and *At San Quentin.* He first played
at prisons in the 1950s, invitations that were issued because of "Folsom
Prison Blues," as was recording at Folsom. The concert albums reignited
Cash's career. *Folsom* included a rerelease of "Folsom Prison Blues" (and

getting caught by Jenkins's son for plagiarism) and *San Quentin* included Cash's (number 2 pop) hit, the Shel Silverstein–penned "A Boy Named Sue." The two albums had the effect of forever linking Cash to prisons, helped by producer Bob Johnston's interview with the Associated Press: when asked which prison Cash had been incarcerated in, Johnston said that he "was not sure whether it was Folsom or San Quentin."[5]

That remark, added to the song and the prison concerts, cemented the assumption that Cash was a rehabilitated criminal who had done time—a story that had *some* weight, given his brushes with the law in the 1960s.[6] He had spent seven nights in jail, including his two most famous arrests: one for drug possession in El Paso and the one in Starkville, Mississippi, that he immortalized in his song "Starkville City Jail." But as Cash himself said, "Jail don't count;" spending a night in jail for drunken revelry was different from being sentenced to prison for a crime. Yet the perception that he had served time never went away. In *Cash*, he wrote that "How much time did you spend in prison?" was one of three questions generally asked of him. And as he answers, this question arose both from his appearances playing in prisons and from his consistent use of subject matter relating to criminality.

> There are those who just don't want to accept the non-felonious version of me, and on occasion I've had to argue with people firmly convinced that whatever I might say, I once lived a life of violent crime. To them all I can offer is an apology: I'm sorry about this, but that line in "Folsom Prison Blues," the one that still gets the biggest rise out of my audiences, especially the alternative crowds— "I shot a man in Reno just to watch him die"—is imaginative, not autobiographical. I sat with my pen in my hand, trying to think up the worst reason a person could have for killing another person, and that's what came to mind. It did come to mind quite easily, though.[7]

Still, Cash's alleged criminality gave him credibility to prison audiences. And even in his denial, one must note his willingness to trade on his darkness, "it did come to mind quite easily," suggesting that he might have turned to crime had his life gone in a different direction.

Cash never fully disavowed his possible criminality because it gave his relationships with prisons and prisoners perceived authenticity, driving the success of his prison concerts in particular. In playing for prisoners as an outsider, Cash seemingly knew that he needed to develop or maintain some connection to them; this line between empathy and participation is one of the most powerful aspects of his prison concerts. There are at least two types of perceived authenticity involved here—the implied and somewhat misdirected one related to his background, plus the notion of playing live in front of prisoners. Yet, as I've already discussed, being authentic is a strategy, and one that worked particularly well when it came to prisons.

Arguably, Cash's first true coalescence between his search for authenticity and his artistic success came with the live prison concerts. As Jay Orr, historian with the Country Music Hall of Fame, notes, "Those two albums made a statement about who Cash was, I think, to an audience beyond the country audience. He suddenly was an important American recording artist, not just a country artist."[8] With his early work, authenticity may have been the motivation in trying to capture the mind of a prisoner ("Folsom Prison Blues") or describing how it felt to be tempted on the road ("I Walk the Line"). But when he moved to a more old-fashioned idea of authenticity as he reintroduced America to historical folk songs, such an experiment did not quite catch on with his public. *At Folsom Prison* and *At San Quentin*, however, combined the perception of criminality—a personal authenticity—with a live public expression of playing for the dispossessed, an effort to do good, drawing attention to the plight of the prisoners. As listeners perceive and as his prison audience seemed to have felt, the concerts were real, the commitment was real, and Cash had been in jail, adding up to an artistic and commercial success. Prison concerts also represent an ideal form of informed simplicity—the concept of playing in front of prisoners is easily imagined, though the practical aspects and the complex nature of performance and recording belies its simplicity.

I argue that Cash's search for authenticity as well as his audiences' search for the authentic Cash came to fruition when he stepped on stage at Folsom Prison and then when his audiences sat down and played the record. The darkness that connected the performance at Folsom to "Folsom Prison Blues" (itself a link to the sorry movie that inspired it) also connected Cash to the folk and political concerns inherent in the 1960s and to the story of black-hattedness that he encouraged, both directly and indirectly, also in the 1960s. It was a midcareer springboard to his ultimate reputation.

To see how strong a hold this idea of authenticity had on audiences, one only need visit the museum at Folsom Prison. The museum's focus is on Johnny Cash, even though there is a talking statue of a prisoner behind bards, articles about prison escapes, and information about the prison itself. But the entrance—and souvenir shop—is dominated by Cash. The museum's docent, Susie Hopkins, told me that visitors often come into the museum convinced that Cash was himself an inmate there. She said they often ask, "If he killed a man in Reno, why was he in a California prison?" They so strongly assume the authenticity of the song that they seemingly question the logic of the justice system itself. I witnessed one group from England visiting the museum, and as two men entered, one explained to the other that Cash had been an inmate. He was startled when he read the description of Cash playing at Folsom to find out he had not been.[9]

This perceived authenticity, fashioned out of an imagined line, a producer's sly manipulation of the singer's history, and Cash's own bad behavior, led to his largest audience, a general public that rewarded such perceptions with a number 1 record. And it's the point at which he moved from wannabee folk singer to folk hero.

PRISONS: AMERICAN STYLE

Cash began his prison playing as a way of doing something for the prisoners, who saw in him a sympathetic spirit. He believed that the American prison system was based primarily on punishment rather than rehabilitation, and punishment whereby prisoners are robbed of America's most valued ideals—liberty, autonomy, and privacy.

American prisons first evolved from European notions of punishment, which were public and monetary for the most part. In the colonial and early national period, America based public punishment on confinement; only in some penal systems, particularly among the Quakers, was rehabilitation the ultimate goal. Because of their aim and form, American prisons have been sources of criticism and wonder to outside observers, who have complained that prisons only punished, did not rehabilitate, and often helped train criminals.[10] A class element was evident from the very beginning, and perhaps this was where Cash's interest lay: prisons were overwhelmingly populated by the disenfranchised, particularly minorities and the poor. But prisons were changing in the 1950s and 1960s, when Cash began playing there. Though he did not explicitly tie his prison activities to the civil rights movement, outside observers have made the connection between prison reform and civil rights.[11]

Cash chose to perform for prisoners because they were powerless, and undoubtedly saw race, along with class, as among the factors that made them so. According to one source, at San Quentin at about the time Cash played there, 30 percent of inmates were African American; 18 percent were Hispanic; 65 percent had less than a ninth-grade education.[12] (One such prisoner at this time was Eldridge Cleaver, author of *Soul on Ice* and a fellow Arkansan.) Such diversity did not always make it into popular representations of prison, which according to John M. Sloop described two main inmate varieties: the white male prisoner who is "a redeemable human being who met with material or social conditions that encouraged a life of crime," and the "prisoner who is innately irrational and immoral, engaging in violence simply for the sake of violence."[13] Cash's narrator in "Folsom Prison Blues" falls into the second category.

Despite efforts at reform, the history of prisons leads most observers to conclude that prison does not do much to change its inmates' lives for the better. As Scott Christianson says, "Today prison is not intended to transform, reform, or rehabilitate people.... [I]n fact most persons tend to assume it will probably make them worse—more hardened, more embittered, more disabled, and better schooled in the ways of crime." He believes that "prison is used to get some people out of circulation ... for a period of a few years when they otherwise might do more damage."[14] But activists would argue that this is done at the expense of inmates' humanity.

Through his prison concerts, Cash participated in the reform movement of the 1950s and 1960s, which arrived in part to make prison easier to bear. His first prison performance took place in 1956 at Huntsville State Prison in Texas, and "after 'Folsom Prison Blues,' the prisoners felt kinda like I was one of them. I'd get letters asking for me to come and play," Cash said. Bob Johnston, his Nashville producer, believed that only Cash could have done the concerts: "I don't think anybody in the world could have done it besides Johnny Cash. I think if I'd have called up here with Elvis Presley or anybody else they would have said, 'no thank you,' but there was something there with Johnny that connected with the prisoners and connected with the guards and connected with *everybody* pretty well."[15]

As the author of "Folsom Prison Blues," and later as someone who was assumed to have done time, Cash understood the complexity of prisoners' perceptions of themselves and of society's perceptions of prisoners. His narrator in the song is as guilty as a man can be, and yet on some level we are supposed to find sympathy for him. Clearly Cash felt sympathy for the men in prison, even if they deserved to be there. As he said in one visit to Cummings Prison in Arkansas: "I think that these men are very, very human. And some people ought to be more careful about how they treat human beings."[16]

FOLSOM PRISON BLUES

America's first exposure to Cash's gangster side came in 1955, when "Folsom Prison Blues" was released (it charted in 1956). The prisoner who narrates the song is guilty and does not want to be reminded of lost freedom, but he feels bad not about what he has done, only that he is imprisoned.

Cash said that after seeing the film *Behind the Walls of Folsom Prison*, he imagined himself as an inmate and wanted others to do as well. His narrator is reminiscent of The Misfit in Flannery O'Connor's "A Good Man Is Hard to Find," who expresses no remorse about what he has done (he says he knew he was guilty because "they had the papers on me") and of course the narrator in Camus's *The Stranger*, who kills an Arab without provocation.[17] The three men share the notion that society finds them guilty but defiantly contend that that does not make them any less human.

"Folsom Prison Blues" joined a veritable country music canon of criminal songs, including the Carter Family's "Banks of the Ohio,"

Merle Haggard's "Mama Tried," and Waylon Jennings's "Good Ole' Boys" (otherwise known as the theme from *The Dukes of Hazzard*). As Cash said, "You know, the biggest sellin' song of the common people in the nineteenth century for 100 years was 'The Ballad of Jesse James.' About a man who liked people and robbed banks. And there's been so many versions of it written and rewritten and parodies of it." He also pointed out that in the twentieth century, "some of the [biggest] songs are the songs about the tragedies and death and prison. Well, the first million seller country record was Vernon Dalhart's 'The Prisoner's Song' back in the '20s. It's just kind of carrying on a tradition, I guess."[18]

Still, in its portrayal of the unsympathetic narrator, "Folsom Prison Blues" is a remarkable song not only for its subject matter but also for its lyrical splendor amid simplicity. It begins right away with the narrator's first impression—"I hear the train a-comin'"—letting us know that our narrator is from the country. There are enough train songs that this is not remarkable, but revealing the accent of the speaker through the lyrics is still crucial. Then we hear that the narrator "ain't seen sunshine since I don't know when," further confirming his southernness but also introducing the fact that the narrator is in jail: "Time keeps draggin' on, but that train keeps a rollin'." The first stanza manages to convey not only the prisoner's predicament but something about his social status and place of origin as well. The audience at this point might be feeling mixed sympathies: the man is in prison and yet seems sensitive enough to notice the metaphorical nature of the train.

In the second stanza we find out why the narrator is in prison. Its lyrical and rhetorical directness regarding violence sets it apart from most previously published music.[19] In "Banks of the Ohio," the female narrator kills her lover because he would not marry her; in Dalhart's "The Prisoner's Song," the narrator does not exactly express remorse, but neither does he express the cold-bloodedness of "Folsom Prison Blues." Sounding deceptively like a nursery rhyme, the stanza begins with a deescalation of sorts: a story about his mother and her caution to be a "good boy" and "don't ever play with guns." Somewhere, though, something has gone wrong, and there's a long distance between his mother's warning and the next line: "But I shot a man in Reno just to watch him die."

That lyric, particularly the word "but," condenses a life gone astray. The distance traveled in that line, particular in the ambiguity of the word "but," is substantial and, more important, leaves the way the prisoner traveled into criminality up to the listener, who in this gap is responsible for *closure*—a term Scott McCloud uses in *Understanding Comics* to explain how readers get from one frame to another by using their own versions of a story.[20] Of course, closure is a part of many songs—indeed, most songs require us to imagine their details or backstory. In the original "Crescent City Blues," Jenkins intimates that the rich folks eating "pheasant breast and Eastern caviar" are a source of envy for the narrator who wishes she could join them. But Cash's narrator suggests that there is some connection, however vague, between his plight and the imagined life of the rich who are living it up on the passing train. There also is the misplaced closure of the audience associating Cash with the narrator. The stanza is remarkable not only for its naked violence but also for Cash's willingness to build sympathy not for the victim but for his guilty narrator, who feels mournfully trapped in a predicament of his own making. The next line about the train clearly refers to class: there's "rich folks eating in a fancy dining car," "smokin' big cigars." Again, he feels bad but not for his victim, and, in a way, not for himself. He knows he "had it coming," he knows he "can't be free." In the rest of the song, he would like to move the train away in order not to be reminded of his predicament.

"Folsom Prison Blues" achieves a form of greatness in a few short stanzas. Though there have been songs about violence and songs about regret (and songs about prison, and songs about trains), "Folsom Prison Blues" combines these into a meditation on class, regret, and naked violence. Much later, Cash called the song "a flight of fancy" but also intimated that it had a deeper meaning: "When I say in my song 'Folsom Prison Blues,' I shot a man in Reno just to watch him die, I meant it. I wanted to let the folks out there know what it feels like in prison. How much poison they put in you."[21] Long after he became associated with prisons, and after the two concerts, he was still trying to swing public opinion to the narrator's side, even though the narrator was unredeemable.

PRISONS, CONCERTS, AND PERFORMANCE

When we listen to Cash singing in his prison concerts, we know we are listening to a performance and so did the prisoners. But concerts were just one instance of a life that itself was performance—in a sense, he was performing all the time as "Johnny Cash." On the artist's end, to perform is to enter another world, where one stands in front of people, saying and doing things outside the commonplace. As Richard Schechner says, "Performance behavior isn't free and easy. Performance behavior is known and/or practiced behavior—or 'twice-behaved behavior,' 'restored behavior'—either rehearsed, previously known, learned by osmosis since early childhood, revealed during the performance by masters, guides, gurus, or elders, or generated by rules that govern the outcomes, as in improvisatory theater or sports." In other words, performance comes not naturally but through a conscious effort—it may seem natural, but it comes from a different place than natural behavior. Schechner adds that "because performance behavior isn't free and easy it never wholly belongs to the performer."[22] One who becomes famous as a performer becomes a celebrity—and celebrity itself becomes a performance. As Andrew Tolson writes, "the public persona of the celebrity needs to project an aura of 'authenticity.'"[23] But by putting his authenticity in quotes, Tolson shows that such a construction is itself unstable.

A prime example of the complicated nature of Cash's performative life came in the way he introduced himself in front of the crowd: "Hello, I'm Johnny Cash." In fact, there was no need to introduce himself, to the prisoners or, indeed, to the listening audience outside the prison; we knew who he was (we bought the album with his name on it). Sylvie Simmons says that Bob Johnston directed Cash to introduce himself as a way of beginning the show.[24] The concert itself features someone asking the prisoners to wait for that signature phrase before cheering, a decision that Streissguth notes came right from Johnston himself.[25] So now the performance has reached a third level—he is playing for the prisoners, for the outside audiences, and to an extent for the recording engineers. And at the San Quentin concert, he was also playing for a television crew. There may have been one Johnny Cash performance but multiple ways of perceiving it, as even the audiences were probably fractured in their generic devotion.

Using the phrase "Hello, I'm Johnny Cash "in many ways raises comparisons with Melville's "Call Me Ishmael," a symbolic name with biblical resonances which suggests a pseudonym, a stage name, a name that will serve for the narrator as he stands in for something else. "Johnny Cash" too may have been a stage name, though Cash used "Johnny" before signing at Sun. Sam Phillips wanted "Johnny" instead of "John" "with an eye to the teenage market."[26] Johnny Cash replaced "John R. Cash," which had been "J. R. Cash," before he had to choose a first name when he entered the air force. Edwards notes that the two names Johnny and John could be viewed as separate identities: "He stages a struggle between 'Johnny Cash' the hell-raiser, hotel-trashing, pill-popping worldwide star and 'John R. Cash,' a more subdued, adult persona."[27] When Cash said, "Hello, I'm Johnny Cash," he was on one level announcing his stage presence but, on another, delivering a line that had no literal purpose—save to the engineers recording the concerts. And yet, his saying it and the way he said it meant something. In a sense, it gave audiences the chance to hear him freshly every time.

Indeed, the prison albums are narratives in their own right: each concert was a story of sorts, with a beginning, middle, and end. A typical performance story begins when the musician first takes the stage, initiating or reinitiating the relationship between artist and audience. Like the author of a book, the artist may already have a relationship with an audience. Like the readers of a book, the audience at a concert may have a relationship to the artist—indeed, probably so, since they have paid money to see and hear the artist. The narrative in a concert consists of at least three elements, all of which are in relationship to the audience: the songs the artist plays, the order in which the artists play them, and the dialogue (or lack thereof) between the artist and the audience. Members of the audience bring varying degrees of knowledge and expectations to a concert, depending on who they are and who the performers are. But no one expects the concert to mimic everyday life; performances provide those in attendance a way to suspend everyday concerns. And rarely are they surprised (and rarely do they want to be). Arguably, those are the reasons that prisons schedule concerts—to suspend everyday life (what Cleaver, a convict at Folsom and San Quentin when Cash performed there, called "madness" and "petty intrigue," suspending which takes a "lot of time and energy").[28]

In performing as a singer, the artist is creating an audience and also removing him- or herself a step further from actual life. And as an audience, we must cross a certain gap to the performer.

There is a real question, however, about what constitutes an audience. The term itself is amorphous and indeterminate. How does an artist know who watches and listens in the aggregate? Artists know only by two measures: what people buy and what people say. But there still is a disconnect between the numbers and the idea behind the numbers. When a performer makes a record, she would be lying if she did not say she hoped someone would listen to it. When a performer goes out on the road, he would be lying if he claimed he did not want crowds to hear what he has to say.

A live performance is often the ideal; the record is a text that can become divorced from its author. Carrie Brownstein of the band Sleater-Kinney says that placing an album out in the world often means losing control of the meaning of a work: "Since my own goals in music lie in forging a connection with people, with an audience, it's disheartening to feel as though my message is misinterpreted or no longer of my own design. . . . At the same time, I cannot wholly ignore those to whom I am trying to relate, who are sharing the experience along with me. It is a precarious position." Brownstein lauds the live performance: "In general, I feel that live performance is the truest and most organic way to experience the tradition of music, for the listener and for the artist. . . . The moment relies on movement, connection, continuity, spontaneity. We are reminded that music is an experience, not merely an object, and thus it becomes difficult to separate it from our own bodies."[29] I would argue that Brownstein's dichotomy is a false one—certainly the behavior of spectators at concerts often suggests a less than full engagement with the "message" of the band, and constant replaying of an album would seem to familiarize listeners with the work rather than alienate them from it. Cash's recorded concerts were complicated by being recorded live. The concert became the album, which people were free to interpret.

Listening to both prison albums, we realize we are being told many stories at once—the narrative as we listen; the idea of Cash giving a concert performance to prisoners or about what prison represents to us; the stories we tell ourselves about those prisoners or about what prison represents to us; the stories we are telling about Cash; perhaps the stories we tell ourselves as well as stories we bring to the playing of the concert itself. The multilayered nature of the prison concerts, combined with the myths about Cash and prisons, helped drive the popularity of the albums. The performance as interpretive text itself unfolded in a delightfully complicated way. When we listened to the live show on a record, it was no longer live; what Cash did and said was mediated by distance and technology. He was not a criminal but was (and often is) thought to be an ex-criminal who was playing in front of a live audience of criminals that was supplemented by a recorded audience: Johnston apparently piped in prisoner yells *after* the concert.

When talking to or reading about people interested in Cash, I was struck by how many had heard the albums in the 1960s, often via their parents who, many said, had little or no interest in country music save for Cash and his prison concerts. This particular audience of non-country listeners may have enjoyed them for a variety of reasons, but I think the power of the concerts came through the informed simplicity of the concept of a prison album: the simple concept of Cash playing at prisons combined with all the imagined backstories and complications to enhance a dynamic performance. One does not have to be a country fan to appreciate the depth and power—and rebellious spirit—of such an arrangement.

But these nuances would not matter save for the main show—Cash performing in a compelling way in front of a dangerous audience that seems to share his bad-boy ethos. The concerts showed Cash's command of his audience; he seemed confident, clearly gearing his dialogue to the men and not to the guards or the warden (or, in the case of the San Quentin concert, to the documentary filmmakers). Cash did what he could to paint himself as a fellow rebel. Before playing "Starkville City Jail" at San Quentin, he asked one of the stagehands, "Will you tune this son of a bitch for me?" and got a big cheer. And he prefaced "San Quentin," a song done from the point of a view of an inmate, by saying, "I think I understand a little bit how you feel about some things, it's none of my business how you feel about some other things, and I don't give a damn about how you feel about some other things." The line was designed to show both camaraderie and strength—he did not want to seem to be cozying up to the convicts. He continued: "I try to put myself in your place and I believe this is the way that I would feel about San Quentin." Then the song began, "San Quentin you been living hell to me."[30]

When Cash had come out onstage there, he said, "there was a lot of tension, a lot of electricity." He deliberately sang songs that hit close to home: "I was *trying* to get things close to the bone. Close to the bone is what it was all about."[31] At Folsom, he began with "Folsom Prison Blues," which is most notable on the record for the sheer cry of enjoyment with which the crowd greets "I shot a man in Reno just to watch him die." According to Michael Streissguth, that response was spliced in—did Johnston feel the presentation of potential violence was not authentic enough?[32] In any case, the concert clearly transformed the song itself. In the earlier recorded version, it was a country blues song, suggesting, at least in its tone, regret. The live version belonged to the rock genre: Cash sang the first two verses a full five seconds faster, backed by a drum and, more important, with a change of attitude. He seemed *happy* to be at Folsom; the song suggested rebellion, that he might as well enjoy his time in prison, and as the first number in his first recorded prison concert, it attempted to establish his camaraderie with his audience.

And yet his audience outside the prison had to believe that the performance was on some level real and dangerous. Such promotion of the danger Cash put himself in continued (and continues) long after the concerts. In a commemorative book accompanying *Unearthed* (released just after his death), Sylvie Simmons and Rick Rubin tried to reify the authenticity of his performance in the prison albums, undoubtedly with an eye toward authenticizing the Rubin projects. As Simmons says, "*At San Quentin* is, if anything, even more untamed and uncompromising than *Folsom*." "They're very edgy records. I remember when I first heard them thinking that it was really beautiful that he chose to be there for the people that society had turned their back on," said Rubin. And Johnston added, "I thought *Folsom Prison* was just the best record in the world, and I think *San Quentin* was the best in the world. There was nothing like them. And there never will be—unless they let me make the third in the Historic Prison Series with Dr. Dre or James Brown in Sing-Sing."[33]

These quotations played into the need for Cash to seem edgy and dangerous. They were, in essence, part of a marketing strategy. But were the performances edgy? Did playing at prisons make a performer tougher? The question becomes interesting when one looks at a later work, *A Concert behind Prison Walls*, which was recorded at the Tennessee State Prison in Nashville in which neither the convicts nor Cash seem particularly menacing. Was it Folsom's reputation that made the performance there seem edgy? As a whole, Cash used the concerts as a way of building rapport with the inmates. They were also great for his career. On the heels of a well-publicized drug arrest, they led to his reemergence as a man of conscience ready for his next act.

OBSCENITY

Playing at prisons was not the only thing that reconfirmed the Johnny Cash story. Johnston's deceptive answer to the AP interviewer gave Cash prison time he did not have, adding to the legendary darkness that began with "Folsom Prison Blues." But two other elements also expanded this reputation: the legendary bird (see chapter 6) and the bleeped-out obscenity in "A Boy Named Sue," Cash's first big crossover hit. Both gave an additional depth to his darkness: as the word "but" expanded the role of the reader in "Folsom Prison Blues," so did the bleeped-out phrase in "Sue" when the narrator's father utters the line "I'm the [bleep] that named you Sue." The restored album, released in the 1990s, retained the phrase "son of a bitch" ending the mystery begun in the 1960s. But listeners could imagine anything in the original bleep, and the mystery was powerful. More important perhaps was the notion that Cash was so dark that one could not play his music on the radio uncensored. The combination of the obscenity and the image of the bird, which bubbled up into popular culture in the 1990s, gave Cash's darkness depth.

The 1990s also brought Cash's explanation of the bird, and other materials emerging posthumously provide additional perspectives that complicate our understanding of its issuance. In 2006, Columbia released the San Quentin concert in its entirety, with an accompanying documentary by Granada, an English television company. The movie is a bizarre mix of concert footage and interviews with prisoners, preceded by a montage of images of cowboys, hinting—but not saying directly—that Cash was the modern-day equivalent of the cowboy. The concert itself was notable for the contributions of June Carter and the Carter Family and Carl Perkins.[34] In all, the concert recording revealed the extent to which Cash's show extended beyond him; the prison documentary, on the other hand, revealed the contexts in which Cash worked (for example, how much like a school stage the prison stage looks—Cash sometimes plays in front of the ubiquitous black music stands).

Although both the concert and the documentary are notable for quirks and oddities, the most newsworthy moments involve jokes told by June Carter and Johnny Cash. After a cameraman bends down to fix something, Cash quips, "You know better than to bend over in here," and starts laughing. A few minutes earlier, Carter, married to Cash for only a few months, had told the inmates to "get your hands out of each other's pockets." How to process such behavior? Cash and Carter were guilty of the dual crime of being insensitive and unfunny, given that prison rape is a serious problem, one that is often ignored or, worse, as in this case, joked about. But beyond our finger-wagging, what do such jokes mean?

There are several ways of confronting them within the contexts of 1969, prison, and Johnny Cash. For one, the jokes engaged stereotypical notions of masculinity and prison, in a place that was hypermasculine (San Quentin is a maximum-security, all-male prison). Both jokes affirmed that a hierarchy of masculinity and power emerge in such a closed environment. As Susan Brownmiller writes, "Prison rape is generally seen today for what it is: an acting out of power roles within an all-male, authoritarian environment in which the younger, weaker inmate, usually a first offender, is forced to play the role that in the outside world is assigned to women." As she notes, "all rape is an exercise in power, but some rapists have an edge that is more than physical."[35] Prison rape as well as the idea of it engages male fears about masculinity. Helen Eigenberg and Agnes Baro observe that prison rape is a staple of prison movies, and Gordon Knowles writes that prison rape remains an ongoing issue.[36]

Cash's joke posited that this type of rape was ubiquitous, whereas Carter's remark actually engaged masculinity more directly, suggesting that such sexual behavior is wrong, was likely humiliating in coming from a straight woman whose presence was already unstable within the prison walls. It's possible, though, that both jokes were indeed funny to the inmates, whose exposure to darkness and obscenity was likely unrelenting. It probably depended, like most jokes that engage stereotypes, on how well the prisoners accepted Cash and Carter.

The jokes also interrogated ideas of obscenity. They occurred only moments after Cash flipped the bird for which he became famous, and just before he uttered "son of a bitch" in "A Boy Named Sue," which became arguably the most famous "bleep" in American cultural history. Such language was not permitted on network television and probably not even in mainstream concerts.[37] But the prison stage was a place where Carter and Cash felt sufficiently liberated to be ribald and risqué, even if their jokes were stale.[38] The prison was cut off from the outside world, and although Cash and Carter acted as emissaries from the outside, it had the power to temporarily cut them off as well, giving them, in effect, permission to break conventional standards. (Of course, in the country music world in which they traveled, the appearance of convention remained important—so much so that it would seem imperative that they get married only three months after Cash's divorce came through).

Finally, these jokes alluded to cultural trends that were current in a world where societal roles were increasingly unstable. However lame they were and however we process them, it's clear that they matter.[39] The jokes and Cash's performances at prisons both suggest that what we learn about prison is what we learn about ourselves. The sheer quantity of prison movies is startling—we've had everything from *The Great Escape* to *The Birdman of Alcatraz* to *The Green Mile* to significant scenes in *Raising Arizona* and *Out of Sight* and even *Alien 3*. Clearly, there is something about prisons that we identify with or fear. Perhaps we see them, as Bo Lozoff does, as metaphoric reminders of our own imprisonment on earth. Perhaps we fear that someday we'll be locked up without reason.[40]

Movies play on this hopelessness and absurdity. Prison movies end only with either escape from prison or release by death, as in *The Green Mile* and *Cool Hand Luke*. Movies mostly posit that there is an abuse of power, either by the inmates against one another or, more likely, by the authorities against prisoners. A movie like *The Shawshank Redemption* suggests, as Michel Foucault does, that everything about prisons is corrupt—the system that put the criminals (or sometimes, an innocent man) there, the guards, the warden, and even most inmates.[41] Watching *Shawshank* today, offers no reason to believe that anything has changed.

These discussions may seem like odd appendixes to a discussion about Johnny Cash, but if we look at his prison adventures as a part of a larger dialogue about prison and its place in culture, their inclusion makes sense. Cash's prison songs and performances were not about the gritty realism normally attached to incarceration but rather about the ability to rise, or think about rising, above such circumstances. In other words, it is not the physical costs of prison that we hear in Cash's songs; it is the psychic cost of imprisonment.

Cash's prison albums turned a country's obsession with prison combined with an imagined idea of Cash's redemption, perhaps combined with their fantasies regarding prison, into an artistic triumph. Perhaps too the albums represented a third way—both for Cash and his audiences—of political and protest engagement compared to the hot-button issues of racial equality and war (*At Folsom Prison* was released only a few months before the tumultuous Democratic National Convention and the Black Power salutes of Tommie Smith and John Carlos.) Perhaps too this third way gave ABC an opening to offer Cash a television series.

Although no one has made the same type of album as Cash, a recent example of a band playing at San Quentin is *Some Kind of Monster*, a documentary about Metallica; the band plays San Quentin in 2003 as part of warming up for their first tour in some time. But they play outside the prison, not inside as Cash did. And when lead singer James Hatfield says he understands some of the pain the inmates feel, after a movie that shows his recovery, we believe him. But he's no Johnny Cash.

4

CASH CHOOSES JUNE CARTER

When Johnny Cash first met June Carter at the Grand Ole Opry in 1956, he predicted, "You and I are going to get married someday."

She laughed, "Really?"

"Yeah."

"Well, good," she said. "I can't wait."[1]

In this conversation, a number of things are on display—Cash's bluntness (and humor), Carter's humor (and humility), and a meta-discourse about marriage that seems spooky given their ultimate nuptials. At the time, Carter and Cash were both married to other people, yet they ended up together in a long-lasting marriage that at least to many observers appeared happy. The conversation also demonstrates that in the 1950s, marriage was the default choice for relationships; it speaks volumes that Cash's reference is to marriage rather than to some other form of romantic attachment.

The exchange is also a rare window into celebrity discourse (which makes it doubly disappointing that James Mangold did not use it in *Walk the Line*): Cash making moves at the Grand Ole Opry and Carter fending them off. A member of the legendary Carter Family, June was more famous than Johnny at this point. Though that would change with Cash's release of "I Walk the Line," she was making thousands a year performing with the Carter Family and writing commercial jingles, including some for Pet Milk and Kellogg's Corn Flakes. Through Elvis Presley, though, she was already well aware of Johnny Cash: "Elvis made me listen to every Johnny Cash record in the business! He's a fan, and, when we stop to eat something in these little cafes, he put his nickels in and I've had to listen to a lot of Johnny Cash."[2]

Although the conversation may seem amusing in retrospect, Carter deflected Cash in a self-protective way, a technique undoubtedly fused from southern gentility (a staple of the Carter Family's act) and years of fending off unwanted advances; it is also somewhat emblematic of her personality. She displayed this mix of directness and coyness even in an interview late in life with Anthony DeCurtis. In discussing her time in New York, studying at the Neighborhood Playhouse, DeCurtis asked her whether she had had a relationship with James Dean. Her reply: "He did give me a rose once, and that's as much as I want to talk about that. OK?"[3] Though we *think* we know what she meant—there was some attachment between the two beyond "the rose"—we do not *know*. In this meta-discourse about celebrities hooking up, Carter took a page from her husband's famous indeterminacy.

Carter and Cash were celebrities who told their story about their marriage in front of reporters and fans, but others recount their own versions of that union. For one, Cash's first wife, Vivian Liberto, disputed everything from Carter's reluctance to hook up with Cash to when his drug use began and even to the authorship of "Ring of Fire," which Carter (with Merle Kilgore) legendarily wrote about her relationship with Cash. Their son John Carter Cash has another story to tell that puts Cash in a less flattering light, and the Carter Family has still more stories about Johnny and June. And outside the narratives told by those close to them are additional stories: for example, the letters that Cash wrote to Liberto during their courtship complicate our ideas about Cash's notions of masculinity and femininity.[4] Like most of the narratives told about celebrities, the primary one commonly told about Cash and Carter is both mythical and mundane, intriguing and cliché, true and untrue. Their decision to marry probably had simple reasons: They loved each another, and the mystery of love between two people is to some degree a private matter, even among celebrities. As Benjamin Kunkel notes, "Because people who live under the same roof don't usually exchange letters, marriage is a silence at the heart of many biographies."[5]

What made Cash and Carter different was that they performed their marriage publicly, perhaps as a way of documenting its authenticity. The two not only toured, performed, and recorded together but also lived together on the road. They each wrote two autobiographies and studied together for their degrees in Bible studies. Cash even proposed to Carter onstage in London, Ontario, in 1968, and they got married in Franklin, Kentucky, a few days later. This publicness likely had three functions: to help rehabilitate Cash's reputation after a decade of visible bad behavior, to legitimize their relationship for a primary audience of country music lovers, and, somewhat ironically to, make normal a decidedly abnormally set relationship by making a celebrity marriage seem down-to-earth. As Michael Streissguth notes, "They were a public entity—June the faithful wife, stage foil, and show partner, and Johnny, the strong husband in the story of Christian marriage and family, around which he built his image in the 1970s and 1980s. The union served each other's needs."[6]

Carter was at the center of this public marriage—she at once served as a media liaison of sorts and as the public practitioner of the idea of a traditional, male-dominated marriage that seemed straight out of Paul's letter to the Ephesians. She treated her audience to a number of details of domesticity and subservience in both media interviews and her autobiographies. From a celebrity biography in 1970—chapter title, "How the Love of a Good Woman Saved Him from the Gutter"—we find out that Carter "presses his clothes, cuts his hair—and everywhere they go, there are always Bibles handy for the kind of inspirational reading Johnny knew as a child." The writer also reports that Carter "makes no pretense to being anything but 'just folks,' yet she has been in the entertainment world all her life."[7] Unpacking that statement—as well as the chapter title—one sees the idea of a public domesticity at work, and it is not likely that her self-fashioning as a domestic heroine was by accident.[8] Hardly "just folks," Carter at this time was thirty years into her career and must have known how well this information would play with an audience seeking symbols of traditional, domestic harmony in the tumultuous 1960s and 1970s. In Patrick Carr's words, "June had this ultra hillbilly persona. But she was a very sophisticated person."[9] One wonders if Carter actually put to work her acting training at W. Sanford Meisner's Neighborhood Playhouse. As its website still says, the goal of Meisner's technique was "to live truthfully under given imaginary circumstances."[10]

Although Cash downplayed Carter's direct influence on his kicking drugs, this sort of caring wifely function is a trope not only in the culture at large but also in country music culture. Cash said in *Cash*, "Knowing what I do about addiction and survival, I'm fully aware that the only human being who can save you is yourself. What June did for me was post signs along the way, lift me up when I was weak, encourage me when I was discouraged, and love me when I felt alone and unlovable."[11] In other places, however, he did acknowledge the importance of her help in getting him off drugs: "When we fell in love, she took it upon herself to be responsible for me staying alive."[12] Still, the Carter-Cash union marked at least a public happy ending of the songs female and male singers alike have sung about their troubled spouses, including "He Stopped Loving Her Today," "Crazy," and "Stand by Your Man." Most of those relationships ended unhappily, but Carter was able to redeem her fallen beau. When it comes to gender roles, country music generally has codified the traditional, though the back-and-forth between Kitty Wells and Hank Thompson (her "God Didn't Make Honky Tonk Angels" was a widely banned answer to his "Wild Side of Life"), the powerful autobiographical statements of Loretta Lynn, and Dolly Parton's and Patsy Cline's prominence have provided counternarratives to country's traditional gender roles—a process of which June Carter too was a part.[13] And Cash's masculinity was a definitive part of his story—his size, his voice, countenance, and body bespeak a traditional American manliness that was often set against Carter's traditional femininity, a posture both of them seemed to keep during their marriage.

This public domesticity also signaled a retention of premodernist ideas in a postmodern era, in the sense that traditional gender roles as espoused by Carter predated the modernist revolution of the early twentieth century; in her view, they came straight out of the Bible. The juxtaposition of traditional gender roles and a world where seemingly every move was televised or photographed showed the tension involved in being country music stars in a rapidly changing world—their audiences had access to the same changing technologies and media forms that marked the era but also were more rooted in tradition—and showed that Cash and Carter were fully engaged players in the game of media participation.

I examine the Carter-Cash marriage in four contexts: traditional marriage, celebrity marriage, Christian marriage, and musical marriage. Through these different lenses, one can see how complicated marriage was for two music stars, and how the simple choice of getting married had complicated aspects. I argue that at least to some degree Cash chose to marry June Carter in order to remain in the country music genre and appeal to an audience that was more conservative than the new fans he had garnered through his prison albums; that Carter performed a type of public domesticity and Christianity, whereas Cash's role in this display was overtly minimal; and that in the context of country music culture the two acted as if they were regular folks who had just hit it big. One can see this not only in the press accounts but also in the way they wrote about their relationships. What is not part of the authenticity debate was whether the two were in love; the question is how authentic was their display of their affection. The Cash-Carter marriage was also an integral part of the Johnny Cash story; without the love story that played out before the public eye—both in the 1960s and in James Mangold's *Walk the Line*—Cash's prominence would have been diminished.

"RING OF FIRE": THE PREVIOUS MARRIAGES

Both Cash and Carter came to their marriage having been married before.[14] At 22, after returning from Europe, Cash married Vivian Liberto, whom he had met while stationed in San Antonio as part of his military service. They moved to Memphis together and then to California; they had four children, Rosanne, Kathleen, Cindy, and Tara. As a husband to Vivian and a father to his daughters, Cash admitted to being inadequate; as a touring musician he spent much of his life on the road, away from his young family: "By the time our second daughter Kathy . . . was born, I was well on my way to living the life of a rambler, and although life is a matter of choices, I didn't feel I had any control over that." He believed much of his neglectful parenting had to do with being a performer: "Being a recording artist meant you had to tour, which meant you had to leave your family. My kids suffered—Daddy wasn't there for school plays, Fourth of July picnics, and most of the smaller but more significant events in the lives of children."[15]

Although the marriage was traditional in structure—Liberto was a stay-at-home mother—Cash's lifestyle was anything but. Liberto writes about Cash's behavior at some length in her memoir and also about Carter's drug use (undercutting the mainstream narrative). It was not only the touring but also the behaviors associated with touring that contributed to Cash's domestic inadequacies; as described by Christopher Wren, his life on the road was far from sedate. Though Wren is not explicit about the singer's private sex life (and Cash is not either), Cash very early on noted the temptations and he acknowledged that "I wrote 'I Walk the Line' when I was on the road in Texas in 1956, having a hard time resisting the temptation to be unfaithful to my wife back in Memphis."[16] Later critics have taken his song as a metaphor for the various lines he walked, but there would have been no need to "keep a close watch" on one's heart or to keep one's "eyes open all the time" if one was not married and facing the prospect of being unfaithful. Still, neither in his nor in Carter's autobiographies nor in *Winners Got Scars Too* are there any accounts that he was unfaithful to either Carter or Liberto, though James Mangold, director of *Walk the Line*, has said that the movie's scenes of infidelity were based on information he learned in interviews with Cash.[17]

That Cash also abused drugs was both a central issue in the breakup of his marriage and a core concern of his union with Carter: "My first marriage was in trouble when I lived in California, and I have to take the blame for that—because no woman can live with a man who's strung out on amphetamines. My first wife put up with me for years after I was hooked, but I'd go home and try to put all the blame for it on her."[18] He made an additional reference to his inadequacies as a father when he recounted that the day after he received honors from the Kennedy Center, his "daughters got together with me and voiced some very deep feelings they'd had for a very long time—told me things, that is, about the lives of girls whose daddy abandoned them for a drug."[19]

If it's possible, Carter had had a much less traditional existence up to that point than Cash, having spent her entire life performing as part of the Carter Family. She grew up in Nashville, and in Richmond, Virginia, where she went to high school, and moved to New York later, where she took acting lessons from Sanford Meisner at the Neighborhood Playhouse. As an actor and entertainer she worked on Jackie Gleason's and Dean Martin's TV shows and eventually costarred with Zsa Zsa Gabor in the movie *Country Music Holiday* in 1958.[20] By her own account, Carter was an ambitious performer whose career was significant and active, both with her family and by herself, long before she hooked up with Cash. And her family remained legendary even in the 1960s, more than three decades since the they had first recorded in 1927. When Waylon Jennings, recording in Nashville early in his career, was invited to have dinner with the Carters, he called it "an even bigger thrill than having my records cut. It was like being given the Holy Grail."[21] Before she married Cash, Carter had married twice and had two children, Carlene and Rose, one with each husband, Carl Smith and Rip Nix. According to both Cash and Carter, they had loved each other for some time before they married. Although much is made of about Cash's jest when they first met in 1956 that he would marry her, at that point he was joking. By the early 1960s, however, both knew they had strong feelings for each other, feelings that Carter said she turned into the song "Ring of Fire" (with Merle Kilgore). Because they were both married, their falling in love indeed did have the potential to be "a burning ring of fire." As DeCurtis writes, the song "is the story of those first, overwhelming feelings of danger, lust and love." He quotes Carter's confirmation that it was about Cash: "I never talked much about how I fell in love with John. . . . And I certainly didn't tell him how I felt. It was not a convenient time for me to fall in love with him—and it wasn't a convenient time for him to fall in love with me." Carter gave the song to her sister Anita to record, but Cash said he knew it was about them and that their divorces would follow and that they would "go through hell" before they could marry.[22]

Anita Carter's version of the song is otherworldly, mystical, and mysterious, with none of the irony of the mariachi trumpets framing Cash's version. Indeed, in his, the narrator sounds pleased about the state of affairs, whereas the narrator in Anita Carter's version sounds almost distraught. June Carter had more difficulty during this period than Cash did. For him, "the 'ring of fire' was not the hell. That was kind of a sweet fire. The ring of fire that I found myself in with June was the fire of redemption. It cleansed. It made me believe everything was all right, because it felt so good."[23] But the lyrics, indicate no such levels of discourse: "Love is a burning thing / and it makes a fiery ring / bound by wild desire / I fell into a ring of fire" does not suggest "the sweetness" that Cash described.

The fact of their marriage, however, soon rendered this issue less important: Cash's and Carter's lives became even more intertwined, both professionally and personally, and the story of their marriage—

perhaps because of their religious devotion—ceased to be a topic of ongoing public interest. Of course DeCurtis's interview, Mangold's movie, and their deaths so close together in 2003 drew more attention. That may have something to do with the way journalism works, that "good news" or no news is itself less reportable. But it also may have to do with Cash's retreat from the front pages of the music industry, fueled in part, some say, by the religious impulses that he and June developed at the height of his comeback.

TRADITIONAL MARRIAGE, CELEBRITY MARRIAGE

Cash's preproposal to Carter gives us some insight into the dominant status of marriage in American culture in the 1950s. It has changed some today, yet according to census figures, more than 65 percent of adults over fifteen have been married. And that Cash and Carter both married again after unsuccessful marriages is easily understood from personal and cultural vantage points. Even in 1992, with divorce rates often hitting 50 percent, a survey among high school students named marriage as the most important goal in life, just edging out finding steady work.[24] In American culture, the default adult relationship is marriage, through which all relationships are categorized: the absence of marriage (single, must try to get married), anticipated marriage (engaged), married, married but in a failing marriage (separated), once married but no longer (widowed or divorced). Of these six possible states, five have definitively to do with marriage, and we assume that the sixth, being single, is an unstable state. So it is not surprising that Carter and Cash ultimately defined their relationship by marriage, even in a celebrity culture that often chronicles the demise of relationships as much as it celebrates new ones.

Nor was it surprising that Carter did much of the public work of defining her marriage to Cash. In American culture, women have traditionally faced heavier burdens of expectation for marriage, even though, as Karla B. Hackstaff shows, "the ideology of gender equality has increasingly contested the reigning ideology of male dominance in marriage."[25] Even in the song "Ring of Fire," Cash construed their love outside of marriage as a "sweet fire," whereas Carter recalled driving fast around

Nashville, wondering about the relationship's viability. For women especially, marriage can be the proverbial double-edged sword. American
culture pushes marriage so insistently on women that it can seem an
end goal in itself. And even the culture at large sees women as the natural consumers of marriage; there are magazines for brides but not for
grooms, fewer groom shops than stores for brides. Of course, Carter's
career was such that these rules did not apply to her, but she did eventually accept a reduced career to become Mrs. Johnny Cash.

At the time Carter and Cash were getting married, women were
acquiring more legal rights and the institution of marriage was under-
going a legal and cultural revolution.[26] This is not to say that marriage's
prominence in American culture was behind the Cash-Carter nuptials,
at least not directly. Indeed, in their world of celebrity, social norms
were often flouted; Cash's rampant drug use was considered something
of an industry hazard rather than a dismissible offense. Still, the institution of marriage itself carries enormous weight within American culture, even among those who shape its content, as Cash and Carter did.

On the other hand, celebrity marriages contain both traditional and
nontraditional elements. By necessity, they combine conservative social
customs with a libertarian streak; neither spouse can really remain at
home, and they often kiss strangers as part of their jobs. These marriages do mean something, but a staple of celebrity marriages is their
instability, and such instability drives celebrity journalism—what would
gossip magazines have looked like in the last few years had Brad Pitt and
Jennifer Anniston remained married? In what Eugene Robinson calls
"Celebrity World" (a world that feels like a small town only with more
up-to-date fashion), women are also the center of attention.[27] Here too
women face the burden of having to serve in multiple, often contradictory roles. In Celebrity World, famous women have to seem both glamorous and accessible in order to remain popular in the public eye.

Marriage is still the goal, but marriage is difficult to manage as a career
move. In theory, women fans can both identify with the domestic every-
dayness of a wife and aspire to the glamour of red carpet fashions and
limousines. But if female movie stars are in happy marriages, perhaps
their fans' vicarious lives are less traditional. With the advent of *InStyle*
and other magazines increasingly geared toward celebrity married life,

perhaps attitudes are changing; still, the treatment of marriage as an end goal is reinforced by celebrity media, particularly by such publications as the *National Enquirer* and the *Star*. Celebrity magazines often gear their coverage toward women. The *Star*, one of the most aggressive chroniclers of Celebrity World, is decidedly feminine in its design and seemingly aimed toward women in its content. Its dominant colors are pink, lavender, and purple, stereotypically feminine colors; it focuses on relationships and fashion, and bases its coverage on stereotypical ideas about women's interests. Articles that deal with relationships are often focused on women and their desires. Some of this is strikingly gender-biased; an article in the *Star* in 2005 had the dubious trend story that women stars from Australia seem to want to have children soon. There were no equivalent stories about men.

Indeed, celebrity magazines and celebrity coverage in general do not focus on men's roles as husbands as much as they do on men's roles in culture. Cash's role as a husband was something we did not think much about when he was on stage flipping the bird or as the author of "Folsom Prison Blues." Yet for the last thirty-odd years of her life, Carter was known almost exclusively as Cash's wife. She had had a prominent career as a musician and actress, but her identity was fused with Cash's by practice *and* by name after they married; whereas Cash remained Johnny Cash, she referred to herself as June Carter Cash (a change from her previous marriages, where she had remained June Carter).

The Cash-Carter marriage displayed some of the usual elements of showbiz marriages but also many elements that bespoke a traditional domesticity, which was the key to its public power and its acceptance by country music fans. According to Carter's own writings and interviews, they had a very traditional marriage, with Johnny the husband and June the doting wife. The two displayed a level of heightened domesticity. When one sees Cash and Carter riding around on their tour bus in *Johnny Cash: The Man, His World, His Music*, those scenes of domestic bliss are normalized by their ubiquity, yet if one thinks about it, the public is never privy to the actual details of anyone's life; reality shows, indeed, derive much of their popularity from the vicarious view of the intimate details of "normal" people's lives. When June Carter married Johnny Cash, she was trading one celebrity identity—as a member of the Carter Family—

for another, as Mrs. Johnny Cash. Indeed, Carter had already been a member of the Cash celebrity family for more than five years before marrying him and often brought her siblings and mother into the band, particularly her sister Helen. Once they were married, she became even more prominent as his wife. In one sense, there was little practical change, given her earlier place as a band member, but her status or stage did change, even if it was only to be called "my wife" by Cash.

And let's not forget the oddity of the mating dance: Cash listening to Carter growing up, the scene at the Opry where Cash preproposes and Carter preaccepts, Cash hiring Carter to be in his band, and—the oddest aspect—Carter cowriting "Ring of Fire" about her love for Cash, but giving it first to her sister to record, and then Cash recording it (probably guessing the story and reciprocating it as well), not to mention the fact that Cash later proposed and Carter accepted on stage. Even the way Carter helped Cash get off drugs bespeaks a world unfamiliar to us; as touring musicians they spent so much time together that she had an unprecedented awareness of his drug use. So even though they did their best to make their union seem normal to their audiences, the very fact of their audiences made such a stance untenable.

But Carter also took an unusual path as part of a celebrity marriage; she subsumed her desires in Cash's. In *Among My Klediments*, her first memoir, she talks about the need to have a clean house and dinner waiting for her husband. As Steven Nock points out, "Doing housework, earning a living, providing for the family, and caring for children are ways of demonstrating masculinity and femininity."[28] But in the celebrity marriage, traditional norms are to some extent subverted. Carter may have believed that a woman should have a clean house and dinner waiting for her husband, but given her chosen profession, she was rarely home; more important, neither was he. . . . Cash said in *Man in Black* that he was not going to tour without Carter, so they hired a nurse to help with the children and continued to tour, even heading to Israel to film *The Gospel Road* when their son, John Carter, was just a baby.[29] Clearly, problematic domestic arrangements in non-celebrity, nonaffluent families are not as easily solved.

Because celebrity marriages can sometimes be performances, even some media people pondered whether their love was authentic. Writing in *Redbook*, Dorothy Gallagher, in an exchange with a sound man, questioned the Cash-Carter public display:

> "June takes my breath when she goes," John had said to the audience when his wife left the stage.
> "Do you think all that was for real?" I asked the sound man.
> "I've seen a lot of people do that kind of thing," he said. "And when people don't like each other, they can't really look at each other. Those two look."[30]

That *Redbook* magazine wanted to confirm the authenticity of the marriage—and especially the performance of the marriage—speaks to both the desire for audiences to believe in celebrity marriage, and their doubts about its reality.

CHRISTIAN MARRIAGE

The Cash-Carter marriage was explicitly Christian, at least according to Carter. In *Among My Klediments* she tied her role as wife to Christian values in a way that was endorsed by the cultural world in which she lived. Indeed, as she recounts, Dr. Nat Winston, the Tennessee commissioner of mental health, suggested that she would have to whip her "problem"—that is, her autonomy—to make the marriage successful. He told her, "You're too independent. . . . If you want your marriage to work, you're going to have to do some switching of your priorities." She mulled this over, and decided: "I would starve, but I would starve by Johnny Cash. I would no longer lead. He would make the decisions, and I would follow him. Mistakes or trials—we would face them all together." She wrote to resign from the Grand Ole Opry, where she had been playing for seventeen years, as a measure of her trust and submission: "There had been security in being with the Opry, but from now on my security would come from God and Johnny Cash. I sent John a copy of the letter."[31]

Her change of heart involved more than leaving the Opry, however. Carter was prepared to leave her solo career behind as well: "Earlier I mentioned that I had always had great ambition. Now I began to realize just how dangerous ambition can be, especially for a wife and mother. There is only one way to be happy—put God first in your life. He has laid down a plan for woman that is a sure way for happiness—God first, husband second, and children next." She believed that "a young wife eaten up with ambition can easily lose this order of things. I speak with authority on this subject, because that is exactly what I did. But through prayer and faith and finally a total commitment to God, I found out that ambition is all vanity." Reading this passage from a nondenominational perspective, and indeed typing it into my computer on a commuter train full of working women, makes it difficult to reconcile her words with modern ideas or even the life and career she led before her marriage. Indeed, she still loved performing after the marriage but put it in a different perspective: "There is nothing quite so thrilling as being on that stage and singing a song with John and being part of his life in every way. But God is first, John second, and third is the sacred trust of raising our children." She says, "I haven't stopped to think about the old ambition in years, and the emptiness is gone."[32]

Carter's ideas about marriage here clearly connect to Christian doctrine; as Michael G. Lawler writes in his book *Family: American and Christian*, "spouses will find the themes and values to inform their judgments about Christian marriage and family specifically in the Letter to the Ephesians."[33] In Ephesians 5, Paul writes about the spousal order of marriage: "Wives, be subject to your husbands, as to the Lord. For the husband is the head of the wife as Christ is the head of the church, his body, and is himself its Savior. As the church is subject to Christ, so let wives also be subject in everything to their husbands." It puts the onus on the husbands not to take advantage of this submission, however: "Husbands, love your wives, as Christ loved the church and gave himself up for her, that he might sanctify her, having cleansed her by the washing of water with the word, that he might present the church to himself in splendor, without spot or wrinkle or any such thing, that she might be holy and without blemish." Some of this behavior should be attached specifically to Christian faith: "Even so husbands should love their wives as their own bodies. He who loves his wife loves himself. For no man ever hates his own flesh, but nourishes and cherishes it, as Christ does the church, because we are members of his body."[34]

Trying to decide whether Cash and Carter were attempting to act out this letter is folly, but one can certainly see the Christian underpinnings of Carter's writings.

In accordance with these beliefs, her submission to Cash seemed complete. In a later section of the book she gave advice on homemaking, on "family worship time," and on how deal with one's husband. She offered a solution to arguing with a husband and controlling one's temper in particular: "If you have a temper try this. Always give thanks to God in all things. If you are so angry at your husband that you can't stand the sight of him, get alone—or pray silently—and say over and over, 'Praise God, and thank You God.'" Such an approach, she suggested, would head off further disagreement: "It's hard for a husband to continue to be mad at you if you aren't throwing harsh words back at him. A sweet smile and a word of encouragement could easily turn the tide."[35]

Without being too obvious here, such an approach did not involve much dialogue and suggested a less than equal relationship. Cash saw arguing in a different (but not contradictory) perspective: "She's the easiest woman in the world for me to live with, I guess because I know her so well and she knows *me* so well, and we get along handsomely. If it looks like there's going to be some tension between us, we talk it out and work it out, or I take a walk and she takes a drive until it's over."[36] In the same section of advice giving, Carter also said she believed that married couples should have a healthy sex life: "I can remember thinking that *sex* must be a dirty three-letter word. But an attitude like that is a hindrance to a good marriage. Sex is to be enjoyed and to perpetuate the human race." There was one area that Carter had more difficulty in reconciling with Christian doctrine—her multiple marriages and, especially, her divorces: "People ask me, 'How can you claim to know God the way you do when you've been married three times?'" Her short answer was that she believed God had forgiven her for the divorces: "It's because of the forgiving grace of God and because of Jesus Christ that I can claim the promise He gave me. Because of the love of Christ and His death on the cross, this sinner claimed His promise, was forgiven, and is a child of God." She does, however, blame her divorces on her "lack of faith": "If I had the faith and commitment in the beginning, I could probably have saved my first marriage. It wasn't that I didn't believe in God, because I have believed in Him since I was a child. It was because I did not ask His help when I needed it so desperately."[37]

She did observe, however, that church institutions had been less will-

ing to forgive than God: "The Christian church has always forgiven mur-
derers, thieves, and other sinners, but just couldn't find it in their hearts
to forgive the terrible sin of divorce. Divorce was high on the scale of
unforgivables, somewhere way up there out of sight. And if you had to
live through it, you also lived with the terrible guilt that was part of it all.
We Christians cannot ignore it any more; there are millions of divorces in
the world today, and unfortunately many of them involve Christian
brothers and sisters." Cash made no mention of such questions being
addressed to him, and Carter may have been describing the more general
trend that Hackstaff references: "Rising divorce rates have often been
blamed on women." Still, she wrote of feeling "such sadness when I see
how easy it is to obtain a divorce these days. In years past, people stayed
married because of guilt, because of hundreds of years of tradition—for
many reasons. But the main thing was that they stayed married." Yet she
also believed that "they can't restore that broken marriage if they've
destroyed it—it's gone. They can't go back."[38]

Carter—echoed by Cash—was earnest and straightforward here, with
no irony; people read Cash's and Carter's faith as folksy, but they likely
meant it sincerely. Though they were nondenominational, Carter's defer-
ence was in keeping with the beliefs of Southern Baptists. Long after she
wrote her first autobiography, the church amended its statement of
beliefs, the *Baptist Faith and Message Statement,* to make the wife's defer-
ence to her husband part of doctrine. Christian Smith quotes the statement as saying that a woman should "submit herself graciously" to her
husband, and that the husband should "provide for, protect, and lead his
family." But Smith goes on to point out that the reality of relationships
with the man as head of the family is more ambiguous: "Most evangelicals are quite comfortable with the idea that the husband should be head
of the family. They believe the Bible teaches this, and they very much
want to take it seriously." But "most ordinary evangelicals are also very
comfortable thinking about marriage as an equal partnership. They stress
the need for mutual respect and participation in the relationship. They
conspicuously avoid talk of wifely submission."[39] This is a crucial paradox—how does one be both subservient (or dominant) *and* equal?

Cash never mentioned the head-of-household issue in any interview
I've read or in his two autobiographies. Part of that omission undoubt-

edly has to do with the gender divide between how much men, compared with women, talk about marriage, which stereotypically at least is very little. But the Cash-Carter marriage was in fact a partnership, even though Carter did give up her solo career to join Cash's band (before they married), and resign from the Opry. And even though Carter may have been absorbed into Cash's career, he continued to value her as a performer: "She's a vital performer, and it's vital for me to have her in my concerts."[40] Both of them ultimately credit God, Cash's will, and Nat Winston (in that order) for Cash's ability to get off drugs, but Carter began the process of throwing pills away in the face of often fierce resistance from Cash. So as Smith postulates, the Carter-Cash marriage was likely more complicated than Carter's account suggests.

On Cash's end, he did express himself directly about his love for Carter but did not write about his spousal role. In *Cash*, he spent three full pages extolling her virtues: "I wish the whole world could know how great she is. She's smart and she's brilliant. She's got a great personality. She's easy to live with, because she makes it a point to be so. She's loving. She's sharing. . . . June is formidable; she's my solid rock. She's my spark plug. . . . She's got charm, she's got brains, she's got style, she's got class." Of course, he also displayed the stereotypical masculine view of women as shoppers: "She's got silver, she's got gold, she's got jewelry, she's got furniture, she's got china, . . . she's got a black belt in shopping." Only one comment references their Christianity: "She and I have become so very close, so intimate. I think it might be because of all her prayer."[41] Did he mean her prayers about submitting to avoid fighting? Overall, the Christianity that they both expressed so readily seemed to apply more specifically to Carter's role in the marriage, which was not inconsistent with the greater responsibility women generally seem to have in American marriages.

THEIR MUSICAL MARRIAGE

Carter represented a tradition of music that grew from both organic and commercial concerns, a tie to some of the beginnings of country music through the legendary Carter Family, which country music historian Bill Malone calls one of country music's "most influential acts." The Carters, led by A. P. Carter and Sara, June's aunt, had a crucial role in recording and disseminating country music, some of which existed in the public domain; other music they wrote themselves. They came to the commercial music scene in 1927 when Ralph Peer first recorded them in Bristol, Tennessee, not far from the current location of the Carter Compound in southwestern Virginia.[42] Some of their classic recordings include renditions of "Will the Circle Be Unbroken?" "Daddy Sang Bass," and "Keep on the Sunny Side!" They remained a vital presence in country music well into the twentieth century, both on their own and as part of the Cash band.

As part of the Carter Family, June sang on stage as soon as she was old enough to walk; they appeared as a group many times at the Grand Ole Opry. In country music, they were royalty of sorts, representing a tradition geared toward, as Malone said, "home and stability."[43] Combine that with Cash's penchant for musical mayhem, and one has either a perfect union of complements or something quite mismatched. In fact, the linking of musical styles, between the remaining Carters and Cash gave the former some modern cachet and Cash a link to tradition—neither of which would matter all that much when the Nashville sound grew in importance in the 1970s and passed them both by. But as Rita Forrester and Flo Wolfe, two of June Carter's cousins, told me when I visited the Carter Compound in 2008, Johnny Cash was crucial in helping to keep the compound going today.[44]

This musical marriage could have been immaterial to the rest of their marriage had Cash not found it difficult to separate his musical life from his personal one. In an interview with Bill Friskics-Warren, he talked about how the Carters became his extended family in all senses, with his parents in California and his difficulties in Nashville kicking drugs: "I was spending a lot of time with the Carters because they were people who truly cared for me, as did June. . . . So it was their love and care for me, and the musical influence, and the musical sharing, eventually, with all of them, that was very binding. And we're all still kind of bound up that way."[45] And as Alicia C. Levin notes, incorporating Cash into the Carter clan gave him a renewed authenticity that enhanced his folk-collecting efforts in the 1960s, making him singularly appreciative of the similar role the Carter family had played (though they were not as self-consciously archival) when they made their recordings in the 1920s and 1930s, the time of Cash's initial musical indoctrination. Cash employed the Carter

Family and the Statler Brothers (soon to be the authors of a nostalgia-draped song themselves, "Do You Remember These") to sing "Will the Circle Be Unbroken?" an old folk song that became a Carter Family staple. In doing so, the families merged—Cash, the Carter Family, and the Statler Brothers—into a musical group that looked to the future by celebrating the past.[46] Leigh Edwards points out that the idea of stability in the Carters' relationship with home was an "extensive fabrication"[47] in the sense that the Carters as much as any other musical group spent time on the road and had complicated family arrangements (including the Cash-Carter courtship). Still, the home they created on stage meshed perfectly with Cash's new idea of bringing domesticity on the road with him.

More important, Cash and Carter made notable music together. The pair won two Grammys: the first in 1967 for "Jackson," and the second in 1970 for "If I Were a Carpenter." Though these songs were not archival in nature and were not written by either Cash or Carter, they do form an interesting commentary on the oddity of celebrity connections. The first, recorded when they were not publicly a couple (it had previously been recorded by the Kingston Trio), spoke of "getting married" in a fever / hotter than a pepper sprout," but he talks about going to Jackson because "the fire went out." Cash and Carter sang "If I Were a Carpenter" right after he proposed to her on stage; the lyric follows the title question with "and you were my lady, would you marry me anyway, would you have my baby?"

Though there's no indication that Cash married Carter for anything but love, part of why he loved her must have involved her level of understanding of music and musical tradition. In other words, theirs was a celebrity marriage that actually enhanced a medium, brought traditions together, and made them compelling listening.

VIVIAN LIBERTO, A GENDERED COURTSHIP, AND ALTERNATIVE NARRATIVES

What the film *Walk the Line* failed to show was that there were *two* love stories. Liberto's book *I Walked the Line*, released posthumously, showed the love story between John and Vivian in a way much more literal and concrete than the visual imagery shown by Cash and Carter in their performances and in their autobiographies. And from Cash's letters, a portrait of a man working through traditional ideas of gender and marriage emerges. What the memoir also displayed was the other side of the Cash-Carter romance—the story of Liberto and Cash's romance and divorce, which offered another view of the role of June Carter.

Liberto's memoir has two parts—a traditional narrative and a reprinting of Cash's letters to her. They include some photographs of letters as well, perhaps as a way of authenticating the material. Both parts go a long way toward destabilizing our ideas about Cash and his two marriages. The letters show him courting Vivian in an openly affectionate but frankly patronizing way. He urged her to "be a nice girl" in a 1952 letter. And he told her, "I always put girls that smoke, drink, and curse all in one class. You know the class." When discussing how they should behave once they were married, he wrote, "Darling, what do you mean that you hope there's nothing wrong with moderate drinking when you're married. . . . But I don't believe in it, so it's wrong for me, and I won't do it at all." These sentiments were part of a more generalized idea of gender: "Women are supposed to be mothers and teachers. They're minding the future of the world. . . . If you're in doubt about something, leave it alone, or as *our* God's Bible says, 'Shun the very appearance of evil.'" And finally, an ultimatum: "It's either our love, or your social drinks."[48] Yet among all these letters are accounts of his drinking, sometimes heavily, and so one can also see a double standard at work. As Liberto pointed out, when Cash started drinking after they married, "all of the things that Johnny had called 'filthy and dirty' and had insisted would destroy our lives were things he began to embrace."[49]

Liberto presented the letters without much comment; that, she saved for June Carter. To put it mildly, she offered a counternarrative that placed the onus on Carter for breaking up her marriage; it contrasts markedly from the one presented by Mangold in *Walk the Line*. She began by describing her first meeting with Carter, claiming that June showed her diamond ring and said, "Look, with every husband, my diamond gets bigger," a reference to her second marriage. Liberto wrote, "If she were the type of woman to judge a marriage by the size of a diamond, I thought, she would judge a man by the measure of his success. And Johnny was ripe for picking." She attributed Cash's increase in drinking to Carter's joining the tour. "With Johnny, I noticed a drastic change soon after June joined the tour. His drinking escalated uncontrollably and he began taking all sorts of pills." In fact, she continued, "The breathless assertions that June saved Johnny from drugs are simply not true. Our family knows it's not true. And it takes the credit away from Johnny, who got himself off the drugs. It was a story that made her look good, and it made them both look good to the world to say that, but like a lot of stories floated out there, it wasn't accurate. I know, and others do too, that she had a drug problem of her own for the duration of their marriage."[50]

She wrote that Cash's daughters told her stories about Carter's own drug taking: "They described her arriving at the breakfast table, incoherent and confused, eyebrow pencil scrawled over her forehead, clearly not 'right.' And as the years went on they would tell me of June passing out or fainting from taking too many pills. Or passing out cold in the middle of them having a conversation with her. Or her saying things that didn't make sense—like the time she was certain she had zebras in her head."[51] John Carter Cash confirms in his own memoir that June Carter did indeed use drugs but places their use later than Liberto does. He also acknowledges that their marriage was not as strong as it seemed: "There *had* been many times when they had nearly given up on their marriage."[52]

Liberto also described a different scenario about "Ring of Fire," Carter's signature song. She said that Cash told her, "I'm gonna give June half credit on a song I just wrote. . . . It's called 'Ring of Fire.'" Liberto even disputes the meaning of the song: "To this day, it confounds me to hear the elaborate details June told of writing that song for Johnny. She didn't write that song any more than I did. The truth is, Johnny wrote that song, while pilled up and drunk, about a certain private female body part. All those years of her claiming she wrote it herself, and she probably never knew what the song was really about."[53]

In short, Liberto contradicted a number of crucial aspects of the Carter-Cash legend, including the dynamic of their relationship, the drug use, and the artistic production of one of June Carter's signature achievements (which *Walk the Line* takes liberties with—it has Carter producing the song in the mid-1960s instead of a few years earlier). Liberto's narration has the ring of truth, but it's not, of course, an unbiased source. Still, there are no unbiased sources in a celebrity marriage or divorce; everyone has a stake in what he or she sees as the truth. In this case, Liberto's revelations were not surprising either in their content or in their production, and they seem unlikely to seriously dent the enduring story of Cash and Carter, which has been told in many outlets and many forms, and in whose service, Reese Witherspoon won an Oscar. But that does not mean they are not true.

CODA

Carter actually did have a second solo career: for *Press On* in 1999, she won a Grammy; *Wildwood Flower* was released posthumously in 2004. She also played Momma alongside Robert Duvall in his film *The Apostle* in 1997. But her attitude about marriage and her role in it changed little over time. As late as 1999, she told *USA Today*: "I chose to be Mrs. Johnny Cash in my life. I decided I'd allow him to be Moses and I'd be Moses' brother Aaron, picking his arms up and paddling along behind him. I stayed in submission to my husband, and he allowed me to do anything I wanted to. I felt like I was lucky to have that kind of romance."[54] The allusion to both brothers in a Bible story and the acknowledgment of Cash's leadership role even in this context remain striking, especially in light of modern conceptions of women's roles and of Carter's own legacy as a performer. At a concert to celebrate her album *Press On*, she said, "I've been real happy paddling along after John, being Mrs. Johnny Cash all these years. But I'm sure thrilled to be up here singing for you tonight." "It was just a choice I made," she said, to Bill Friskics-Warren, who adds, "sounding less like a submissive homemaker in the Phyllis Schlafly mold than like a woman who knows her own mind."[55] Whether she was a devoted wife as well as a feminist, only Carter knew, but the possibility raises one further interpretation that is difficult to dismiss: was Carter's expressed Christian submissiveness a form of humility, traditionally a southern way of deflecting one's own importance? Her pre-marriage reaction to Cash's move-making at the Grand Ole Opry bespeaks a woman who knows the ways of the world and knows how to deflect attention from herself and her own desires. Is any of her rhetoric here in the same vein?[56]

In a review of a 1988 concert, Jon Pareles in the *New York Times* shows that Carter was fully aware of her place both in the marriage and in the larger world: "A few love duets later, she talked about watching Elvis Presley put nickels in jukeboxes to hear her future husband sing 'those low notes,' and said that in more than 20 years of marriage: 'We've had some rough times, too. You do get *The National Enquirer* up here, don't you?' Then the Cashes sang a duet about fidelity, written by their son-in-law Nick Lowe, called 'Where Did We Go Right?'"[57] The self-referentiality on a number of levels is striking. Carter commented on tabloid reports *in order to acknowledge their truth*, dismisses their importance, and then sings a song about fidelity, all while referencing Elvis, who allegedly wooed her—all as a way of drawing attention to the longevity of her and her husband's careers—not to mention that the song was by Lowe, who had divorced their daughter. (Lowe's work shows up memorably on *American Recordings*, where Cash covers his "The Beast in Me.") Can something or someone be postmodern if being a character in a larger drama of celebrityhood is a default mode? Like most postmodern questions, it remains open.

Carter never lost her self-imposed mate-of-an-icon status. Even when she died in 2003, her obituaries celebrated her marriage as much as her career. *People* said that her death "marked both the passing of a legend and the end of a fabled romance." Even the obituary's title, "Johnny's Angel," suggested possession."[58] (Of course, the next article in the magazine was about the growing role of grooms in planning a marriage; it was titled "Groomzillas!")

5
CASH CHOOSES (NOT TO CHOOSE) VIETNAM

In 1969, Johnny Cash told the story about his involvement in the Vietnam War in front of an enthusiastic crowd at Madison Square Garden. He recounted a conversation he had with a reporter after returning from visiting troops in Vietnam. "That makes you a hawk, doesn't it?" asked the reporter. Cash told the audience that he answered, "'No, no, that don't make me a hawk.' But I said if you watch the helicopters bring in the wounded boys, and then you go into the wards and sing for 'em and try and do your best to cheer 'em up, so they can get back home, it might make you a dove with claws." He then launched into a cover of Ed McCurdy's "Last Night I Had the Strangest Dream," a song about ending war.[1]

The image of a "dove with claws" is striking—the symbol of peace fused with a symbol of aggression. On one level, the image makes little sense—Cash later called the metaphor "stupid"—as indeed doves already *have* claws; it's the equivalent of talking about a dog with paws. But as an imaginary symbol, perhaps a small peaceful bird with extended oversize claws, ready to defend or attack as necessary, it works better. Maybe when he described himself as this kind of dove, he meant that he sought peace aggressively.[2]

This problematic metaphor is apt for Cash's own ventures into the world of popular politics in the 1960s and 1970s, ventures that were decidedly ambiguous in their orientation toward the traditional poles of liberal and conservative. Leigh Edwards calls this political ambiguity a contradictory element meant to keep audiences from characterizing the performer: Cash "is striking for his consistency in refusing to resolve binary tensions, in the depth and longevity of his exploration of those binaries in a range of American themes, and in the degree and longevity of this incorporation of that irresolvable tension into his media image."[3] In that respect, Cash was successful. He was an outspoken defender of the downtrodden throughout the decade of the 1960s, but he never fully connected with more prominent forms of protest. *Bitter Tears* chronicled the Native American plight in 1964, and he played prisons in the late 1950s and throughout the 1960s, culminating in *At Folsom Prison* and *At San Quentin*. Only *Bitter Tears* could definitively be called protest; still, because playing at prisons helped bring attention to the plight of inmates there, one could certainly classify the prison concerts as protest albums. He also recast his use of black. Earlier commentators had noted his tendency to wear black, labeling him the "Man in Black." In 1970, Cash redefined the label to denote into a crusader who wears black to protest injustice of almost every sort. (Later he refined it as indicative of his religious faith.) Such liberal-seeming associations allowed general audiences to at least commercially endorse him—he sold more albums than practically anyone else in the late 1960s.[4]

But soon after Cash visited the troops in Vietnam, he played at the White House and, despite not playing songs that Richard Nixon requested, said he would "stand behind him." He was also associated with country music, and although he did not always confirm that association, it was generally considered a politically conservative genre. And in 1974 he wrote and recorded *Ragged Old Flag*, whose title cut is unabashedly patriotic.

Such political stances seem more profound in retrospect. But as Jim Hightower quipped in the title to his book, "There's nothing in the middle of the road but yellow lines and dead armadillos," and Cash's famed ambiguity sometimes got him in trouble with his audiences. For the generally liberal audience that adopted him because of the prison albums, there was little liberal about his Vietnam stance, especially given the tenor of the discourse coming from popular music artists and critics. In other words, Cash may have been liberal but not in the terms of the liberal consensus at the time. On the other hand, his prison concerts and endorsement of Native American rights and the decidedly democratic nature of his television show may have given his conservative, classic country audience pause. At the same time, Cash in this period seemed hyperaware of his audiences, perhaps because of his raised national profile in an era when the relationship between politics and music itself had become important. Indeed, many of our mental pictures of the 1960s include not only seminal political figures like Martin Luther King Jr. and John F. Kennedy but also Bob Dylan, Jimi Hendrix, and Janis Joplin. And many locate the end of Memphis's importance in the music world not by the diminishing importance of Sun and Stax production or the death of Elvis Presley but by the assassination of King in 1968.

An example of this hyperawareness came at the 1969 Madison Square Garden concert, where Cash unsubtly used his songs as a sort of biography of himself and his region, highlighting the differences between him and his audience by assuming New Yorkers' lack of geographic and agricultural knowledge of "the flat black delta land of Arkansas." Cash knew his New York audience would receive his stories about Vietnam differently and more receptively than did audiences in the South. In his recorded prison concerts from this period, he did not mention Vietnam at all. At least with some audiences, Cash was a man involved not only in a "war on war," as the band Wilco put it, but also in a war with himself over what his stance should be. Indeed, the "dove with claws" remark shows a man likely worried about alienating his primary country music audience but also willing to break with the rank-and-file patriotism and war support of most country musicians. Cash's politics reflected in many ways his indeterminacy and perhaps fluidity as a musician. One cannot know whether this was a strategy to appeal to many audiences, though over time, it certainly has had that effect: Republicans *and* Democrats and their related institutions have seemed to love him, whatever his actual politics.

One measure of a noncountry, East Coast audience's engagement with Cash and his politics was his increased coverage in the *New York Times*. Although the *Times* and Cash might seem an odd pairing, they both benefited from it; Cash received the more universal recognition he sought, and the *Times* could show its open-mindedness about the culture beyond the eastern establishment. Like other observers, the *Times* saw Cash as authentic, and Cash tried to show that his mixed politics was less a reaction to his primary audience than a definitive ambiguity. That this did not work underscores how difficult the political climate was, even for an entertainer with two hit albums and a national television show. It also might have hinted, if Cash had read the coverage, that his ideal audience might not be a country one but one that saw the greater symbolism of what he meant to do.

This is a difficult chapter when it comes to authenticity and choice—it requires speculation into the motives of Cash and his relationship to his audience. If he was a product to be sold to various demographics, he faced a real problem, because his newfound popularity had introduced or reintroduced him to a number of audiences. Was his ambiguous belief real? On one level, of course—that's how we know about it. Was it calculated? That's a tougher question. Did Cash take his audience into account when making a decision rather than consulting his beliefs? We run into trouble in analyzing a performer, because deciding what is real and recognizing what is performed naturally come in conflict. As the popularity of Cash's prison albums represented a rare moment of cultural unity when they climbed the charts, so did he represent an instability of cultural unity in a country made fractious by a controversial war that seemed to shape not only Cash's political efforts in regard to war but even later political discourse related to him.[5] And you might notice that this chapter is not about a "choice to" but rather "choices to" or "a choice not to." Cash could not choose without alienating one of his audiences. So he did not. The failed metaphor of a dove with claws also suggests that there was nothing elemental about his decisions here. His new success and a political environment placed him beyond any path toward informed simplicity.

CASH AND THE POLITICAL 1960s

Before the 1960s there is very little record of Cash's political background but enough biographical and creative material to let us know that he had at least already thought about class. He moved at an early age to a government colony, part of a New Deal program that allowed farmers to apply for land and support. Ray Cash, Johnny's father, was a lucky recipient of one such parcel in what became known as the Dyess Colony. Tom Smucker, in his obituary of Cash in the *Village Voice*, speculates that he never forgot the government program that gave his family sustenance in a difficult time: "If you look at Cash's work, you see the New Deal all over it. There are all the country virtues of family and hard work and religion, and the post-war energies of upward mobility and modernization. But

there's also the New Deal feeling for social justice, national unity, tolerance, and progress."[6] Although the New Deal has had a fairly traditional
left-right reception in the East and West, as Catherine McNicol Stock
discusses, radicalism in the Midwest and South has a number of different
strains that complicate traditional definitions of left and right.[7] Smucker
observes, that although Cash embraced the government's aid to his family's cause and the liberal sentiments behind it, this New Deal background
did not fully prepare him for the complexities of balancing his positions
on the Vietnam War with the political leanings of his long-standing country audience and his new broader one.

In the 1960s, Cash's main causes were prisons and Native American
rights. His decision to play in prisons reflects a reform element in his political leanings.[8] He was not specific about what he would do to change the
prison system, but his empathy and his commitment to that empathy
showed that he was aware of the injustice inherent in the American prison
system and that he had a desire to change the lives of its inmates. And it
was his sympathy with Native American causes that led him to record *Bitter Tears* and to bemoan the record industry's decision not to play it more.

Though Cash did not often discuss race outside of Native American
concerns, the stands he took led to difficult relationships with some of his
audiences. In his autobiographies, he left out a particularly telling incident
about his relationship to his southern audiences. At one point in the 1960s,
the Ku Klux Klan spread a rumor that Cash's wife, Vivian Liberto, was
African American. According to David Ragan's *The Great Johnny Cash*
(one of several fawning biographies published in the late 1960s and early
1970s), the rumor about Cash's wife "spread like a roaring forest fire
throughout the Southern states—and had its intended effect": some book-
ings were canceled, and record sales were affected. Christopher Wren
relates that some Klan members made death threats, including one in
Greenville, South Carolina, and that a Klan "wrecking crew" attempted to
grab Cash in Nashville. There was no obvious reason for the either the
rumors or the KKK reaction, though Wren speculates that it was "probably in retaliation against his outspokenness on behalf of American Indians, whom the Klan also worked hard to hate." Whatever the cause, Cash
responded by announcing he was suing the Klan for $25 million, saying
publicly, "What I resent is the attempt to make my children ashamed that

they were born. If there's a mongrel in the crowd, it's me, because I'm Irish and one-quarter Cherokee." (He later retracted this statement; though he believed he had Cherokee ancestry, he could never confirm it.) As Wren writes, Cash "recognized in the charge a calculated move to undercut his popularity where it was strongest, among white Southerners." He later decided against suing.[9]

Cash's response was based not only on his sense of justice but also on the possibility that his career might be affected. Obviously, the incident implicates the southerners who started and believed this rumor and suggests that the climate Cash faced when undertaking his protests about Vietnam in the late 1960s might not have been receptive to them. But it also suggests that he was aware of both commercial and social consequences associated with his politics. Why did he leave this incident out of both autobiographies? One can only speculate that he was still sensitive to audience reaction, but the awkward nature of his defense probably was a factor as well. Edwards notes that Cash's power dynamics—in both this and another incident when he was robbed at gunpoint in his Jamaican plantation house—were unstable.[10]

Because Vietnam triggered the most fervent protests of the 1960s, which began with students in mid-decade and spread to the entire country, everyone was seemingly forced to take a stand one way or the other. The protests largely came from the East and West Coasts; the South was less opposed, though as Gregg L. Michel points out, some southern college students did protest."[11] According to Dewey Grantham, "Though opposition to the Vietnam War damaged the Reserve Officer Training Corps in much of the country, ROTC programs continued to flourish in the South during that long war," perhaps because of what Grantham calls "the region's traditional military spirit."[12] But although southerners in particular were more likely to support the Vietnam War, New York City's Hard Hat Riots and subsequent protests in 1970 against antiwar demonstrators showed the tendency of the working class in general to be less radical in politics—though certainly rioting constitutes a radicalism of its own. Cash's background places him firmly in both groups, southerners and the working class, and yet, as his "dove with claws" remark suggests, while he may have been from them, he was not necessarily of them ideologically.

By 1969, given his cosmopolitan life, Cash had spent a great deal of time outside the South. And in writing "What Is Truth?" about the travails of youth in a world that looks only at surface appearances, he suggested that he understood the issues at play in American culture at the time. The question is whether Cash's ambivalent viewpoint about Vietnam was directed toward keeping his country music constituency or whether it reflected a true ambivalence about the war or some combination of the two. His protest against the war while supporting the troops, his complaints about prisons, his embracing of Native American causes all bespoke a man who understood injustice and cared about it. "Man in Black," written in 1971, is itself a protest song, done very much in the straightforward style of writers such as Harriet Beecher Stowe and John Steinbeck, and folk singers like Woody Guthrie, Joni Mitchell, and Bob Dylan. As the second stanza says, "I wear the black for the poor and the beaten down / Livin' in the hopeless, hungry side of town / I wear it for the prisoner who has long paid for his crime / But is there because he's a victim of the times."[13] Such lyrics were not so much a call to arms as a call to notice—again, radical in fashion but perhaps not in execution.

When Cash wrote about the Man in Black, he was deliberately reinventing himself. He had worn black at for at least a dozen years before he wrote the song—seemingly because it was cool, in the performer-having-to-look-cool sense; now he wore it because it was cool to protest. In his reinvention, Cash turned the semiotics of color to his advantage, switching his costume from the sympathetic bad man to a portrayal of the protester. Does this reinscription of the Man in Black make it less authentic? Or does it make him a more savvy observer of media participation in meaning making?

Whatever the answer, Vietnam clearly rattled Cash, as it put him in conflict with some audiences and, more important, set up clashes between his own competing values: peace, patriotism, Christianity, loyalty, freedom of expression. Any choice had consequences. That's why tracing his attitudes about the war is so tricky—he seemed to change his mind often before eventually settling on the stance that the dove with claws seemed to represent.

VIETNAM, THE *NEW YORK TIMES*, AND JOHNNY CASH

We know about Cash in this period because he generated or provoked lots of material—two autobiographies, two autobiographies by his wife, several biographies, and almost endless media interviews. But oddly enough, one of the best ongoing interpreters of Cash at the time was the *New York Times*. The *Times* holds an ambiguous and evolving place in American culture and history: it's an eastern media institution that leans left or center, depending on who observes it. To many, including observers from the right today, its stand on the Pentagon Papers in 1971 marked it as leftist. But in other ways, especially in its view on culture, the *New York Times* can be conservative; it seems always to be struggling with this perception because of its self-appointed and often culturally appointed place as the American newspaper of record. More important, it serves not only as a symbol of the liberal elite but also as a marker of how culturally important a subject or figure is. In other words, having the *New York Times* recognize you means you have arrived in the eyes of a certain audience. This fact bears mentioning because it parallels Cash's later relationship with National Public Radio, which engages a similar educated and culturally curious demographic.

Cash's relationship with the media was largely positive. He created an image that was compelling, and he had the gift of seeming forthright when dealing with members of the media. To a large extent, his image was that of an authentic man in a media-driven world. Part of his authenticity came from the fact that he spoke with a southern accent and wrote and performed a startling array of songs—some funny, some mournful, and some God-fearing. It also came because he did not sound like anyone else, spoke his mind (or seemed to) on controversial topics, and acted like a villain without actually being one.

When it first seriously chronicled Cash in the late 1960s, the *Times* was struggling to be modern; Cash's reemergence coincided with the newspaper's efforts to cover popular culture more completely, and the story of its coverage of Cash overlaps with the indeterminacy of Cash's politics. The *New York Times* certainly regarded Cash as a relevant figure in the late 1960s; its reporters wrote about his records, his concerts, and his visit to the White House, in addition to several feature stories.

The *New York Times* and other media outlets rediscovered Cash just after his new audiences did. He was almost unrecognized by the media in the mid-1960s, with only thirty-six mentions in the *Times* between 1965 and 1967 and no articles about him specifically, save for a brief mention that he had been arrested in El Paso for drug possession. But between 1968 and 1970, he was mentioned more than 250 times, and more than a dozen articles specifically about him appeared, including full-length features in both the *Times* and the *Times Magazine*. There were another 200 mentions between 1971 and 1973.[14]

This attention reflected not only Cash's newsworthiness but also a conscious effort by the *Times* to position itself as more nationally oriented in its coverage of popular culture. The interests of both were served equally with this attention: the *Times* sought an audience outside of the North, while Cash sought one outside of the South. Choosing Cash as a subject came as a result of the growing national reputation initiated by his two prison albums and, more than likely, the perception that he was different from other country musicians. The *New York Times* likely read his indeterminacy as a type of authenticity.

The *Times* coverage of Cash was also part of its efforts to define culture more broadly in the wake of the exploding changes in popular culture. In 1962 it created the position of cultural news editor, under the aegis of the news editor, who was supposed to expand the role of the *Times* in covering cultural events beyond theater and movie reviews. In 1968, the newspaper hired a dedicated stringer to cover rock and folk music (even though one editor wrote in a memo that the stringer, Mike Jahn, "looks like a werewolf").[15] So when Cash reemerged in 1968, the *Times* was more prepared to receive him than it had been in the earlier phases of his career. And although it treated Cash with respect, it treated his fans somewhat differently; in a number of the pieces, the writers clearly felt superior to Cash's country music audiences, apparently saying that only they truly understood Cash's intellectual ("real") appeal and that traditional country fans were not as savvy. One can see here why reception or audience interpretation plays such a large role in understanding Cash—a New York media institution had to reinterpret and explain a southern icon to its favored audiences of liberal and eastern tastemakers. The same actions that led the Ku Klux Klan to target him made him a liberal darling.

Cash may have been "country" to the *Times*, but he was "a singer of country songs" or a "deep-voiced country and Western singer." That is, the *Times* contextualized him as a different sort of country musician, almost always avoiding the straight terms "country singer" or "country star." Obviously, the *Times* separated his identity from his function—he might have been singing country songs, but he was no country singer. According to Tom Dearmore in the *Times Magazine*, he was "the first angry man of the country songsters"; an accompanying caption noted that "Johnny Cash has broken the mold of Grand Ole Opry-type country-Western and is pounding out his own folk form. Darned if folks don't like it." The implication was that Cash's folk leanings put him in a category diffe-rent from country. Dearmore also wrote that Cash's work moved "away from the rackety, say-nothing song types that have prevented many peo-ple from taking his field seriously. Unlike the comical, cowboy-hatted, spangle-decorated country warblers of early fame, he comes to his mis-sion with a fierce and looming personality and black attire."[16] In the space of these few phrases, the *Times* writer essentially dismissed an entire genre, basing his view partially on appearance; apparently, Cash's black attire had its desired effect. Because he wore black, Dearmore seemed to think Cash had separated himself from the genre (even though wearing black was not really uncommon among country musicians).

A more benign but still pointed separation came in a review of Cash's 1968 concert at Carnegie Hall. Robert Shelton, famous for his chroni-cling of Bob Dylan, pointed out that Cash's appeal cut across many audi-ences and genres: he was greeted with "an audience part country people and part hipsters and pop musicians rediscovering an old path beneath the faddism of pop music." Shelton's self-justifying purpose was to pull Cash from the country singer context and refashion him as someone with broader (and presumably more compelling) interests. The review implied that country singers sing songs that do not resonate beyond their particular group, but Cash does—after all the *Times* is writing about him! In general, the *Times*'s attention was both negatively disposed toward country music and positively disposed toward Cash. Dearmore placed him within a broader context of American musicians: "Cash is some-times like Paul Robeson toned down and countrified, sometimes like what Dean Martin would be if he were melancholy, but he really is unlike either, or anybody else on records."[17]

Still, Cash's relationship to his native South posed problems for the *Times* writers. Some of this criticism was on the silly side, focusing on surface issues: in one article, Michael Lydon wrote about Cash in a way that emphasized his physical oddity and southernness: "Handsome Johnny Cash, as fans call him, is too big to be trifled with ('biggest man I know,' says his wife, June Carter, batting her false eyelashes), 6 feet 2 and 250 pounds, with ploughboy shoulders." The false eyelashes, the ploughboy shoulders, the "handsome" moniker all bespeak a playfulness that perhaps borders on disrespect for either Cash or his audience. In a sense, Lydon justifies this attitude with his choice of Cash quotations: "Ain't nothin' too weird for me. . . . I guess I've never been normal, not what you'd call Establishment. I'm country."[18] (The playing off Johnny Cash's countryness started early. The anonymous author of a *Time* magazine profile in 1959 wrote about "Daddy Johnny Cash" having to "hit the road to rustle up some cash"[19]). Still, his background did endear him to one critic; in writing about Bob Dylan's *Nashville Skyline* album, William Kloman pointed out that Cash's influence on Dylan was profound: "Johnny Cash, it seems, has taught Dylan where the *real* folk live," a reversal of the commonly authenticant hierarchy that put Dylan over Cash.[20]

Other writers took a more reflective approach to Cash's interactions with his audiences. Dearmore acknowledged his devotion to social causes but thought it did not go far enough: "Cash's most serious shortcoming is that he leans excessively on the Depression, which is fast becoming ancient history. He sings about the poor of yesterday, but not about the poor of today (with the exception of convicts and Indians, who are a tiny fragment of the whole)." Dearmore also raised the issue of race, which Cash rarely addressed: "There are few hobos today, but there is plenty of misery for Cash to interpret outside the prisons and the reservations. The poor in this period of richness are more controversial because they are raising a commotion and are disproportionately black." Dearmore here identified Presley and Dolly Parton as performers who have done more. Probably correctly, Dearmore identified Cash's charitable focus as an audience issue: "Cash will not talk much of the contemporary poor, of civil rights and civil wrongs, of black people and Chicanos. Perhaps many of the down-South country folk who buy his platters would rather not hear about those subjects . . . but possibly in Cash there are recondite sympathies that will one day surface in song." Though devoted to his current audience, Dearmore suggested, Cash still might move beyond it. The implication was that those listeners might never be ready for such a change—but the rest of America and the *New York Times* would be.[21]

One incident in particular demonstrated acutely the odd place Cash occupied in the mind both of the *Times* and perhaps of America in general. A series of articles detailed his encounter with Richard Nixon, who invited him to the White House to perform in 1970. For some reason, someone made public Nixon's, (or, as Cash said later, Nixon's secretary's) request for several songs, including "Welfare Cadillac," written by Guy Drake, and "Okie from Muskogee" recorded by Merle Haggard and cowritten by Haggard and Roy Burris. Both songs emphasized traditional values: "Welfare Cadillac" was about a family that bought a Cadillac with welfare checks, and "Okie from Muskogee" suggested that many Americans did not share the views of protesters (one line from "Okie:" "We still wave Old Glory down at the courthouse").[22] Cash said that he would not sing either song if given his choice. At the concert, he did play Nixon's third request, "A Boy Named Sue," about a son who seeks revenge against his father for giving him a girl's name, but he also played "What Is Truth?" one verse of which goes like this:

> A young man sittin' on the witness stand
> The man with the book says "Raise your hand"
> "Repeat after me, I solemnly swear"
> The man looked down at his long hair,
> And although the young man solemnly swore
> Nobody seems to hear anymore
> And it didn't really matter if the truth was there
> It was the cut of his clothes and the length of his hair!
> And the lonely voice of youth cries, "What is truth?"[23]

The song was written in the storytelling mode that helped bring Cash back to the national stage. Here, however, here the concern was not with a boy named Sue but with a young man who had the stereotypical hair of a hippie.

Apparently, Nixon was not pleased by the choice.[24] But Cash also said this about Nixon: "We elected our man as President, and if you don't stand behind him, get the hell out of my way so I can stand behind him." By printing three articles about this incident, the *Times* showed how important it thought Cash was. As an aside, in the *Penthouse* interview, Cash talked about having a cup of coffee with H. R. Haldeman and John Ehrlichman during their trials (Cash's attorney at the time, James Neal, was also the government's prosecuting attorney); he claimed to be both "sick and ashamed" about Watergate but "really liked Haldeman as a person," indicating that the personal in politics often trumped the political for Cash.[25]

As a whole, the *New York Times*'s bifurcated treatment of Cash and his supposed southern audience coincided with an eastern intellectual disdain of the South. This undoubtedly occurred partly because the *Times* and other eastern media outlets saw southerners as backward. For those who tend to lump together all inhabitants below the Mason-Dixon Line, a southern accent is a southern accent. But anyone who is from the South or has lived in the South for a time knows that being southern is a complicated identity. As Willie Morris, a native of Mississippi and editor of *Harper's,* writes in his wonderful memoir, *North toward Home:* "The literary and publishing worlds of the city [New York] were perilous vantage points from which to understand the rest of America. There was a marked sense of superiority, amounting to a kind of distrust, toward other American places. This had always been true, and it was likely to become more so, as the older regionalism died in America and as the cities of the East became more and more the center of an engaged and argumentative intellection." Morris believed that when the eastern media looked beyond New York, they saw nothing but "a vast and grassy steppeland populated by hillbillies and the descendants of the original Forty-Niners."[26] Perhaps this provincialism was replaced by other attitudes in the 1970s, as Grantham writes: "The depiction of a savage and benighted South in the national media during the 1950s and 1960s was replaced by the image of the sun-belt South."[27] Nonetheless, in the period when Cash returned to public prominence, the belief that the South was backward lingered.

And yet, for the *Times* to recognize Cash as cool made the *Times* cool. It allowed the newspaper not only to praise some country music, but to claim that it was not regionally biased because it wrote positively about a southerner and country musician. To its credit, its overall coverage of country music increased after the cultural news editor was hired. And it is worth repeating that during this same period, Cash was hardly mentioned in the *Tennessean,* Nashville's primary daily newspaper; as Robert Oermann told me, Cash received little coverage there until the mid-1970s, when Oermann became the first full-time reporter. The irony is that institutions like the *New York Times* likely treated Cash better than the media outlets that represented his core fans. Cash had become a national figure who represented the political conflicts and confusions of the nation.[28]

A disdainful attitude toward the South and country music still exists, although Cash often escaped it. Yet, even at the end of his career, he couldn't escape the northern perception that he had a limited audience. In a *Daily News* review of his 1994 Carnegie Hall concert, Bill Bell marveled at the diversity of the audience: "It was an interesting audience, too, and a demonstration of Cash's across-the-board drawing power, with a lot of biker and banker types, and surprisingly few folks dressed for a night at the rodeo."[29] It's no wonder that the *Times* rediscovered Cash, as this generation has again. Unfortunately, the lack of attention paid to Cash in his home genre verified the *Times*'s view of him as an anomaly in country music.

Ultimately, the coverage revealed a lot about Cash too. His search for diverse audiences and his efforts to take a position that acknowledged student protest, troops in Vietnam, and even the Nixon administration seemed to be successful at least in the long term, although what effect this had in the short view is less clear. We know Cash's career declined in the 1970s; was it because of his ambiguous politics, his renewed and public religious faith, a combination of both, or neither? Was it because of his affiliation with commercial interests? The audiences the prison albums brought him would likely not have taken well to either religious profession or open support of Nixon.

As Leigh Edwards notes, Cash's politics remained a mystery to most people—or rather, most listeners assumed that his politics were their politics.[30] The documentary filmaker Robert Elfstrom said that, at least with him, "John was pretty apolitical; I don't know where he was politically. It never really came up. At one point he told me he never voted. I don't think he knew a Democrat from a Republican." Chris Willman confirms Cash's ambiguity in his fascinating book *Rednecks and Bluenecks*. He cites those close to him such as Kris Kristofferson, his daughter Rosanne, and Merle Haggard who claim him as a liberal. Rosanne Cash said, "Dad was always a Democrat. But he never registered, you know. He never affiliated with a party, but he was definitely liberal in his social and political views." But Willman also cites Bill Malone, who noted, "It's hard to find anything in either Haggard or Cash that's brave or radical. . . . It amazes me when people try to make Cash out as either a liberal or an outspoken radical."[31]

In bits and pieces, however, Cash indicated his preferences. In one article, he mentions being against the action of the contras war in the Reagan era.[32] And after one of the 2000 presidential campaign debates between Vice-President Al Gore and George W. Bush, he told an interviewer that "Gore stomped him."[33] Still, both liberals and conservatives claim him. In 2004, after his passing, the American Gas Association and Nissan Motors sponsored a reception at Sotheby's, where part of Cash's estate was going up for auction later that year, for the Tennessee delegation to the Republican convention. The implication that Cash would have supported Republican ideas outraged liberal fans, who conducted a protest outside the reception and expressed outrage on the Internet. One commenter on *Daily Kos,* a liberal blog, indicated that in a *Time* interview the year of his passing, Cash had expressed outrage at the Bush administration's behavior: "He also gave an interview to *Time* in 2003 in which he wearily lamented the direction of our country under Bush and his Iraq obsession."[34] But the interview itself revealed this "weary lament" only indirectly, if at all; Lev Grossman and Cash had this exchange:

LG: Do you watch the news?

JC: Yeah, quite a bit.

LG: Do you feel pessimistic about the way things are going?

JC: I just wish we would . . . I wish we would . . . mmm. Not going to get into that, Lev.[35]

The interview implied but did not express disapproval. And as Rosanne Cash posted on her own website, there were two parties—one approved by the family and hosted by the Tennessee Republican senator Lamar Alexander, whom Rosanne called "an old family friend of Dad and June," and another that "seemed to play rather fast and loose with the image of my Dad on their invitations and party plan. As soon as we found out about this, it was stopped."[36] Edwards notes that counterprotesters in 2004 wanted to focus on keeping him nonpolitical.[37]

So the politics of Johnny Cash remain murky, complicated by family ties and changing definitions of "liberal" and "radical," and embraced by everyone, both conservative and liberal. Cash's rebellion against the record industry echoes elements of radical discourse against what many saw as an oppressive establishment. It was this essential conservatism of Nashville that often led him to distance himself from the genre of country music. If Cash is the Man in Black, he remains a symbol of protest but also one of indeterminacy: while black can mean many things, it's also hard to read. If we take into account both his dominant audience and the degree to which he threatened to alienate them, we have to count him as a radical of sorts—though probably not a radical with claws.

Cash's childhood home, early Sunday morning in 2007. The house now has an owner and is no longer in disrepair (but the only sign that Cash ever lived here is the fact that the owner wants payment to photograph it).

This modest monument is located at the center of Dyess, Arkansas, where Cash spent most of his formative years.

Cash's head floats above the iconic quote from Sinatra on the wall of Landry's in downtown Memphis, where rockabilly stars used to shop.

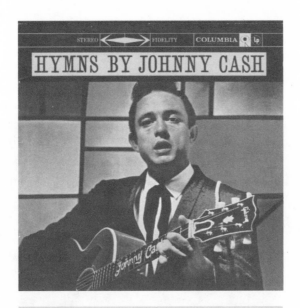

(Above) The seriousness of his effort in Hymns is signaled by the cover photo of Cash as earnest young man against a modern stained glass window background. Courtesy of Sony.
(Below) Even in this effort to win over folk fans, Cash (or his promoters) can't avoid the darkness, as Cash plays a man about to rob a train. Courtesy of Sony.

Ralph Peer first recorded the Carters in Bristol, a small town located in both Virginia and Tennessee. This mural celebrates the 1927 recordings of the Carters, Ernest and Hattie Stoneman, and Jimmie Rodgers.

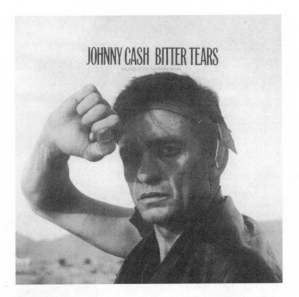

(Above) On the cover of *Bitter Tears*, his stern look and leather headband (and black sleeveless shirt) are meant to paint a serious portrait of Cash as Native American. Courtesy of Sony.
(Below) Cash and Carter before their marriage, a year before the release of *At Folsom Prison*. Both are smiling, but Cash looks sickly. Courtesy of Sony.

Cash and Carter performing. Cash wears black, but the outfit is not subtle—and not out of character for a country performer. Courtesy of Sony.

Cash with Carter on the tour bus, symbol of the wandering life. Photo by Joel Baldwin.

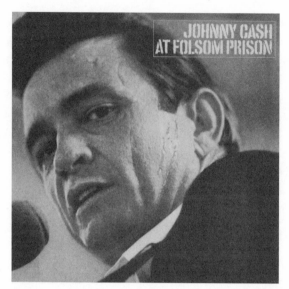

The closeup cover shot for *At Folsom Prison* shows a sweating, older Cash, his face definitively masculine. Courtesy of Sony.

Cash performs, probably at a college, in the South in the late 1960s (note the audience member on the right waving a Confederate flag). Photo by Joel Baldwin.

Cash looks at the camera as he signs an autograph on a woman's hand, in a photo that reveals his understanding of the way the camera serves him (and he serves the camera). Photo by Joel Baldwin.

Cash as commodity—a Johnny Cash T-shirt and hat share a window display with Jack Daniels products and other items.

A worn mural in Nashville near Broadway uses the iconography of his later career and familiar black-dominated color scheme.

Cashanalia in the Folsom Prison Museum shop.

Shades of brown used in the interior and Hank Williams's ode to authenticity at the Country Music Hall of Fame in Nashville together represent the bedrock of country music—closeness to the land and the need for singers to be real in their expression.

The distinctively aged wood of the Carter Family Fold exterior, with its retro-looking sign.

Johnny Cash—ever iconic and mysterious. Photo by Joel Baldwin.

CASH CHOOSES TELEVISION

If the images could come out of television, what would happen
if I went into the television, and it was turned off?
—Johnny Cash, introduction to his short story
"Holografik Danser"

During the taping for television of, *The Johnny Cash Show*, Cash used to like
to have the cue cards held upside down, according to Chance Martin, his
lighting director during the 1970s. Turning the cards upside down was a
way to tease the producers about their nervousness over allowing a relative
amateur to host a show and, according to Martin, a sign of the tension
never fully resolved between Cash and the producers. "Hollywood wanted
a certain type," Martin said, that type being a more mainstream than
country-oriented artist.[1] Viewers, however, do not notice this tension; they
see a show that may be low on production values (even for the 1970s), a
little cheesy but earnest, and yet remarkable in the scope of its music
guests, which ranged from Bob Dylan to Glen Campbell to Derek and the
Dominos, from Joni Mitchell to Roy Orbison to Ray Charles—hardly the
country orthodoxy about which ABC complained. As Bill Friskics-Warren writes, "Often cited for its singular contribution to that era's South-
ernization of American culture, 'The Johnny Cash Show' offered dazzling
evidence of Cash's commitment to reaching out for the tie that binds rather
than divides people."[2] In Rodney Clapp's description, Cash's show was "democracy as parade, finding a common direction and hope for hippies and rednecks, convicts and preachers, lineworkers and corporate executives."[3] Cash
seemed country, given the obvious signifiers of the show's origin in Nashville, the nature of its humor, and of course his voice, but learning his musical tastes from the show's content would be harder. If one posits that Cash's
indeterminacy was in part the source of his perceived authenticity—that
some of his appeal came from the inability of a public to pin him down—
then his eclectic and democratic guest list is one more exhibit.

But the cue cards may reveal also a more personal tension that Cash felt as host. For most of his career, he alternated between rebelling against the industry that made him a star and carving his own path. Becoming a host meant switching from the rebellious hellion of his drug-fueled 1960s to a more responsible role. In his television show, he welcomed America into a faux living room, offering his viewers entertainment from musicians of a variety of genres and education in the form of his *Ride This Train* segments. A host's actions are very different from those of a rebel: a rebel makes others uncomfortable, whereas a host is supposed to make them feel comfortable, even if the host himself is uncomfortable, which Cash seemed to be.

Yet the television show gave Cash the national audience he had always sought. And he used it as a bully pulpit of sorts, revisiting his folk past, inviting all sorts of performers on, but basing the show in Nashville not Los Angeles. Once acquiring the audience he wanted, he was faced the dilemma of how much of himself to be. As in his decision on Vietnam, such a question was trickier than it might have been in 1959 or would have been in 1979. Cash had managed, as a southerner in a difficult time to be from the South, to capture the nation's attention with his prison concerts and "A Boy Named Sue." Could being himself, or rather presenting his interests to the nation at large (the television audience is even more diffuse than a genre audience), work?

But appearing on television was only one among Cash's choices. His participation in visual mediums was hardly unusual for musicians, who have historically tried their hand at acting and hosting. Besides *The Johnny Cash Show*, he had other television and movie credits: he had acted in a number of TV shows and films, had written (at least in part) a movie, made commercials, narrated and acted in a special on trains, and guest-starred on other television shows, including notable turns on *The Muppet Show* (where he sang "Jackson" with Miss Piggy) and *The Simpsons*. On the Internet Movie Database, Cash is listed as having had twenty-three acting roles—in movies like *Door to Door Maniac*, the made-for-TV version of *Stagecoach*, and dozens of appearances on television as either a musical guest or an actor, including stints on *Little House on the Prairie* and *Dr. Quinn, Medicine Woman* with his wife, June Carter. His "Delia's Gone" video appeared on *Beavis and Butt-Head*, and in probably his best role on television, he did a guest stint on *Columbo*.[4]

Though his dramatic career was extensive and diverse, it was at best a mixed success—a surprise given his striking and iconic visual presence, in part clearly the source of his endurance on the public stage. Cash was least successful on television and in movies, not only in popularity but also in execution. At his best, he was a B actor, full of effort and intensity but without the ability to shed his self-consciousness as a performer. He seemingly could not pretend to be someone else; even being a different version of himself as a television show host was difficult. To know one is being observed, let alone filmed, forces an alteration of one's behavior or as Richard Peterson notes, is an order to "act naturally." Cash's best performances were those where he acknowledged them as performances, as in his familiar "Hello, I'm Johnny Cash" and also in the performer's patter that accompanies all concerts. In other words, Cash seemed at his best when he did not have to pretend he was not performing.[5]

Cash's visual performances shaped our perceptions of him; accordingly, this chapter's focus is not only on his choice to do a television show—an obvious one because of its potential to reach a larger audience—but also on his choices to participate in visual culture as a whole. Although the television show was the most prominent of these decisions, Cash's visual presence in American culture had several distinct components: his persona, best captured in stills and record covers; his music performances; his television and movie appearances; and his videos. Each aspect represents a specific choice among choices that overlap in their intent and effect. But at their heart, these choices about visual culture represent ontological debates about both performance and visual expression—we know performances are not real, and we think photographs are. Yet Cash seemed at his most real when performing, whereas the famous shot of the bird, in which he grimaces while spontaneously giving the finger, has been manipulated and misinterpreted far beyond its original context.

As did other decisions that displayed a complexity beyond initial appearances, so did Cash's choices in the visual realm reflect the informed simplicity of performing. The complexity of production, the decisions before filming begins, and the required self-reflexivity and distance while repeating the same material every night require the appearance of simplicity in the face of complexity. These components show how the visual material of an icon evolves over a career, and Cash's performances and personas showed contradictions: highly confident when presented in the direct gaze of photography and documentary, he somehow became less himself and yet not enough of anyone else when faced with the prospect of acting. In a career that was undoubtedly aided by a strong presence in front of the camera, his lack of mastery was surprising. His musical performance became more naturalized, but other kinds of performance never did. What tied these other performances together was essentially a lack of control on his part—he did much better when he controlled the terms of performance, less well when he had to negotiate his performance with the needs of others. Such negotiation took place in all his artistic production but was least able to be smoothed out in the visual mediums. And yet it was a lack of control that also led to the bird, one of the most enduring images of his career.

PERSONA AND MUSIC

Cash's most successful visual performances were those most closely aligned with his musical career. His photographs, for album covers and promotional materials, captured a man whose visual presence was consonant with his recording career—large, sometimes intimidating, unforgettable.

He *was* a large man, one whose size was an inherent part of his identity. Robert Oermann said he was physically imposing: "It was like meeting Lincoln. But he wasn't intimidating. Although he knew he was Johnny Cash, he never acted it."[6] The Lincoln comment is borne out by early TV performances, where Cash was a lanky dark-eyed presence with slicked-back hair, statelier than most others of his time. Michael Streissguth notes that "to innumerable fans, his is the one face missing from Mt. Rushmore"—a construction is at least partially visual in nature.[7] Combined with his voice, Cash had a presence that went a long way in explaining his iconic nature. Though photographers would have an interest in making it so, his presence always seemed to fill the frame of any photograph. Especially as his career progressed, he loomed in the lens, never more so than when his photograph was taken alone, and he gave the camera neither a smile nor a frown, just a stare. In the bird picture for example, one might focus on his extended finger, but Cash remains an imposing presence in the background. He dominates even some early photos, such as the one for the album cover of *The Fabulous Johnny Cash*—one is drawn to both his hands and his head.

Look photographer Joel Baldwin shot Cash during his peak years. He found Cash to be very cooperative (as witnessed by the hundreds of photos of virtually the same shot found in the *Look* archives at the Library of Congress). "In those days, they let you into their life," Baldwin said. "They loved being promoted like that. They ended up trusting you." One striking feature of photos is how they hew to the Johnny Cash story—there are images of him staged next to railroad tracks and signs, one leaning on an old pickup truck, another in the cotton fields, and several hunting and fishing. All of these images are associated with "country" or rural activities, or those referred to directly by Cash. Baldwin said both he and the art director chose the shots.[8]

There were three main image phases of Cash's life. In the early phase, he was seemingly all ears, hair, and limbs; he did not seem particularly threatening, and in fact looked a little bit goofy, as his photographs intimate he was eager to please. The second and most prominent phase was Cash at his most iconic, his hair longer and over his ears, his body filled out, a large presence. We think of this Cash when we think of Johnny Cash, the quintessential iconic figure. Then there is the last phase, the elderly Cash—seen most prominently in the "Hurt" video but elsewhere as well—his hair diminished and white, his face puffy, and his body indistinct.

One might argue that the way we look at celebrity changes reflects on our own obsession with aging. With Cash, the changes marked not only body type but popular perception. At his youngest he was just one of many rockabilly stars, as his clean-cut image reflected. The cover of *The Fabulous Johnny Cash* suggests little darkness, only star power, though his live performances imply an edginess. In one such performance at the Town Hall Party in Southern California (it was clear from the audience that it was a working-class population more attuned to Buck Owens than to pop musicians), Cash went into something more than an aside about being idle after moving to California; neither lighthearted nor funny, just mildly disconcerting, it was an odd moment, and perhaps an anomaly, but it did suggest his struggle to be both real and a performer at the same time. That changed as the 1960s progressed, especially in his thematic albums, which suggest a more serious, rugged Cash (not coincidentally, drugs were beginning to take a toll). At the Hammerstein Ballroom in London in 1966, a poster showed a wraithlike Cash, on the verge of a breakdown. But even his recovery in *At Folsom Prison* and *At San Quentin* suggested someone dark and deep—the consequence, undoubtedly, of Columbia's savvy marketing campaign. Cash sported a pompadour on the cover of *Folsom*, still appearing a relatively young man; *San Quentin* displayed him outlined in blue light. Cash in his middle to late age was an icon whose presence in American culture represented a number of contradictory forces—redeemed sinner, southerner, protestor, man of tradition. The images from this later period, which one would expect to be unified, given his status as the Man in Black, are surprisingly diverse. Clothing varies from blue jeans to a ruffled shirt and (my favorite), a turtleneck with a blazer, (in a *New York Times* feature around comeback number one), with the article titled "Ain' Nothin' Too Weird for Me."[9]

Surprisingly, these changes seemed not to undercut his iconic image but to enhance it. His presence was not diminished, perhaps because his face had reached the stage where character seems to be etched into it—he could have been thirty five or fifty—but it's a bit weathered and ultimately masculine (in sharp contrast to Presley's face, even before he acquired the name "Fat Elvis"—in his comeback special in 1968, Elvis remained pretty).

Cash kept this face—though he abandoned his slicked-back hair around the end of the 1960s—until decline seemed to hit him suddenly in the 1990s, when his health problems multiplied. In David Kamp's view, he seemed to grow old overnight, his looks remaining distinctive but decidedly different from his previous image—his face flaccid, his hairline retreating.[10] In his American Recordings albums, his photos show this deterioration: he is clearly aging on the first two albums, *American Recordings* and *Unchained*; on albums three, four, and five he is, if not exactly hiding, certainly shading his features; even partially hidden, they are certainly less distinct, with the darkness of the photographs meant both to indicate a symbolic darkness and to hide the aging performer from more direct examination. Admittedly, it is difficult to watch an icon age, and Cash's decline in vitality made it even more so. Still, at the close of his life, he remained a transcendent icon, unapologetic in his aging, unafraid seemingly of further transformations.

When he died, his portrait on *Time*'s cover showed an aging Cash but not the one featured so starkly in the *National Enquirer* photos of him at his wife's funeral, where he looked like a man far beyond his age of seventy-three—white and puffy and in a wheelchair. The *Time* cover suggests a compromise between portraying a man as he was and as how his audiences might want to remember him: the hair is still black, but the face is etched with age. It is okay to grow old, it seems to say, as long as we can remember what you looked like when you were young.[11]

The most crucial element of Cash's visual relationship to music was his image as the Man in Black. Black was important in Cash's career because he was able to manipulate its ambiguity for his own uses—first as a symbol of cool, mixed with the suggestion of black as a villain's color, then as a symbol of protest. But Cash did not always wear black, and even when he did, it was often *part* of an outfit, not the whole outfit itself. His willingness to call himself the Man in Black showed his willingness to traffic in his own visual currency.

Despite some initial awkwardness (something *Walk the Line* does get right), once Cash grew into his role as a performer, it was his most comfortable form of visual participation. Early performances featured him as rail thin, with ears that protruded, and a head twist after he uttered each line—something he never lost. Still, he sounded more assured than it looked. Even in the dynamic San Quentin performances, he did little moving around, sometimes stepping back to strum his guitar. But he was often seated for his performances—including that of "A Boy Named Sue"—reading the lyrics from a music stand. He sounded rebellious but did not especially look it—at least not while performing, and not in the way that Elvis, Jerry Lee Lewis, and other rock-and-roll stars did. In other words, Cash was more folk in performing than he was rock—singing with feeling, letting his voice rather than his body carry his performance. He spent so much time performing that such a role became second nature, normal, as opposed to the other visual roles in which he made himself participate. The rebel and the aging patriarch seemed like two stages in a life bound to clash with mainstream notions of normality.

MOVIES, TELEVISION, AND VIDEO

Being on television or in the movies was a crucial aspect of being a music star in the 1950s and 1960s, and Cash's active participation led to his becoming host of *The Johnny Cash Show* from 1969 to 1971, which began as a summer program and then came back as a midseason replacement. He also hosted a four-show series in 1976 on CBS, titled *Johnny Cash and Friends*.

One of his problems on television, whether his own show or a special about trains, was that from our current perspective but also the perspective of the antiestablishment, the shows were (for lack of a better word) *showbizy*, with the mannerisms and touches of what the network thought to be current and cool; these seem dated now and probably seemed a little dated then. The difference between the Beatles or the Doors appearing on Ed Sullivan and Cash hosting his own show was that Cash was part of the means of production—a producer, not just a performer. The difference between "hosting" and "performing" is significant. Witness how Bob Dylan's reputation is enhanced in a scene that figures prominently in both Martin Scorsese's documentary *No Direction Home* and Todd Haynes's film *I'm Not There*: the press conference in which Dylan calls himself a "song and dance man." Cash was aware of this difference, and his rebellious spirit manifested itself in flipping the cue cards upside down.

Though Elvis Presley was perhaps the most prominent example, performers from Roy Rogers to Lyle Lovett have acted in movies and TV. In the 1960s, Glen Campbell, Andy Williams, Roy Clark, and Buck Owens all either had their own shows or had served prominent roles. Others in the same era were more successful in the visual mediums; Frank Sinatra's movie career often met with critical success (particularly in *The Manchurian Candidate*, 1962, and *From Here to Eternity*, 1953). Dolly Parton had a few successful roles (such as *9 to 5*, 1980), as well as those less so (*Straight Talk*, 1992). Others, like Willie Nelson, had careers similar to Cash's, appearing in movies, including *Honeysuckle Rose* (1980) and *Dukes of Hazzard* (2005). And the Grand Ole Opry show, *Louisiana Hayride*, and *Hootenany* were televised, the 1960s equivalents of MTV's *Total Request Live* or its *Unplugged* series.

But Cash's television prominence came only after a failed movie career. On the heels of Elvis's increasing reliance on movies to make a living, Cash headed to California in 1958 in part to become a movie star. It never happened. For the most part, his film career consisted mostly of (rarely memorable) television productions. He did have an early prominent role as a kidnapper and bank robber in *Door-to-Door Maniac* (1961)—a forgettable thriller, yet, Cash's performance was one of his best. He played one mood—unrepentant evil—and played it well. The movie begins with a robbery scene in a dark alley with Cash gunning down a policeman. The movie then switches to suburban California; as a narrator recounts the backstory, we see Cash strumming a guitar while his girlfriend gets ready to go to work. (His obvious southern accent is never explained, even though the robbery takes place in New Jersey.) In the rest of the movie, set around a plan for his partner to rob a bank while he holds the bank's vice president hostage, Cash becomes increasingly violent. We see no humanity in the character, just a hardened criminal. But as a young star, Cash was captivating; he had a real screen presence in this movie.

Also an important part of Cash's movie legacy was the documentary by Robert Elfstrom, *Johnny Cash: The Man, His World, His Music* (1969), perhaps the single most mesmerizing film about him. It stands equal with Christopher Wren's biography *Winners Got Scars Too* in truly capturing Cash at his height of his first comeback in the late 1960s because it shows Cash's appeal by letting the singer, his music, and his world speak for themselves.[12] *The Man* is striking in two respects: lack of narration and thematic coverage. Elfstrom takes us from subject to subject, place to place, using songs, interviews, and images to guide the viewer without narration. By the end, an alternative but convincing view of Cash has been constructed: that he is complicated. We see little of the darkness that is at the center of the Johnny Cash narrative (and the movie *Walk the Line*), but rather a man who engages a variety of people and ideas.[13] He talks to fans, aspiring songwriters, Bob Dylan, producers, and reporters with equal ease. Elfstrom reveals Cash's complexity through a loosely thematic organization; the documentary covers Cash's involvement with the country music genre, Native Americans, prison, the South, farming, celebrity, religion, travel, rural life, the home, and family. These are all part of the Johnny Cash story, and Elfstrom's framing and emphasis of them is well placed.[14]

TV roles that did not require much emoting were the ones that served him best. He did well in *Murder in Coweta Country* (1983), where he played the local sheriff who is trying to bring the rapacious southern landlord (Andy Griffith) to justice. June Carter played a crazy soothsayer with abandon proportional to Cash's reserve. Cash had only two modes of acting here, either determined or righteously angry (though still quiet), and did both well, though occasionally with the split-second delay in getting out his lines which often marks his work. The oddest things about the show was the makeup, which made him look as if he were wearing mascara, and the outfit he wore as sheriff, which looked not unlike a leisure suit from the same era as the movie.

After that, Cash occasionally appeared in movies without much fanfare. His own turmoil in the mid-1960s may have had something to do with how abbreviated his movie career was, but more likely it was his love of music—he toured constantly in that decade. He never gave up his visual performance career, however, even though he shifted it to television. Many music or variety programs were showcasing musicians in prime time, including *The Ed Sullivan Show* (which memorably introduced the Beatles to a national audience) but also, among others, *Shindig*, *Hullabaloo*, *Hootenanny*, and *American Bandstand*. Because music had become so popular and youthful, the popularity of music shows then seems analogous to reality shows today.

Given Cash's popularity in the late 1960s, it was not surprising that ABC gave him a television show—at least no more surprising than reality shows about Ozzy Osborne and Jessica Simpson today. When he made this move to the television screen, Cash was coming off the crest of the comeback that produced his two popular albums and number 2 hit, "A Boy Named Sue." The live albums, combined with his own intriguing story and the success of other pop music shows, probably made offering Cash his own show easy.

What he did with the show may or may not have been on ABC's agenda: he used it as a means of communication between two often separate worlds: country and mainstream. He introduced his country crowd to performers like Bob Dylan, Louis Armstrong, Mahalia Jackson, Creedence Clearwater Revival, Eric Clapton, and Joni Mitchell; and he introduced the mainstream crowd to every possible country musician, including Roy

Orbison, Merle Haggard, Tex Ritter, and Roy Acuff, and playing duets with Bob Hope and Kirk Douglas. In all, he hosted 58 shows. The overall effect, according to Friskics-Warren, was a form of inclusive musical community: "Cash's guest list proffered a vision of community that bridged faiths, races, and musical genres, the counterculture and the cultural mainstream."[15] This variety, however, went against network wishes, writes Marc Weingarten: "Right off the bat, Cash sent a message to his viewers that he wasn't going to abide by the usual network policy of booking well-known nightclub hacks when he hired his old Sun labelmate Carl Perkins to be a regular on the show and recruited Joni Mitchell (who performed Cash's 'I Still Miss Someone' with the country legend) and Bob Dylan to sing some duets with him for the very first broadcast."[16] In another account suggesting that Cash had some trouble with the network in choosing his guests, Blaik Kirby writes that ABC initially balked at having Pete Seeger on: although his appearance would "testify to Cash's intention of putting art ahead of politics. Seeger was [almost] banned because of his [leftist] leanings; Cash himself is a firm believer in the obligation to serve his country, in Vietnam if need be. In today's conditions that makes him a hawk."[17] It seems clear that Cash's attempt to make viewers believe in his ambiguity was working, for better or worse. This ambiguity did not always endear him to his critics, who harped on his image as being too Hollywood, but it shows that any effort to characterize Cash politically was a fool's errand—Seeger and Dylan were notably counterculture, if still mainstream in their own way. (It's also interesting to note that both Seeger, the man who tried to prevent Dylan from going electric, and Dylan were on Cash's show.)

Contrast Cash's show with *Hee-Haw*, which offered an exaggerated form of southern hospitality, an idea mocked by northerners in the era of civil rights. So Cash opened his home in Nashville—rather than Los Angeles, where he had lived for most of the 1960s—to Americans and showed them the diversity of musical taste a southerner might have. As modern commentators have recognized, his repertoire was notable (though others like Ed Sullivan had a similarly diverse performer list). By today's standards, the show was neither visually nor topically sophisticated, probably largely because of being filmed in Nashville rather than New York or Los Angeles. According to Albert Govoni, Cash himself had something to do with the production. The show began with a shot of the crowd with a sped-up version of "Folsom Prison Blues" playing, because as Cash said, "one of the most exciting moments in my life is when I'm waiting in the wings to go on. There's nothing in show business more magical than that moment when you're looking out there at the performer's back, with the audience reacting like crazy." He said he wanted "the camera to capture that. I want the television audience to feel what the performer feels when he walks out on that stage with the studio audience applauding like hell." Cash said the production values and elements of the show were deliberately low-key because "I don't go for a lot of that flashy stuff. That's just not my line. The show is coming out of Nashville, where people sing songs. Sing songs—that's what we're going to do on this show." But "when the show started," wrote Kirby, "it was criticized for having too many guests and too much slapstick, inappropriate to Cash's own quiet image. [Now] it will have no more than two or three guest performers, and they'll be the ones Cash wants."[18]

The reviews were generally good, however. Cleveland Amory, writing for *TV Guide*, liked the candid opinions Cash offered. In one episode that he cited, Cash had said he supported the president, showing that he might be part of the "Silent Majority." That did not bother Amory: "Everyone applauded, and we did too—although we happen to be a member of the Noisy Minority. To our way of thinking, candid personal opinions not only make shows like this more interesting and individual, they also help make them seem, if not actually alive, at least a little less taped." And Amory appreciated the star himself. "We also happen to like Mr. Cash. It is true that he talks a good deal of the time as if he was eating, and he swallows an occasional lyric. But he is quick on the drawl when he needs to be, and the majority of the time, either silent or noisy, he can, as the occasion demands, sing up a storm or down a ballad." Still, Amory could not help adding what he must have thought was a clever countrified remark: "The audience doesn't just applaud the show; they root, hog and die for it."[19]

Viewing the show today gives a different perspective. Although it had admirable aims, it was not without its shortcomings: the lighting was not particularly good, and the sets (which Cash referred to on camera as his "home") looked makeshift and, well, a little cheesy. They were supposed to provide at once a background for singers and a sense that the show was "down home"; one had the motif of a country field; another had a series of ladders, set off by shadowed lighting; and where Cash played duets with his guests, the scene was supposed to represent a living room. When Dylan played with Cash, they sat by what looked to be a fake brick fireplace. Whatever the tension involving cue cards, Cash clearly used them, with the timing often a little off and the conversation seeming scripted. Despite this awkwardness, however, there were moments of transcendence, including a wonderful solo rendition by Ray Charles of "I Walk the Line." Though game, Cash was not a natural host and had the odd habit of looking away (perhaps toward the cue cards) after his guest answered a question. Overall, watching the show today is both surreal and entertaining.

But it likely had its desired effect of broadening the audience for Cash and country artists. Mark Jacobson acknowledges that in effect it changed his definition of what cool was:

> When I was in college, a snot-nosed Berkeley radical, Cash taught me that not everyone born in places like Kingsland, Arkansas, where people work with their hands and talk like LBJ, was a beady-eyed racist standing behind a luncheonette counter with an ax handle. No hippie, Cash was a whole new kind of South; he had Dylan on his TV show and sang songs like "Singin' in Vietnam Talkin' Blues" and "What is Truth" which struck exactly the right populist pro-vet/antiwar notes. But beyond that Cash taught me it was possible for a white man inflamed with the Pentecostal spirit— some damn Jesus shouter!—to be not only smarter than a wiseacre like me but *cooler*, too.[20]

Cash himself was of two minds about the show. In the 1970s, he cooled on it. It was "all right the first year," he said in *Man in Black*, but he realized that he "was just another piece of merchandise to the network, a cog in their wheel, and when the wheel started squeaking and wobbling they'd replaced me with another cog." He repeated for authenticity's sake the common criticism about network television's lack of quality, part of the difficulty was ultimately his loss of control: "I felt as if they were stealing my soul. To get ratings, they immediately started putting guests on my show that I couldn't—if you pardon the expression—relate to."[21]

In *Cash,* he wrote that his open statement of his Christianity got him in trouble. He said he made the profession as a result of the letters he received asking whether he sang the gospel songs as a Christian. His answer: "Yes, in short, I meant the words I was singing. When I actually came out and said the words, 'I am a Christian' on TV, that was the context: introducing a gospel song." According to Cash, "ABC didn't like it"; one of the producers told him he should not be talking about religion and Jesus on television. He responded:

> You're producing the wrong man here, because gospel music—and the word "Gospel" means " the good news about Jesus Christ"—is part of what I am and part of what I do. I don't cram anything down people's throats, but neither do I make any apologies for it, and in a song introduction, I have to tell it like it is. I'm not going to proselytize, but I'm not going to crawfish, and I'm not going to compromise. So don't you worry about me mentioning Jesus, or God, or Moses, or whoever I decided to mention in the spiritual realm. If you don't like it, you can always edit it.[22]

In *Man in Black,* he wrote that he did not like the way "the outside influence from the East Coast and the West Coast crept into the format of the show," or the "cabaret and café society people that I felt and looked out of place with." When the producers canceled his "Ride This Train" segment, he told them he was "going to Australia": "If I can't choose my guests and most of them from the country music community from here in Nashville, and if I can't continue to do the shows from Nashville, tell headquarters that it's just fine with June and me if the TV show isn't renewed for next year."[23] To move from Nashville and a southern idea, he thought, would undermine what seemed to be one of the show's unstated goals: to invite the nation into the South.

Whatever Cash's mixed feelings, the show seemed to embody many of the aspects of his career—the ambiguity of genre, the place of religion in his life, and his unwillingness to abide authority. Its cultural impact is harder to measure. It was a show without an automatically dedicated audience: country viewers would not necessarily like all of it, nor would the mainstream like the low production values. Perhaps the way it just missed both audiences was what made it cool. More important was what Cash was trying to do. His efforts had everything to do with his avoidance of being put in "the bag" he often referred to; he wanted to cross genres and audiences and to educate as well as entertain. That it steadily lost popularity had to be disappointing. Although it placed Cash more prominently in the public eye, the television show in a way marked the beginning of his slow slide to a prolonged stretch of national cultural irrelevance.

A few years later, in 1974, he appeared on *Columbo*, which may have been a last attempt to retain his place as a relevant artist in an entertainment world that was gradually turning away in two directions—toward a more vibrant and interesting American rock genre and toward whatever youthful trends Nashville was embracing. (The episode was directed by Nicholas Colasanto, better known as Coach on *Cheers*.) Cash played a country and gospel singer, Tommy Brown, forced by a spiritual wife (played by the well-known actress and director Ida Lupino), to sing gospel songs in order to build a large church. Brown murders both his wife and his ex-girlfriend (under age at the time she was with him) by drugging them, jumping off the plane he's piloting, and letting it crash. After a typically dogged and idiosyncratic investigation, Columbo solves the crime.

As in most episodes of the series, the point is not the destination but the journey. We know from the start that the perpetrator is guilty and that Columbo will find him. This journey is delicious especially for two scenes. In the first, Cash is performing with his band only hours after burying his wife, with several bikini-clad women eagerly watching as they play Kris Kristofferson's "Sunday Morning Coming Down." The implication is clear—Brown is a ladies' man who has wasted little time after his wife's death in pursuing new avenues of romance. Columbo too watches Brown perform, clearly entranced by what he is hearing. The other scene takes place at the end, when Columbo catches up with Brown, in essence having given him the chance to escape, which he does not do. Brown asks Columbo, "Why did you let me go up to the mountain? You know, I could have escaped." Columbo replies, "A man who has a voice like yours can't be all bad." In between, Brown has tried to seduce one of his own employees and attempted to charm Columbo. Thus, though Columbo does catch Tommy Brown, Brown also in part ensnares Columbo, who by the end is not only a Tommy Brown fan but one who could explain to another listener that country music is a lot like folk music.[24]

Cash's natural and easy manner in this role represented the height of his acting career. He went on to a number of forgettable cameos and multiepisode roles: on *Little House on the Prairie* (1976) he played a scammer posing as a preacher; in four episodes of *Dr. Quinn, Medicine Woman* between 1993 and 1997, he and Carter played a preacher and his wife in recurring roles. In both shows, the viewer could not get past the fact that Cash was acting. The best actors get beyond themselves, even their personas, so that even if we are on one level aware that it is Al Pacino or Robert de Niro playing a part, we are involved in the character as well. Cash as an actor could never quite lose himself enough to let us forget that it was Johnny Cash acting.

His last significant work on network television was his stint on *The Simpsons* (1997) as the voice of the coyote appearing to Homer when he is hallucinating. The perception of *The Simpsons*' creators that Cash would likely be in someone's drug trip is a testament to his status as an icon but fully within the context of his roots in popular culture and image as "cool" among young people.

His most well known visual performance in the last decade was video. Cash made a few videos for MTV; the two that stand out most were his "Delia's Gone" and "Hurt." The first introduced a number of new listeners to Cash and his old oeuvre of unrepentant violence; the second in effect offered a valediction and a goodbye.

For "Delia's Gone," two of the new listeners included Beavis and Butt-Head, the iconic animated characters and critics, who both say Cash frightened them. They also noted that he was cool. Butthead, in fact, said, "I bet this dude scores a lot because, like, he wears black."[25] The video shot by Anton Corbijn, features Kate Moss as Delia and shows Cash, as menacing as ever, with two dogs and a shotgun. There is no smiling, nothing that provides much solace.

"Hurt" (which I discuss in chapter 8) was one of Cash's best performances. Just as Kurt Cobain's acoustic "All Apologies" on MTV's *Unplugged* was taken as a prescient final goodbye, so has Cash's acting here been taken as almost literal—a way of expressing regret and the uncertainty of his fate. He convinced viewers that he believed life was tragic and full of regret, though those who knew him said he felt at home with his lot.

There is still a little mystery about why Cash turned out to be limited in his abilities as an actor, given such an impressive performing background. Perhaps it had something to do with what Waylon Jennings said about the similarities between himself and Cash: "Looking at John was like catching a reflection of myself: driven, restless, searching for acceptance."[26] In performance, Cash never looked completely comfortable, and I do not think it had anything to do with either not enjoying performing or not wanting to be filmed. It had more to do with an odd, small deficit of confidence, a need to please, which somehow made it into his performances—an asset when playing to the crowd while on stage but a hindrance when performing for the coldhearted camera.

THE BIRD

Although Cash, his producers, and other artistic associates planned many of visual contexts, perhaps his single most memorable image was the result of an instantaneous decision. Its impact has grown, less because of Cash's decisions than those of his audiences.

The famous bird first took flight in San Quentin—but where he aimed it is still an open question. His finger was first directed, depending on who tells the story, either toward the cameraman who was filming for a documentary or the warden who let Cash play and record in the prison. Since the warden was not actually standing on the stage, it sure looks as if the bird was aimed at the well-known rock photographer Jim Marshall, whose portraits of Jimi Hendrix and Janis Joplin are legendary. Of course, this bird has flown long past its original context, later showing up on posters and T-shirts, and then appearing again in a somewhat more official capacity in a 1998 advertisement celebrating Johnny Cash's Grammy for Best Country Album, *Unchained*. (Cash and Marshall sued Urban Outfitters in the 1990s for using this image without their permission. The case was settled.)[27] Overall, the meaning of Cash's finger is unstable as a sign because of factors surrounding its origin, its subsequent use as a mark of rebellion, and its reinscription as an ambiguous symbol close to its everyday meaning of "fuck you." Still, in its instability, there are real lessons about the nature of performance and the semiotic journey of decisions, big and small.

Because of its ambiguity and instability, the finger can be read as an imperfect metaphor or analogy for Cash himself, for what he meant both in American culture and to his numerous audiences. Although the finger has retained its basic meaning all these years, it's hardly unambiguous. The reason the metaphor is imperfect is that the meaning of Cash doesn't match up with the finger's ostensible use as an obscenity, either humorously or seriously. One could never reduce Cash to such a simple meaning. Indeed, his bird is all the more powerful because of his own complicated identity as rebel, Christian, redeemed sinner, southerner, liberal, country music legend, folksinger, song collector, activist, writer, husband, father, and farmer. What the finger does stand in for is the way Cash himself, as a semiotic subject, a sign, is both unstable and constant. More important, the meaning of the bird and Cash is audience-dependent. One can choose to read the bird as an aggressive gesture or as a sign of affection and Cash as a rebel or as a Christian or as an activist.

Cash's bird also represents a kind of choice that we encounter all the time but that rarely carries much weight in analysis: the instantaneous choice. A word, a gesture, even an errant thought could change our lives, can live on beyond either the moment or the intent. Cash's songs are full of narrators who make such choices. In our own lives, we may end up as either heroes or villains if we make snap decisions. Cash's bird was a choice whose reverberations are still being felt some thirty-five years later. And although very little stands in for Cash as a symbol—indeed, what could?—the indeterminate nature of the bird and its status as a symbol of rebellion makes it an ideal semiotic doppelganger.

Its authenticity as a symbol is as murky as other Cash symbols, however, since no one can agree on how it came to pass or even who was its original target. Just as we do not know what the bird means, we have difficulty understanding what Cash means. And when he disappeared from public consciousness as a recording artist, his reputation as an artist among the population remained intact. So when the bird emerged again on T-shirts and posters in dorm rooms in the 1990s, it matched Cash's reemergence. Even if we don't know how the bird came to be, we still believe in its authenticity.

Giving the middle finger has a long history, probably dating back to Roman times. Indeed the Romans had a name for it: *digitus impudus*, the impudent finger.[28] According to this interpretation, the finger is supposed to be phallic in nature, which certainly dovetails with the vulgarity "fuck you." The finger is also a specific type of gesture called an emblem. Emblems fall somewhere between speech-accompanied hand movement, where meanings are often dependent on speech, and sign language, where movements are precise and their meaning has little ambiguity. As David McNeill says, "For many individuals emblems are the closest thing to sign language they possess."[29] Yet the meanings are not quite stable. Though altering the gesture itself—moving the OK sign in a circle, or giving the finger over your head—doesn't change it as a sign, an emblem can often be read in different ways.[30] In terms of semiotics, where the signifier is the physical sign and the signified its meaning, gestures often contain a very specific signifier but a more unstable signified. We think we know what a finger means, but such meanings are more fluid than they seem. Cash's middle finger, for example, is a sign whose signifier is clear but whose signified is indeterminate.

Part of the bird's indeterminacy comes from its status as a performance: its vitality and its distilled nature make the image ripe for reinterpretation and further context; yet its meaning may be fleeting because the context is temporal. We can look at a picture of someone doing just about anything and divorce it from its original context. In the case of Cash, there are any number of contexts in the way the sign was produced, all of which may add some insight and some that may confuse. There is also the matter of the audience(s) and their roles.[31] Because Cash himself as a subject is rich in meanings that overlap and often contradict one another, trying to understand his audiences' perceptions is crucial.

Indeed, taking his finger as a subject specifically and Cash himself as a subject generally means one has to acknowledge ambiguity both as a primary feature of any interpretation and as the way his audiences participate in choosing some meanings of Cash over others. The first way the audience created such meaning came in its informal (and illegal) adoption of Cash's bird as a symbol of general rebellion between the time Marshall first took the photo in the late 1960s and the time Rick Rubin legally reprinted it as an ad for American Recordings in the late 1990s.

Its instability as a symbol, however, seems an inherent part of its makeup. Almost everything about it seems indeterminate, even its genesis. There are two stories about its entry into popular culture—one from

Cash, officially recounted in the liner notes of the rerelease of *At San Quentin*. In his version, the recipient of his gesture was a TV crew on hand to film the show; he writes: "I yelled, 'Clear the stage! Can't see my audience.' Nobody moved so I gave them the bird." But Marshall has a different story—or stories. According to one article, Marshall recalls, "I said to him, Johnny, let's do a shot for the warden.' I guess flipping the bird was his natural response." On his website, however, Marshall is more uncertain: "I forget why he flipped the bird in this picture. It might have been directed at the television crew who was filming there, or I might have suggested doing a special shot for the warden." When I talked to Marshall in 2004 and asked which story was true, he said, "It was some of each. It was thirty five years ago. I don't fucking remember." (Marshall didn't say this in either anger or exasperation—just matter-of-factly.)[32]

Some of each . . . the phrase is entirely appropriate, given how long ago the event took place and its unknown intent. One possible interpretation is that Cash meant it as a joke, a form of mock aggression. According to Mary E. Ballard, Shavonda Green, and Caroline Granger, mock aggression is "behavior that resembles aggression but lacks intent to harm" and is essentially the opposite of aggression in its intent and result. They specifically cite "giving the finger" as a form of mock aggression, which they say is "typically accompanied by positive emotions and almost always has positive outcomes."[33]

Cash's mock aggression was a form of humor that resonates with us, because it naturally provides a form of harmless tension. It suggests that the relationship between the two parties is strong enough to survive an obscene gesture. In the case of Cash and the cameramen, it could suggest the same thing, or perhaps humor dependent on the always shifting power relationship between the media and Cash—he knew better than most how to handle the media but still depended on them for publicity. If his bird was aimed at the warden—the person responsible for giving Cash permission to play, record, and film at San Quentin—well, he was not on stage, so presumably he did not receive the message. Or perhaps the warden stood in for the prison system itself. In the late 1960s, a time of intense rebellion on almost every front, the warden might have represented The Man, and Cash all those who wanted to flip him off.

Still, there is good reason to believe that whatever anger is displayed in the image, the intent was to be funny. According to author Robert Oermann, who talked with Cash about it after it was republished in the late 1990s, he meant the bird to be funny; he would never have used it in any seriousness with his mother-in-law, Maybelle Carter, on the stage: "It was a joke. He was doing it to be funny. The bird photo had Mother Maybelle in the background. I wouldn't angrily give the finger with my mother-in-law in the background."[34] For a moment consider the surreal landscape presented here: Cash on a stage in a California prison, recording a concert in both music and video, the already legendary rock photographer Jim Marshall taking pictures, film running, and Maybelle Carter, the queen of mountain music, on stage—not to mention June Carter's presence. Into this mix of country royalty, commercial possibility, and social activism comes the bird.

Indeed, there's some irony in the fact that distilled out of this event were both the live recording of "A Boy Named Sue," Cash's last real breakout hit (which originally contained a bleeped-out vulgarity that invited speculation as to what the words were) and the bird, one of two enduring visual images of Cash (the other being his status as the indeterminate Man in Black). Marshall was unsure how the bird even made it past this moment. He told me that the image was not published anywhere (though "there were a few prints around"), yet somehow made it onto T-shirts and posters, which as I recall, started showing up in the 1980s in record stores. These uses violated copyright laws; Marshall and Cash never saw any money from them. At this stage, then, the finger became an unadorned sign of rebellion, even as Cash himself had become musically irrelevant to many people. With its meaning in doubt, the notion of authenticity shifts back to the audience, which has become the caretaker of its meaning.

The bird reappeared officially thanks to Rick Rubin, who added the infamous text, "American Recordings and Johnny Cash would like to acknowledge the Nashville music establishment and country music for your support."[35] The image even more tightly focuses on the bird and clearly trades on any number of Cash images—the young vital Cash, the rebel Cash, the antiauthority Cash, and the DIY Cash—which come in the midst of a time when Cash was both musically vibrant and physically breaking down.

The Rubin version seems a more unambiguous image than the previous one, for here Cash is giving the finger to "Nashville." Still, the wording carries enough ambiguity that apparently there were those in Nashville who did not know they were the targets. Some of that has to do with the image Cash then had in Nashville. As Oermann said, "Nashville as a community embraced him. Radio is a corporate entity that rejects the legends and spits on legends and creates media Prozac for housewives. Music Row deeply and profoundly respected him." Oermann acknowledged, however, that Cash's iconic status increased once he began recording outside of Nashville. He said, "You have to leave Nashville and trade in your iconness, icon status with the rest of the world, so Nashville will stop taking you for granted."[36]

The bigger truth, however, is that the image only partially represents Cash as he was in 1999; it is more indicative of his status in the early 1960s. Even the places the image appeared—in *Billboard*, a music insider's magazine, and in a limited run of promotional material (Marshall says 5,000 copies were produced)—show that the dispute was a limited internal one. It also shows how fleeting the music business is: Columbia in Nashville had released him from Sun and allowed him to make all the albums he had been denied at Sun.

Yet, there is truth to this use of the bird. Nashville, like all the pop apparatus in this country, tends to discard its older stars. Cash had been dropped by Columbia and Mercury before Rubin gave him new life as a recording artist. Still, I think the bird shows an assertion of artistic vitality more than a true "fuck you." Because at least part of Cash's appeal is his rebelliousness, American Recordings, produced this advertisement along with the marketing for previous albums. But the bird reflects only a partial aspect of Cash's oeuvre, which contained a great deal of religious material. Cash and Rubin knew that rebellion was the hook to getting new audiences. Both birds are performances: the first, a joke, aimed at a system that largely loved him; the second, at a system that ignored him but still loved him—done by a master marketer who loved having Cash on his label.

Overall, the bird reflects the complicated way Cash is perceived in American culture, and the way Cash himself participated in it. The bird reflects a partial metaphor for the way he made decisions. You could never explain with a simple answer why Cash did what he did, because he was deliberately ambiguous; there are always multiple factors involved in trying to decode his intentions. As a thirty-seven-year-old man with a new wife and four kids from a previous marriage, Cash made and unlikely rebel, demographically, at least; on the finger adjacent to his bird is a wedding ring. Standing on the stage at San Quentin and playing in front of prisoners was rebellion, yet he was taping for an album, so he was not performing without commercial considerations. And he knew Marshall was taking pictures, so even the performance of the finger itself was not without intent.

We are drawn to him because of this ambiguity, this uncertainty. Yet the more we know about him, the more unknowable he becomes. If Cash was a mainstream performer in the 1950s, and a little less so in the 1960s, and completely country in the 1970s and 1980s, his tonal shift is surprising—to the fans of alternative music in the 1990s. Much of that occurred through Rubin and the machine that put Cash out in the 1990s. So selling Cash as a marker of rebellion is part of his history but also an explicit marketing strategy.

The slipperiness and somewhat inauthentic nature of the bird as a symbol also normalizes it within the realm of other rebellious rock symbols. Like many other rock symbols—"the Street-Fighting Man" and the trashed hotel room, the Mohawks and excessive zippers, the flannel shirts and the Nazi slogans—the bird is a sign of posed rebellion inscribed on a landscape where real rebellion is scarce.

We love rebellion or the image of it in our rock stars. It stands in for our own often never realized and thwarted rebellion. Accordingly, rebellion is often an audience-created marker. We make our symbols to suit ourselves as we did with the bird specifically and Johnny Cash generally. Johnny Cash is especially appropriate as a symbol because he constantly reinscribed familiar symbols and ideas with different meanings: country music, black, the finger, southern, Christian—these are words whose signifieds seem relatively stable, but they become unstable in Cash's hands. He was aware of this process, trafficked in his own symbolism, a man aware of the semiotics of his person, his clothing, his fingers, his voice, and the power that each of these, together or apart, had on his audiences. In the end, the finger represents a compact of sorts between the man and his audiences to codify his rebellion with our rapt attention and our interpretations. It was also a gesture that captured some of the essence of Cash's appeal—iconic, rebellious, reinvented, and now, with the passage of time, part of a tradition.

7
CASH CHOOSES HIS FAITH

I only hope . . . that someday John and June will
write a book for ALL the world to read . . . all about
THE MIRACLES OF GOSPEL ROAD. John and June
. . . PLEASE do this. This old world needs to learn
of this kind of miracle today . . . and who could
tell it better than you "born again Christians"
in the service of our Lord and our God.

—Virginia Strohler, *Our Kinda Cash*

At about the same time that Johnny Cash released his comeback album
with Rick Rubin in 1994, he put out the CD version of another large
project—a sixteen-volume recording of the New Testament with the
noted religious publisher Thomas Nelson. The timing of the two projects typified Cash's life after his religious reawakening. He traveled two
distinct but overlapping paths: one devoted to popular music and the
other to religion. He chose this religious path more than once—in 1959
when he released his first gospel album for Columbia, and again when
he renewed his faith in the 1970s. He may have helped derail a vibrant
career by declaring his faith on national television. But as the Bible
recording suggests, it was a choice he kept making again and again. The
choices to declare his faith on his television show and to make *The Gospel Road* place this chapter after Vietnam and before Rick Rubin.

Still, many if not most people did not know about Cash's deep religiosity (let alone the fact that he recorded the entire New Testament). The
question is how much this lack of knowledge was attributable to Cash's
desire to keep his religious and secular paths distinct and how much was
due to his audiences' willful ignorance. Are the two paths distinct
because Cash made them that way, because we want to read him that
way, or both? Although Cash never negated or denied his Christianity in
his popular music, he also found a way, or perhaps his audiences found
a way, to use it as a marker of his authenticity as country musician or a

southerner rather than as a pure expression of religious faith. Many of his fans saw one artist and one career; Virginia Strohler, who served as his fan club president for years with her husband Charles, saw no discrepancy between Cash as country musician and as gospel star. But many of his audiences found it hard to reconcile his dark side with his explicitly religious material.

Some of this confusion may have resulted from the fact that country music has strong links to Christian-oriented music. Because gospel music comes from many of the same roots as folk and country music, the majority of Cash's modern audience—those not familiar with songs like "It Was Jesus," an uncomplicated pop song about, well, Jesus[1]—may have believed his Christian music to be separate from his country music or perhaps a form of folk music. Country fans, on the other hand, knew that Jimmie Davis's "I Was There When It Happened" and Hank Williams's "I See the Light" (which Cash covers with great delight in his *Columbo* episode) were essential parts of the country canon.

Alternatively, later arriving audiences may have read some of his more directly religious songs as different aspects of his musical oeuvre—perhaps some as a form of Goth music, a perception earned by Cash in songs like "Folsom Prison Blues," "Ring of Fire," and especially his covers of "Rusty Cage" and "Hurt." One cut from his Rubin work, "Down There by the Train," on its surface seemed to be just another of his many train songs—but it is an explicitly religious metaphor. And "Kneeling Drunkard's Plea" in a rollicking way confirms the power of religious faith, but in a duet with Tom Petty it feels more like a story song. In these songs and others, Cash invited his audiences to imagine him as a rebel, iconoclast, sinner, or criminal, which gave them the impetus to view his religious music as an extension of songs about sin, revenge, and self-mutilation or as an expression of American ideals and history.

In other words, recorded by someone else—someone who had not made a movie about Jesus, written a novel about Paul's conversion, and recorded the New Testament as Cash did, not to mention invited Tammy Faye Bakker on stage in the 1990s—the expressions of religious faith might have served as one aspect of a multifaceted career (perhaps part of *Love, God, Murder*, Cash's anthology from 2000). And it was, yet even with Cash's real and prominent faith a very public part of him, somehow our perception of him has not fully acknowledged the depth of his faith.

Cash chose (or rechose) his faith for many of the reasons that others choose it—because he was a believer and because he needed it. A focus on the contexts for this explicit choice and, most important, some of the ways Cash communicated it to new audiences not so inclined to accept faith in a public setting requires a broader discussion of the way religion functions within American culture.

Cash sought what he defined as an authentic Christianity, as stripped down and basic as his music. In other words, as he did in choosing places to live, music to record, and content for his television show, he matched his idea of simplicity with the appropriate type of Christianity. That meant a nondenominational evangelicalism, and his expression—from singing songs to a stripped-down version of Jesus's story in Israel (*The Gospel Road*) and his story of Paul (*Man in White*)—focused on the meat, not the sauce. His emphasis on the simple over the complicated both unified Cash's religious oeuvre and confused his listeners—if his faith sounds like songs in which he sins, what makes them different? In other words, if God is another spoke on the wheel with Love and Murder, aren't they equal—and part of a commercial strategy? In Leigh Edwards's words, "he and his record companies incorporate his saint-sinner persona into their marketing and his media image"[2]—but only to the extent that there seems to be a relationship between the music and his Christianity. In other words, the recording of the Bible and the deep religiosity did not reach all of his audiences, and so whether Cash wanted it that way remains an open question.

CASH AND EVANGELICALISM

Cash did not readily self-identify as belonging to a particular denomination for some of the same reasons he did not like his music to be classified in a particular genre. We know he was evangelical mostly through his association with Graham, whose religious organization is called the Billy Graham Evangelical Association. Cash's willingness to do revivals and the traditional nature of his faith also marked him as an evangelical. And as Rodney Clapp notes, "Currently the de facto Protestant mainline in the United Sates is evangelicalism. In power centers as well [as] much of its heartland, America speaks with a southern, evangelical accent."[3]

Perhaps some of his reluctance to be "boxed" came from evangelical Christianity's reputation, particularly in recent years, of being associated with the religious right. As Christian Smith notes, however, evangelical Christians are much less unified than they are popularly portrayed, and, especially, often diverge from the writings of their leaders.[4] Smith and Randall Balmer have pointed out that within American evangelical religious practice there are different groups with different political beliefs. Graham today is virtually apolitical (earlier in his career he was a vocal anticommunist and anti-segregationist); Focus on the Family's James Dobson, who is one of the most powerful political figures in America, is the unofficial head of the religious right; Jim Wallis, editor of *Sojourners*, is decidedly liberal.

Still, evangelical Christianity's reputation, at least in popular perception, is right-leaning. When I explained to my students that I wanted to interview Billy Graham as part of this project, one student, with a decidedly negative tone, asked, "Why?" *His* question made me question my own surprise regarding the depth of Cash's faith. As someone who follows politics and the place of religion in American culture, I am sometimes suspicious of expressed religious faith in a public setting. Perhaps my suspicions come from the academic crowd I run with, a crowd that expresses skepticism about such faith. As Balmer writes: "We live in a skeptical, post-Enlightenment age where belief has become unfashionable; the liberal and ecumenical trends in Protestant theology, further, have blurred doctrinal differences in the name of unity, toleration, and inclusiveness."[5] And Stephen L. Carter points out that despite the often growing presence of religion in American culture, many people would "prefer to pretend it is not."[6] Perhaps this is one of the reasons why we do not think of Cash as religious: the content of his darker songs and his open-mindedness seem at odds with our stereotypical ideas of religious believers who speak in public, evangelicals such as Dobson, the late Jerry Falwell, and Pat Robertson, who have led us to believe that their faith and conservative politics represent all evangelicals. That construction would necessarily leave out someone like Cash.

The instability of evangelical Christianity's reputation is matched by the lack of consensus about what constitutes evangelical Christianity. There are some generalities, as Balmer describes: "Beyond general—but by no means unanimous—agreement on personal conversion, the importance of Scripture, and the expectation of an apocalypse, evangelicals contend with one another over the rigor of those beliefs and the appropriate expressions of piety. Evangelicals unite instead behind a charismatic leader, a common spiritual experience, or a set of doctrines—and, more than likely, some combination of the three."[7] They find common ground in belief but not in the expression of it. Cash himself in *Man in Black* indirectly connected to these beliefs: "I have more tolerance for people of other religions who traditionally reject the divinity of Jesus than I do for those people who claim to be Christians, yet disclaim and deny His virgin birth, His resurrection, or any of His miracles."[8] This was a classic evangelical view in its insistence on keeping the focus on the core beliefs of Christianity, and an emphasis on being a real Christian, rather than one who alters the core beliefs. But he also wrote a song that praised the "great super preachers" that "go crusadin' on" in "Billy & Rex & Oral & Bob."[9]

Something else Cash shared with evangelicalism was its seeming contradiction between current ideas of media and culture and tradition. Like popular culture generally, evangelical Christianity relies on modern forms of communication such as television, and even can be self-referential in the way it construes reality. When attending a Southern Baptist service in San Antonio in 1986, I was treated not only to a concert but also to the taping of a commercial for the church, as well as a lip-synced music performance. Was a church that needed to attract parishioners more real because it taped its commercials in front of a live audience? Although I suspect that my experience was atypical, the direct links between expression of faith and the daily realities of life, including the search for the money needed to run a church, seemed to be symbolic of a greater truth about the way evangelicalism confronts its needs directly. More important than the money is the notion of revival that puts on stage the direct desire to have people come to Christ, rather than some denominations' more subtle entreaties to find within oneself the means necessary to become committed.

Another evangelical link to Cash is this idea of choice. Graham's magazine is called *Decision*, emphasizing the role each person has in making a commitment to Jesus Christ.[10] Such an emphasis dovetails with Cash's conception of how he came to Christ, by conscious choice—which, I believe, was one of the reasons he tended to discount the role of June Carter in bringing him to religion and getting him off drugs. His recovery and his faith were his own. But put another way, evangelicalism is not much different from the music that Cash first recorded, generated by a combination of doctrine and on-the-ground experience. People called to evangelical preaching often rely on a mix of scripture and a vision of the world around them. Cash never had an orthodoxy surrounding his music, and it is not surprising that he did not have one for his religion either.

CASH'S RELIGIOUS HISTORY

Cash had a long, intense, public history of religious behavior that invited speculation, probably because he also had a history of bad behavior. We know that he ended up as a man of faith, but his beginnings probably had much to do with his ultimate religiosity. He was raised as a Christian by devout parents. Many of the songs he sang growing up were hymns (disc four of *Unearthed* is titled *My Mother's Hymn Book*). As he said while touring with *The Gospel Road*, "I've always sung gospel and religious songs . . . I've been a converted Christian since I was 14, but I did a lot of backsliding."[11] Tom Smucker suggested in the obituary he wrote for Cash in the *Village Voice*, however, that Cash's religious background was tempered by his family's inclusion in a government program that gave them both land and a house. Religious devotion in this modern era has often meant a more conservative political outlook, whereas Cash and his family saw early on that salvation on earth might also be aided by the government.

Although it is hard to gauge the depth of Cash's faith in his early career, he said the first songs he wanted to record were religious ones, as he recounts in *Man in Black*, primarily a hymn he wrote, "Belshazzar." But as he recounted, Sam Phillips, the head of Sun Records said, "I love those hymns and gospel songs, too, John, but we have to sell records to stay in business. We're a small company and can't afford to speculate on a new artist singing gospel."[12]

Cash did leave Sun for Columbia in part to be able to record religious music, but there were other reasons as well. The 1960s marked a tumultuous time for him, and finding religion in the mid-1960s was one of his ways out of it, at least temporarily. According to *Man in Black*, he did not do much active practicing of faith from the beginning of his career until he was born again in the early 1970s. He mentioned attending church sporadically when he lived in California, but the main narrative that the memoir focused on was his growing dependence on drugs and then turning to God for help: "Only I could do it, and I had to lean on God—like He knew I'd have to." And he did so, in 1967. But, backsliding on a trip to Vietnam in 1969, he described his temptation in terms of demons:

> "You deserve to enjoy the trip. Have a couple of capsules of Dexedrine," said a demon called Pride.
> "It's *your* business and nobody else's," said Arrogance.
> "Right. Nobody will know," said my old tormentor Deception.[13]

In the traditional Cash narrative, his religious devotion was intimately tied up with Carter and getting off drugs. Carter's faith may have had something to do with Cash's rediscovering his, but according to him, her influence was oversold. In his first autobiography, *Man in Black*, he described drug addiction as a form of evil. But he explained later:

> After I had managed to overcome my pill habit and things started to go good again, I had to realize that it was the prayers of a lot of people that pulled me through. And so I felt like it must be for a purpose—that God had some purpose on earth for me. So when June and I got married we decided to do things differently. We had both been converted when we were younger, but we'd given our bodies to the devil, and we'd really been through hell. So we decided to try to go back—to try to feel that touch of God we'd felt so long before.[14]

In *Man in Black* he replayed a conversation with Carter about deciding to join Evangel Temple in Nashville. She talked about being raised a Methodist; he described being raised a Baptist. Although he was not sure that he believed in the totality of Evangel's doctrine, he decided to join the church anyway, not wanting to "nit-pik" about "what's right or what's wrong with this or that church" and saying, "I need a spiritual foundation here on the earth that we have to walk around on. I need a spiritual anchor that I can reach back and grab hold of when I begin to drift. I'm human, and I need all the help I can get."[15] Note here that the simple reason for choosing faith and the dismissal of labels echo Cash's determination as a musical artist not to be classified. For if genres are bags, so are denominations.

According to Charles Paul Conn, author of a religious biography of Cash, the exact day of his true rebirth into Christianity was May 9, 1971, at a Pentecostal church outside Nashville, where he responded to an altar call, which is often part of the process of becoming born again. According to Conn, on that day "Johnny Cash stood up, stepped into the aisle, and walked a few short steps to the wooden altar. He knelt heavily on the deep-red carpet and in his own words, 'made complete dedication of my life to Jesus Christ.'"[16]

Christopher Wren, who had spent a significant amount of time with Cash in the late 1960s, told me that Cash did not seem particularly religious when he saw him then. But soon he announced on his national television show that he was a practicing Christian in response to questions he said had been mailed to him about the Christian content of many of his songs—itself an indication that audiences were confused about the relationship between country music and Christianity; otherwise, they would have assumed either that he was Christian or that it was just part of the oeuvre. His public admission, Cash intimated, had something to do with ABC's decision not to renew the show. Cash knew the peril: "Any combination of religion and TV, or religion and secular celebrity, makes for dangerous ground, full of traps and pitfalls, marked out with lines that can be too fine to see, and that's especially true for the man standing in the glare of the spotlights. I should know; I've crossed a few lines myself and found trouble on the other side." His policy, he said, was in general not to "cram anything down people's throats, but neither . . . [to] make any apologies for it."[17]

Christianity colored much of his life after his declaration of faith. Cash was part of a larger movement of religious revivalism. As Stephen Prothero notes, two very prominent movies about Jesus—adapted from stage musicals—appeared in 1973: *Jesus Christ Superstar* (score by

Andrew Lloyd Webber and Tim Rice) and *Godspell*. In 1972, Cash himself appeared at Explo '72, a religious festival attended by more than 80,000 at the Cotton Bowl in Dallas, which some labeled "Godstock"—a festival notably different from the Newport Folk Festival where he had played a few years before.[18]

After recommitting to religion in 1971, Cash undertook four prominent public forms of faith. The first was making *The Gospel Road*, a film released in 1973, which he funded himself. He approached Robert Elfstrom a few years after they made *Cash: The Man, His World, His Music*. "He called me up and said, 'Bob, I want you to make a film about Jesus.' I responded, 'Jesus who?' He responded, 'Jesus Christ.'" Elfstrom said Cash wanted to work with him again because he was comfortable with him: "I wasn't a feature film director or an actor or any of those things." Cash told Elfstrom that *Gospel Road* was motivated by his bad experience with network television: "He didn't like doing the TV series," Elfstrom said. Cash told him, "Bob, you know that live television steals your soul. It isn't clean money. June and I want to do this with the money." Elfstrom did the movie—and played Jesus despite being "not particularly" religious himself (and blond and blue-eyed). ("We had everybody but Jesus. 'Bob, why don't you do it?' he said. If he'd found a better one, a hippie going down the road, he would have used him," Elfstrom noted.)[19]

The film did not do well with secular audiences but remains popular in evangelical circles (promoted by Graham himself).[20] It features Cash standing on an Israeli mountain with a Bible in his hand, narrating the life of Jesus in Israel and singing, while a largely silent cast of characters act out a story. As he did with *The Man*, Elfstom directed a taut, well-paced movie. Unlike Mel Gibson's *Passion of the Christ* (2004), which overwhelms the viewer with violence, *The Gospel Road* is constructed on the idea that the story of Jesus is indeed a story that can be told quickly and simply. The film is a bit hokey in places, as Cash walks and talks to the camera a little too much, and sometimes the action seems a bit overacted—almost a necessity given that the only dialogue comes from Cash's mouth. This particular oddity, however, pushes the movie beyond simple docudrama. Overall, it is an effective dramatization of the life of Jesus and is much better than reviews indicate. Moreover, the film reflects the ethos of Cash's religious faith. As Edwards notes, its focus on Jesus' advocating for the poor connected with Cash's "class advocacy."[21] It's Cash and Bible in the real holy land, Israel—the site for the Bible—and it is the Bible's words that are spoken, not lines invented for the actors. Again, the simple idea and concept led to a more complicated artistic expression.[22]

Despite or perhaps because of this emphasis on authenticity, the reviews were decidedly mixed. One reviewer wrote: "At times, 'Gospel Road' becomes overly dramatic. Cymbals crash and modern city scenes flash across the background as Jesus dies on the cross, for example. But most viewers will find Cash's vision of Jesus warm, personal and valid."[23] Another reviewer, Richard Mial, was less kind—in fact, sarcastic: "'The Gospel Road' . . . is pretty boring, even with all the sunset photography, and the country songs sung by Cash, his wife and Kris Kristofferson." Mial pointed out that "Cash narrates the movie with all the rough hewn sincerity that sold thousands [of gallons] of Amoco gasoline. . . . You expect more from Jesus, but you just don't get it." He went on to mock the heavy-handedness of the crucifixion scene: "When Jesus is on the cross, the background scene shifts from a deserted village near Jerico [sic] to large American cities (it can happen here, you know)." Overall, he concludes that "there aren't any new insights here, and the film was viewed by fewer than 30 people at the 7 p.m. show." He quoted the ticket-taker: "We're competing with *Godspell*" (which was playing at another cinema).[24]

As the empty seats indicated, the movie did not recoup the $500,000 it reportedly cost, at least not in the theaters. Some of its lack of success may have had to do with Fox's limited promotion. George Vescey quoted Hal Sherman, the company's coordinator of national promotions: "It's good quality but it has a very strong fundamentalist opinion. In the south, people take the Bible more literally than in New York, Chicago or Los Angeles. Theater owners resist this kind of picture because traditionally people go to church on Sunday and they want entertainment from the movies." Sherman said the studio would "schedule it where we get requests."[25] Sherman confirms what we suspect: the media believed that audiences for *The Gospel Road* and probably other religious material produced by Cash would be the same as for his country music. In short, they saw Cash's new turn as a turn away from the national audiences he once commanded.

In the same period, Cash began to attend religious revivals hosted by Graham and others, a practice that continued as long as he was able to undertake music tours (he attended a revival with Graham as late as the mid-1990s). In 1974, at one hosted by James Robison of Hurst, Texas, Cash came and sang two songs, but according to one account, his witnessing was the crucial part. He talked about his seven one-night jail stays and how much life had changed since he found God:

> My life, you could cut the last 14 years into two seven-year slices. The last seven years I've been a milk-fed Christian trying to grow. Every day has been a new and rewarding experience.
>
> Out here in that world that I live in, the entertainment world, which I love, there [are] a lot of people that don't exactly share my faith. I'm some kind of weird freak, I guess to a lot of 'em and I'm a terrible contradiction, because they read all that truth about me all those years, and they don't understand Johnny Cash going right. I threw the script away they had planned for me—the script that said I was supposed to die along about October of 1967. But that's when I was born.[26]

Part of Cash's strategy in talking about both faith and his past was to reveal the seeming contradiction between his life before and after being born again, to make it seem real. But more important, he spoke to the notion that his religious faith had confused his friends in the entertainment business—and therefore probably his audiences as well.

He took this approach even further with his first autobiography. *Man in Black* was ostensibly the story of his life and career, but it focused on his drug and alcohol addiction and then his redemption, told from a religious point of view. Cash was unrelenting in his description of what he considered sinful behavior, and the end of the book has a laser focus on his religious commitment. At the beginning of the second-to-last chapter, he wrote: "I have learned that a Christian cannot perform a totally secular concert," but as he says, he didn't perform an entirely religious one either. He did not dismiss his performing life but made clear that it took second place to Christianity: "What an obligation Christians have to those who are seeking—even to nonbelievers who are not seeking; and the entertainment world is the front line for spiritual battles."[27] This approach changed—his 1990s religious beliefs were more subtly displayed. Perhaps after almost twenty years of wandering in what constituted the entertainment desert—two recording companies had dropped him, and he was playing smaller and smaller venues—fighting such religious battles became less important in the entertainment world itself. In the same chapter, he published a letter he had written to Graham from Las Vegas, asking him to crusade there. And the last chapter begins with a request to appear at the revival of James Robison in Fort Worth, and ends with Cash connecting turbulence on the plane with flying over his brother Jack's grave. Rita Forrester, June Carter's cousin (A.P. and Sara Carter's grandchild), has indicated that Cash still was affected by Jack's death even in his later years.[28]

Published in 1975, the book marked the third reinterpretation of the Man in Black—from cool musician to protest artist to redeemed singer. *Man in Black* is essentially a confession of past drug use and a narrative of conversion. Its oddity is that Cash downplayed almost everything but his drug use (much like the Ray Charles biopic, *Ray*, 2004), on which he spent so much time that he diminished other aspects of his life and career in order to serve the greater purpose of announcing his faith.[29] This balance changes in his second autobiography, *Cash* (1997), a book that places his religious faith in more context. One could certainly expect *Man in Black* to be a religious work, given that it was published by Zondervan, which says on its website: "We are an international Christian communications company that provides resources for people of every age and in every stage of life as they seek a richer, more fervent, more enlightened relationship with Jesus Christ."[30] The book was in a way a punctuation mark on the third phase of his career, one that began with *At Folsom Prison* and concluded with this newfound focus on Christianity.

As with anything new about a celebrity, Cash's religious belief received a lot of attention in the 1970s because it stood in such contrast to his well-known bad behavior. In an interview with *Penthouse*, asked whether he was becoming more "radical," Cash said he was just trying to become a "good Christian." He said his religious philosophy was simple, that there were three types of Christians, "preaching Christians, church-playing Christians, and practicing Christians," and "I'm trying hard to be a practicing Christian. If you take the words of Jesus literally and apply them to your everyday life, you discover that the greatest fulfillment you'll ever find really does lie in giving."[31] Again, although he did not talk specifically about authenticity, the implication was that practicing Christians were the real Christians.

In this same period, Cash participated in making a Christian comic book about his life, which took the same earnest tack but has a friendlier face and, unavoidable in retrospect, was a bit of camp, especially when reading the text about religious devotion set in comic book font. The Cash comic indicates his dialect by omitting the "g" from every present participle and gerund, and the sentences end with an exclamation point—or three. Example: "SOMETIMES GOD SEEMED A LONG WAY OFF . . . BUT I NEVER STOPPED SINGIN' . . . AND HE NEVER STOPPED LOVIN'!!!" Font and grammar aside, the work demonstrates the narrative of Cash's life as a triad of music, temptation, and realization of God's power. In one early episode about his life in Germany in the air force, the narrative shows him first playing music for other people, then noticing that "JUST ABOUT EVERYBODY IN GERMANY DRANK BEER" and later regretting that he "IGNORED CHURCH!" and remembering "THE SONGS I USED TO SING . . . ABOUT **JESUS!**" It shows the temptation of women for Cash at the beginning of his career (women in the 1950s are pictured wearing halter tops and short skirts to enhance the temptation) as Cash thinks: "IT'S GONNA BE **TOUGH** LIVIN' A CHRISTIAN LIFE IN **THIS** *BUSINESS!!!*" The true temptation comes through the pills: the comic book has DECEPTION depicted as a moving image coming right from the pill jar.[32] I'm trying not to poke fun but to show how deeply committed Cash was to his religion in 1976 and how a simplified version of it was presented to his young audiences.

In this period, Cash was less guarded and unabashedly direct in his religious belief; later he seemed to become more aware of the effect his words might have on his audiences, though he answered direct questions about his faith openly. He did not see his faith as contradictory to his love of country music or his performing: "See, I do what I do no matter where I am. I'll be what I am and if it turns people off, they can [listen to] somebody else." The fact that he would give an interview to *Pent-*

house and play in Las Vegas showed that he tried to demonstrate that being a Christian did not change his being the star that audiences had gravitated to in the 1960s. And he felt no need to proselytize: "I'm not so much of a gleaner because if you really want to get into religion I believe that if people sow the proper seed, the Holy Spirit will do some work as time goes by." The most passionate part of an interview with Don Cusic came when Cash responded to Paul Harvey's charge that country music was "pornography": "I don't think that is fair at all. I just don't think that it is fair to the people who love music. You can take any kind of music you want and use it as a vehicle for obscenity. . . . To say that country music is decadent or rock n roll music or rockabilly is decadent is just a ridiculous statement." He believed that audiences tend to make whatever they want out of the music: "I really think it is what the people make it in their own minds and their own lives. I don't make it rotten or a vehicle of sexual expression or thought." Cash here suggested that the audiences who listened to popular culture participated in meaning-making, a belief that seemed to guide him at many points in his career. Perhaps the most interesting (and unexplained) comment came at the end when he said he loved country for the "music's sake: It has nothing really to with sex, except the fact that I feel very virile. I really get into the music and the beat."[33]

For his next public Christian act, Cash wrote the story of the Apostle Paul in *Man in White* (1986). The novel recounts the story dispassionately and forthrightly, letting the power of Paul's conversion's serve as the focus, keeping the book in line with the simplicity of his other religious concepts. *Man in White* comes from what Graham called a "Paul obsession" that Cash had in the 1970s which also led to the song, "One of These Days I'm Gonna Sit Down with Paul": "I will ask him about his journeys / And he will tell me about them all."[34] Billy Graham's biographer Marshall Frady called Cash "an especially energetic disciple of Graham's," and Graham agreed: "He's been studying the New Testament all the way through, he's on St. Paul now—he's just finished the letter to Timothy and he's starting on Titus." Graham added: "I tell you, Paul has become all Johnny wants to talk about here lately. He thinks Paul, eats Paul, sleeps Paul, I expect dreams Paul. He even wants to make a movie with us on Paul now. He wants to play Paul himself. We've had to tell him we just can't do it if he insists on that, and I hope he'll finally agree not to. I like Johnny a lot, but Johnny Cash playing the role of St. Paul wouldn't quite—you have to watch out sometimes, you know, you can lose your balance and perspective if you get too absorbed in a thing."[35] What's left unsaid is that Cash never fully escaped from his reputation—almost every biography, even now, recounts his drug troubles—and though Graham clearly loved Cash, he carried a certain wariness about Cash's faith. More important, he worried about Cash's reception as Paul in front of a religious audience—the flip side of his mainstream handlers' worries about Cash as a religious man in front of a secular audience.

We might ask why Johnny Cash identified so strongly with the Apostle Paul. His *Man in White* is inconclusive about this, but one could certainly speculate that he saw a parallel between himself and Paul and their religious transformations. Leigh Edwards believes that Cash saw a parallel "saint-sinner dichotomy" between himself and Paul and therefore "accentuate[d] Paul as an individualistic hero who achieves his religious goals and refuses to be defined by his society, preferring to define himself though his interaction with religion."[36] Why too as a religion-oriented performer did he so insistently play for secular audiences? And where does all this fit into how we view Cash as a cultural figure? Arguably, his complex handling of his religious faith—intellectually, musically, and emotionally, though these responses overlap—shows the same complexity and indeterminateness expected of Cash in other matters. The introduction to *Man in White* is vague; Cash cited Paul's ability to get things done directly—the book jacket cites Cash's interest with the transformation. It may be that Paul's transformation from torturer of new Christians to a primary author of Christianity is an imperfect metaphor for Cash's own revelation. Even in *The Gospel Road*, Cash never saw himself as Jesus—instead he told Jesus's story. So as a teller of Paul's tale as well as a more open proselytizer for Christianity, Cash could begin to do some of the work Paul did, as he tried to do in *The Gospel Road*, *Man in White*, his gospel music, and his less well-known Christian forays. And what could be more Paul-like than trying to sell Christianity within the secular entertainment world? (His country audience, of course, as witnessed by Virginia Strohler's request, certainly might have been receptive.) Cash said in an interview, "Paul had become my hero. He was invincible. He made it his life's mission to conquer and convert the idolatrous, pagan world over to Jesus."[37] He also told *People* magazine (article title: "From *A Boy Named Sue* to a Saint Named Paul): "I got excited about him. It started coming to me what this man was up against—to take the gospel of Jesus Christ into a world that already had more gods than they needed, or could even remember. It was a very tough selling job." The book was better reviewed than the *The Gospel Road*. As Mary Campbell wrote for the Associated Press: "'Man in White,' though it is the first novel Cash has written, has a style that compels one's continued attention."[38]

Though clearly written from passion, *Man in White* does not seem as passionate as its author is about the subject, but it does reflect his idea of informed simplicity—the purpose of the book's lack of adornment is to get at the truth of the Apostle Paul's story, which of course is complicated. At this point in the mid-1980s, Cash had not had a hit in years, and he took a notably defiant tone about his faith, though he's certainly not defensive. In many ways, the book is not a particularly important one, either in the general scheme of religious history or in how Cash will be remembered; not a single person I talked to about him even knew that he had written a novel, let alone one about the Apostle Paul.

The last prominent religious act, outside of his music-recording career, was to record the entire New Testament, which was first released on tape and later on CD. If possible, this rendition has even less tone than the novel—Cash performed a no-nonsense reading from beginning to end. If simplicity is authenticity, then this version certainly qualifies as authentic. But not everyone accepted Cash's transformation. When I went to Nashville for research, I stayed across the street from a Lifeway Christian Store and, as it happens, the whole Lifeway corporate complex. They did not sell Cash's recording there, though they did sell James Earl Jones's reading of the Bible as well as books on the religious lives of UCLA basketball coach John Wooden, NASCAR driver Darrell Waltrip, and soccer player Michelle Akers. I did not know what to make of this; it seemed strange that one of Nashville's heroes could record the New Testament and yet it would not be sold in this Christian bookstore only a few blocks away from Ryman Auditorium, site of the Grand Ole Opry, and close to the Country Music Hall of Fame. The assistant manager told me, "Just because someone is from a place, doesn't mean they are popular here," demonstrating again that three decades later, Cash's passion for religion had not eclipsed his dark 1960s reputation.[39]

Cash participated in a few other religious acts as well. He recorded an electronic Bible which he helped sell at Christian merchandising conventions at least as late as 1997. He wrote a preface for a 1991 religious self-help book, Arthur A. Smith's *Apply It to Life*. He described Smith's faith in glowing terms, in a way only someone deeply committed to religion could: "Arthur is a living testimonial to the fulfillment of this promise. He has long walked in the Light. He has been an exemplary disciple of the Lord for the thirty years I have known him, and he has often shed much light on my path during times of adversity. But now, with this work, the matured, wounded and healed, tested and tried Arthur A. Smith shines in the full spiritual light of day." Smith's purpose, Cash continued, was to show "us how we can apply to life the lessons in the parables, the teachings of Jesus, and the experiences of great men of God such as David. The classic story of the prodigal son becomes, in the light of Arthur's writing, a lesson for the church today on unity, usefulness, and vision."[40] Smith clearly did not show the same reluctance as the assistant manager in allowing Cash an association with a religious book.

Yet, after announcing his faith on *The Johnny Cash Show*, Cash learned quickly that religious expression might indeed hurt his secular career. One can also see in this announcement a commitment to meta-discourse on the part of both Cash and his audience. Both in the show in 1971 and his autobiography in 1997, he explained to his viewers and readers how he lived his Christianity, making public what often is private in order to make it real. As was true of his marriage to Carter, this perceived authenticity came from transparency and public disclosure. In particular, his efforts at both were a way of ensuring that the public saw the "real Cash," a source of his appeal to audiences. And given religion's place in American culture, it was not enough for him to be religious—he had to explain it.

That was due in part to the nature of Cash's legacy as a celebrity— although at least some of Cash's power came from his authenticity, it also came from his rebellion. So in an audience that wanted a simpler narrative, Cash's religious beliefs may have caused a disconnect with his previous image. He left it to the audience to interpret what was a straight-forward statement—he said he was a Christian, and some wanted to believe he was something else; audiences in a more straightforward time with a more straightforward author would have taken him at his word. If we do not associate Cash with Christianity, we have both ourselves and Cash to blame. If we would rather our public figures be discreet about their religiosity, in Cash, we have got our wish: he framed his reli-gion in a way that made us believe it might performance, or perhaps part of the genre in which he was performing. In other words, there seems to be no question that Cash's faith was authentic—what is more open to question is whether his relationship with the public regarding faith was authentic, and whether he used his image of a complicated, rebellious musician and performer as a buffer for his faith. Cash did use figures like Graham and James Robison and, more important, Christian doc-trine itself to help keep the tribulations of pop stardom at bay. In doing so, he fashioned himself as a religious believer and one not afraid to become vocal about his beliefs. But his self-fashioning never quite took with the public at large, which never lost Cash's idea of himself, also consciously formed, as a rebellious iconoclast.

Cash in some ways did not choose his faith—he was born in a reli-gious household, and he says never he truly lost his religious devotion. And as part of Christian faith, one often believes one is chosen as much as one chooses. What he did choose, and choose completely, was a form of encompassing religious faith that in turn changed the way he looked at and interacted with the world. One can argue whether, choosing God or being chosen, is more powerful, but what Cash *did* choose were the connections between his faith and his music, both of which were passed on to his audiences.

No matter how he fashioned himself publicly, then, his multidimen-sional response would not have disappointed authenticants or casual fans. His choice of faith would have seemed to end effectively an existen-tial crisis that had dominated his life since he graduated from high school. In some ways, this choice was the most crucial of the second half of his life, yet it coincided with his least productive and least successful musical period. And since his identity was so tied up in music, such a state had to raise doubts about his future in the music profession, inducing an existential crisis of a different kind. In contrast to his marriage to June Carter and his explicit indeterminateness when it came to the Vietnam War, Cash seemed to have mixed feelings about using public discourse as a way of authenticating his faith. Or perhaps the audience had its own mixed feelings about rewriting its own expectations of a new kind of a Man in Black.

CASH'S MUSICAL AND RELIGIOUS HISTORY

Cash's musical career was intimately tied to his religious life in a way that should have left no doubt of his faith: he put out several albums of hymns, beginning in the 1950s; many of his songs have religious components; and his three-album set is titled, *Love, God, Murder.* Many of his rural and small-town associations placed him distinctly in the country music genre. What also placed him there was his religious music; there is a long-standing connection between country music and religion, with strong geographic ties between the two.

Though country music is popular all over the country, rural areas appreciate it more than cities do. Religious faith often works the same way—the red states are more openly devout than the blue states, though I would be neglectful not to say that blue staters are often religious (and often enjoy country music too). So it's not surprising that scholars have made the same connection as Jimmie N. Rogers and Stephen A. Smith: "Religion and country music also remain prominent symbiotic cultural institutions in the South."[41] Thus some of the demographic connections are clear. Among other connections, Cash himself explained in 1974 that "simply, country people are honest in their expression of feeling, and God comes through in their songs."[42] Honesty here stands in for authenticity.

But there are different ways of interpreting this honesty. The contrasting attitudes can best be summed up by two iconic quotations, one from comedian Bob Newhart and the other from the famed country songwriter Harlan Howard (responsible for "Busted" and "I Fall to Pieces," among many country standards). As a staple of his comedy routine, Newhart often tells audiences, "I don't mean to denigrate country

music—for those who like country music, denigrate means 'don't like.'"[43]
Howard's famous definition reads, "Country music is three chords and
the truth." Newhart indicts country music's audience, while Howard
praises the work that country music does, simple as it might sound. It's
a running joke in popular culture that talking about one's woman, dog,
or truck constitutes a large percentage of the content of country songs
(add 9/11 and patriotism, and the percentage would go higher). On their
surface, these songs often do not have layers of irony or abstraction;
their content is often startlingly direct for those unaccustomed to it.
Other genres of music such as hip-hop and traditionally defined pop
often have these elements of straightforwardness as well, as does plenty
of rock music—but the kinds of rock and roll that critics like needs
interpretation or shies away from direct expression. That is what rockism is all about.[44]

Having said that, one must add that anyone who reads country music
so directly misses a great deal of nuance and subtlety that exists beyond
the first level of expression. That subtlety often is in the layered nature of
a song in itself, and always in the complex understanding one must have
about the nature of the way audiences connect with not only country
songs but songs as a whole. Aaron Fox and Cecelia Tichi believe that it is
a mistake to read country music so simply. Fox compellingly argues in
Real Country that country music (particularly the classics) is "a vital cultural tradition." His book in fact is a testimony to the "richness, gram-
maticality, and rhetorical brilliance of even 'average' working-class Texas
English discourse," and it makes the case for "respecting the beauty, skill-
fulness, and power of a dialect that is so often stereotyped as 'illiterate'
and 'ignorant'"—a direct refutation of Newhart and an endorsement of
Howard.[45] Our mistakes, then, come mostly from underestimating the
discourse involved in the way country music transforms emotional
responses to complex situations into more easily digested lyrics. But it is
also the case that southerners have never fully recovered in the national
mind from their regionally slow acceptance of civil rights, and since
country music is often associated with the South—and is an overwhelmingly white genre—it shares, fairly or not, some of the South's legacy
regarding race.

There are more genre- and geography-based reasons for the links between country music and religion. Gospel music has a long tradition within country music, whereas it has almost no tradition within mainstream rock music.[46] Part of this has to do, perhaps, with the greater integration of religion into the daily life of the more rural populace that in general listens to country music, whereas rock and roll music began in an era when public faith was less prominent and when, in its rise from country, blues, and rhythm and blues, it lost the religious content in order to appeal to a wider, largely teen demographic. But from the beginning, religion has been a part of country music. Country Music Television, the country equivalent of MTV and home of country videos, used to host religious shows; try to imagine MTV doing the same. (CMT no longer does so—perhaps because it is owned by Viacom, the same company that owns MTV.) And the Southern Baptist Convention produces a weekly radio program called *Country Crossroads*, which, as of 2005, appeared on more than 400 country stations (down from 1,500 in 1993) to demonstrate "the strong, religious heritage of this nation [and] to inform people that Christianity is relevant, that Christ can make a permanent difference in our lives." As Rogers and Smith go on to point out, as of the early 1990s the stations that carry the show are much more prevalent in the former Confederate states (their term, not mine), which have an average of 60 stations per state, as opposed to the non-Confederate states with an average of 21.[47] *Country Crossroads* is also syndicated as a television show.

Part of the prominence of religious content in country music, compared with other genres, has to do with its relationship to rebellion. In general, rock and roll celebrates rebellion within the music in a way country music does not; country musicians tend to rebel *outside* the music—witness the hard living of Cash, Hank Williams, George Jones, and Waylon Jennings. Still, as Cash himself pointed out, rebellion was not only the province of rock and roll; "Folsom Prison Blues" is just one such work in country music. Barbara Ching writes in *Wrong's What I Do Best*, however, that the decidedly rebellious trend in country music, is not the music that gets played on the radio.[48]

Part of the reason has to do with Howard's statement about three chords and the truth. Religious belief carries this same commitment to a powerful truth and is earnest almost by definition; one has to believe what one says when expressing thoughts about God. There is also a strain of redemption in both Christianity and country music, occcasionally at the same time. Country music requires sinners—or a loss of faith or will or morals—who need to be redeemed. This aspect does mark Cash as country; his work presents unrepentant sinners whose fates may be sealed but for whose lives he wants us to feel sympathy. ·

For most of his career, his religious songs delivered the gospel in definitive vernacular. For example, "The Greatest Cowboy of Them All" describes the "the man who rode the donkey / He's the greatest cowboy of 'em all." Another song about Jesus is "I'm Gonna Try to Be That Way": "He never done anybody wrong, um um / He tried to help everybody 'long." Or in "He'll Be a Friend": "Well God told Noah to build an ark / He said it's gonna rain, gonna be dark." Just as he did with his vernacular tellings of American history, Cash tried to use songwriting in an everyday, decidedly southern voice to reach his audience. In "God Is Not Dead," he even addressed the famous *New York Times* headline: "It isn't God, but man that's dead / When love is locked outside."[49]

In the last part of his career, especially with Rick Rubin, his albums are laden with religious material. Some of the songs feature clear displays of faith; others are a mix of story and religious belief. "Kneeling Drunkard's Plea" is the latter; "Why Me Lord" is the former. Although many mainstream reviewers chose not to focus on the Christian content, at least one Christian magazine took note of it in Cash's music. Arsenio Orteza, writing in the Christian publication *World*, said about *Unchained*

> that the album's biggest root is gospel seems to have gone unremarked upon by the same journalists who still haven't given the gospel music of Mr. Cash's friend Bob Dylan serious attention. But gospel predominates, both overt (. . . "Spiritual," & "Kneeling Drunkard's Plea," & "Meet Me in Heaven") and subtle (the title song and "Rusty Cage"). Songs originally made famous by Jimmie Rodgers, Don Gibson, Hank Snow, Dean Martin, and the alternative rockers Beck and Soundgarden, are unified by Cash's gospel sensibility, elevating *Unchained* to the level of art.[50]

Orteza was correct in noting that religious material in Cash's albums was not mentioned as much as were the other parts of Cash's trilogy of

Love, God, Murder. The irony, of course, was that Cash was no longer part of a country world that would appreciate religious content, and the rock/alternative/Americana world that he lived in then was generally uncomfortable with direct expressions of faith. The title track begins with Cash reading the Bible over what sounds like a radio with excessive static, evoking radio shows from the past. The song itself is an explicitly religious telling of Revelation.

But Cash deflected the religious content. He must have known that when someone hears him sing about the Man coming around, they most likely think about Cash himself (the Man in Black) rather than Jesus or God. Indeed, here Cash might have been performing a mild version of what Bruce Lincoln, when referring to George W. Bush's religious stance, calls "double coding." Lincoln writes about Bush's use of religious imagery: that "the practice lets him convey things the faithful love to hear, while also letting them feel that they enjoy a privileged relation to him by virtue of sharing biblical reference points. At the same time, it lets him veil these things from people who would be put off by the biblical language or might challenge its propriety."[51] If it makes Americans uncomfortable to display faith, why not code it both ways? Cash went further in the case of "The Man Comes Around." In several accounts, including his liner notes, he explained that the song came to him in a dream about Queen Elizabeth, during which she called Cash a "whirlwind," which becomes "whirlwind in the thorn trees." I do not think Cash was trying to deceive, but he did divert the reader from the song's religious content when he referred to Queen Elizabeth, hardly a symbol of piety. "The Man Comes Around" is prototypically Cash—difficult to pin down because of both the song's content and Cash's discussion about it.

PUBLIC RELIGION AND ARTISTIC EXPRESSION: CASH'S DILEMMA WRIT LARGE

In recent years, Americans have more explicitly discussed what determines appropriate public expression of faith, especially given a president, George W. Bush, who reportedly said that God wanted him to be president, and a Hollywood actor, Mel Gibson, who spent considerable cultural and economic capital to make a docudrama about Jesus.

Though contributing to the upsurge in the debate about the place of religion in public life, Bush and Gibson were involved in familiar controversies, as the public place of religion has been an issue from the beginning of American history. The separation of church and state happened after a long history of religious behavior within the public sphere, starting with the Puritans and Pilgrims and the theocracies of the Massachusetts Bay Colony. That the framers of the Constitution decided to separate church and state probably contributed to the attempts to regulate the presence of religion in public affairs, but their efforts have done little to stop it from being a source of controversy in everything from Christmas assemblies in public schools to the displaying of the Ten Commandments in courthouses to public prayer in government-sponsored activities.

Following the 2004 election, commentators were quick to point out that faith had influenced backers of Bush, in a way that probably helped lead him to victory. According to Dan Gilgoff, Bush's campaign targeted evangelicals as the single group that would give him the popular majority vote he did not have in 2000: "Between new evangelical voters and those who had voted for Gore in 2000, Bush picked up nearly 6 million new evangelical votes, about twice his margin of victory."[52] The notion of what place faith has in the public discourse has never been more under discussion. Among books addressing this question generally are Jim Wallis's *God's Politics: Why the Right Gets It Wrong and the Left Doesn't Get It* (2005), and Thomas Frank's *What's the Matter with Kansas* (2004)—and, more specifically, *A Man of Faith: The Spiritual Journey of George W. Bush*, by David Aikman (2004) and *The Faith of George W. Bush* (2005) by Stephen Mansfield.

The issues at play here are the presence of religion in public life, the public expression of faith by individuals, and the divide between church and state; related questions include how much should faith influence public policy; how vocal should political leaders be about religion; how vocal should cultural figures be about religion; what is the public tolerance for such issues, and how should that influence political and cultural figures?

Johnny Cash was a singer and Mel Gibson is an entertainer, and they do not belong in the same category as George W. Bush, who was charged with leading America according to its laws and, many would say, its principles. But Gibson does and Cash did matter in the public sphere, if their attention from the public is any criterion. And at least according to gate receipts, *The Passion of the Christ* received quite a lot of attention—it grossed more than $370 million.[53] It does say something about the religious nature of American culture that the third most popular movie of 2004 was a story about Jesus. The success of *The Passion* validated Gibson's particular worldview and allowed those with similar ideas a place in the debate. But it also was a risk for Gibson, who had earned a great deal of cultural capital as an actor and director over the years, to spend it on one film.

For Cash, it was a similar transaction; the writer of "Folsom Prison Blues" and "I Walk the Line" spent his cultural capital on *The Gospel Road*. Tom Cruise chooses to spend his on an affirmation of Scientology. When actors and musicians do try to transfer their influence outside the way they made their reputations, they cannot know what they are going to get. In the case of Cash, Cruise, and Gibson, their hopes were that the public would translate their interest into religious devotion. That being said, though, it's not clear that the motives of Gibson and Cash were transactional. In the case of *Gospel Road* and *Man in White*, Cash could not have expected his work to reach a wide audience—but thirty years later, Gibson's did. What had changed? For one thing, Christian groups were much better organized in their efforts to get people out to see Gibson's movie. For another, the movie aroused controversy, which made people want to see it. And Gibson was an actor in and director of successful movies before, probably made a better movie than Cash did.

On the other hand, Cash's faith, while ever present and conspicuous, was tolerant and sympathetic, which has not always been true with those who express their faith so publicly.[54] One trait that Cash did share with other evangelicals is that he was personally and explicitly Christian; his faith was an essential part of his life and music—but he also made it clear that faith didn't necessarily dictate his art:

> I put God and my family first. God is the basis for all living. We try to live our lives so that we reflect our Christianity and be a credit to our Christian faith. I think the world needs Christian entertainers. Some have asked me if I was going into full-time Gospel

Singing. Well, God hasn't yet given me those great gospel songs to write or sing. The Lord called me 22 years ago to be an entertainer. I try to be the best entertainer I can and also to live the best Christian life I can. We try to combine all form(s) of music into our lives and show that it all works thru Christianity.[55]

Cash stated here that religion would not trump art—performing and being an artist meant presenting the best material he had. Faith has an often contentious and sometimes negative relationship with mainstream popular culture generally and music specifically. But the reasons are not simply a discomfort with public displays of faith in a secular society or the humanistic legacy of separate church and state. Most people profess to have some faith but do not express it in a public forum. Accordingly, some Americans hold a grudge against those who do express their faith in a way that seems publicly exclusionary. It's one thing to be religious or to celebrate one's faith in a public fashion, but those publicly identified as being "religious" but who are not religious figures are perceived to have separated themselves from a portion of the public with an unbridgeable gap.

It is clear that some public figures understand this—Jimmy Carter, Bill Clinton, George H. W. Bush, and Ronald Reagan all went to church, but most citizens probably did not attach much significance to it. The second President Bush has said that he believed God wanted him to be president; according to Richard Land, a Baptist preacher, he said so at a meeting at the Texas governor's mansion shortly before he decided to run for the White House. That a presidential candidate would think this way is not acceptable to a large portion of the public.[56] And sometimes musical groups and public figures are inadvertently caught up in this disagreement. After his initial foray into controversy on his television show, however, Cash never seemed to use his faith as a way of separating himself from others or as a means to criticize. One of his reasons was more personal than theological—as he said openly, he did not like to be put "in a bag." Part of his power as singer and entertainer—and man— came from his mystery. In a way, his religious side added to that mystery and power; without the "God" portion of Love, God, Murder, love and murder would be less mysterious.

CODA: SUFJAN STEVENS

Another artist who fits Cash's profile has emerged—a mainstream singer, difficult to classify as to genre, whose music has distinct Christian elements. That musician is Sufjan Stevens, the independent darling and provider of the unofficial soundtrack for Brooklyn coffeeshops in 2007. Stevens has put out several albums, the most famous being his two state collections, *Michigan* and *Illinois*, part of a proposed fifty-state album project.

Another part of his oeuvre is *Seven Swans*, which is notably Christian in content, with songs about Abraham; the Transfiguration, a turning point in Jesus' life; and "All the Trees of the Field Will Clap Their Hands" (the title a reference to Isaiah 55:12): "If I am alive this time next year / Will I have arrived in time to share? / And mine is about as good this far. / And I'm still applied to what you are. / And I am joining all my thoughts to you. / And I'm preparing every part for you."[57]

While Stevens seemed open to discussing the Christian content of his albums before releasing *Illinois*, as commentators have noted, his reluctance has grown since then because he senses the hostility of his audience, the college crowd Cash also sought, toward religious content. As Randall J. Stephens and Delvyn Case write, Stevens has "joined the ranks of a handful of other artists and bands—Danielson Familie, Damien Jurado, Pedro the Lion, and Starflyer 59—which have earned respect and critical acclaim almost in spite of rather than because of their Christian faith."[58] Stevens has shied away from such discussions. As Nick Sylvester notes, "So Stevens apparently believes the 'Christian artist' stamp is a deal breaker. Likewise his publicist, who reminded me that 'Sufjan has asked that the topic of religion not be discussed in interviews from this point on.'"[59]

Stevens's fears are legitimate. Given the climate in the country, religious expression now has connotations that it did not a generation ago. Yet artists who work on religious material that is clever and nuanced, or direct and sincere, may find ways around this feeling. Cash's Christianity displayed directly in *Love, Murder, God* did little to dissuade his listeners from being loyal.

And just as Cash learned later in his career, Stevens knows he can't avoid discussions of his material: "I do have to reckon with the material I'm singing about. And I want to be responsible for what I'm singing about. But I can't be responsible for an entire culture, or an entire church. I can't be responsible for Christendom. I think that when people react reflexively to material that is religious, they're reacting to the culture of religion. And I think an enlightened person is capable, on some level, of making the distinction between the institution of the culture and the culture itself."[60] In the world of independent music, though, where authenticity is a watchword, acknowledging the theological aspects of his work may ultimately be problematic. As Stevens said in an interview: "I don't think music media is the real forum for theological discussions."[61]

Andree Farias, writing in *Christianity Today*, may have the most appropriate response for the dilemma faced by Stevens and Cash: "Indie heads need Jesus, too."[62]

8
CASH CHOOSES RICK RUBIN

In 1993, at the now departed Rhythm Café, a dinner theater in Santa Ana, California, Rick Rubin approached Johnny Cash, wondering if Cash would consider recording with him. There was some hesitation on both ends—Cash called his daughter, Rosanne Cash, who knew more about Rubin than he did; and Rubin consulted Tom Petty, who was a bridge between all sorts of musicians and genres.[1] Both Rosanne and Petty urged Cash and Rubin to work together, and so a partnership, one that accrued benefits for both sides, was forged despite differences in age, in faith, and, arguably, in genre.

Johnny Cash, was not exactly washed up at the time, though he was on the verge of being forgotten as an active musician. He was continuing to perform, if only at casinos, county fairs, colleges, and various other small and medium venues. He remained interesting, even though he had not produced anything as a solo artist that reached mainstream consciousness for almost two decades, and he was without a record contract. In his own mind, he was done. As he says in the commemorative book that accompanied the posthumously released collection *Unearthed*, "Before Rick Rubin came along ten years ago, I had declined to the bottom of the ladder . . . at Mercury/Polygram in Nashville. It didn't hurt me all that much because I expected it. I expected it when I saw that there was no interest in my recordings, and since there was no real purpose to having a recording career, that it would all fade away. I was kinda ready for it to happen."[2] The partnership changed all that and gave Cash a new recording life. As David Kamp says in his fine article about the Cash-Rubin partnership, "Cash, re-energized and alight with inspiration, was afforded a happy ending to the recording career he'd effectively given up on."[3]

Given Cash's affiliations with country and Rubin's with rap, the collaboration seemed novel and perhaps unworkable, but it might not have been so regarded thirty or forty years earlier. There was a place in public consciousness then for all types of music, and almost every genre was played on the radio. As critic Barry Mazor observes, radio used to be a lot more diverse; on one playlist, in the 1960s, "could be the Rolling Stones, the Supremes, Buck Owens, and Sinatra."[4] In the era before specialization really took hold, a particular producer working with an artist might not signal genre at all. Although Jack Clement is most associated with producing and performing country music, he considers himself "jazz."[5] Producer Bob Johnston, responsible for both of Cash's live prison albums, served as the head of the Nashville office of Columbia but also produced Bob Dylan, Leonard Cohen, and Simon and Garfunkel, not to mention Patti Page and Burl Ives.[6] Cash's producer in the early 1960s, Don Law, who preceded Johnston at Columbia, recorded mostly country artists, but he had grown up in England and had produced blues musicians as well, including another legend, Robert Johnson. And Cash's original producer at Sun Records, Sam Phillips, was well known for embracing variety.

But since the 1960s, music has fractured into multiple genres and subgenres. *Billboard* has nine basic genres on its charts but dozens of subgenres, including nine under country alone. In 1993, Rubin was only beginning to shed some of his affiliations with rap; he was best known for producing Run-D.M.C., LL Cool J, and the Beastie Boys. When he approached Cash, the musical landscape was much different from what it had been Cash moved to Memphis in the 1950s. These questions about genre are at the core of the oddity of Cash's decision to record with Rubin. Indeed, this strange pairing in part inspired my study of Cash—I could not understand how a country musician would want to record with a rap producer. But as *American Recordings* demonstrated, he and Rubin did have an overlapping interest in their common emphasis on songs rather than on genre, an emphasis that placed the collaboration closer to pop than to rock, country, or folk.

Rubin in fact takes credit for the introduction of the rap *song*: "My biggest contribution to rap was the structured-song element. Prior to that, a lot of rap songs were seven minutes long; the guy would keep rapping until he ran out of words. 'It's Yours' [by T LaRock] separated it into verses and choruses."[7] Despite Cash's long history of association with country music, Rubin saw him as Cash saw himself—as someone who could not be categorized easily. And so what Rubin proposed was to record a mix of Cash's own songs and songs whose sensibility would fit Cash's. That they ended up with such an eclectic mix was a sign of Rubin's broad knowledge of music, Cash's willingness to experiment, the arbitrariness of genre, and the universality of song. When Cash recorded a song, it became a Cash song, easy to recognize as his and uncertain as to genre. It would be hard to determine that "Rusty Cage" was originally a metal song by Soundgarten, or that "Hurt" came from Nine Inch Nails; neither band had any connection to country music (in much the same way that bands like Ratt and Led Zeppelin had no connections to Cash and yet ended up in the same storefront window). Underneath most of the songs he recorded, however, were the Cash tropes of murder, heartbreak, salvation, and love; they would have to be in order to fit within the Cash oeuvre. Indeed, when choosing songs, Rubin obviously took into account Cash's past, part of the story that he had been telling for almost forty years. As Michael Streissguth notes, "Rubin collared the bad-boy image, the Cash of Folsom Prison, the Cash who abused drugs and mistreated women, the Cash who might have shot your uncle just to watch him die."[8]

But choosing the songs was only part of this process; there was also the reinvention of Cash as a musical star, which took a sixty-two-year-old singer and put him though some of the same paces one might have used with an unestablished artist—recording a video with model Kate Moss, sending him to small intimate venues to perform, and creating a new logo, the now familiar C A S H that graces all products from the Rubin-Cash partnership. These strategies were explicit appeals to authenticity. Playing an acoustic guitar at a small venue is the way many new recording artists begin, and these artists, before they have the chance to be "ruined" by big-time production, often record their first works in small or private studios not unlike the casual atmosphere of Rubin's living room, where he recorded Cash. But these were not two unsophisticated artists at the beginning of their careers; each was an *authentikos* undertaking a deliberate performance of the authentic mode of production.

They were fabricating authenticity, which, to them, was signaled by a stripped-down production that focused on Cash playing songs. As he told *People* magazine, "This was the dream album I always wanted to do—just me and my guitar singing songs for you."[9] Of course, this is exactly where authenticants meet the *authentikos*—on the bridge of an acoustic guitar.

And yet, from this deliberate recasting came a series of great albums that indeed captured Cash's spirit; they are among his best work. Rubin used the singer's collective memory as well as his age as signs of authenticity, employing genre confusion, Nashville disillusionment, and a lingering bad reputation as marketing tools. Although it truly paid off only when Cash died, this recasting did give him a new life as a recording star. This act was not intended for the core of Cash's longtime fans, who would be familiar with the thematic hooks; rather, it was to attract new fans, the modern authenticants who would be intrigued by this mix of tradition and innovation, wrapped in rebellion and authenticity.

Yet Cash's reinvention reached only two of his four main audiences—classic country, college radio, NPR, and mainstream listeners—and even with total saturation of college radio and NPR, the first American Recordings album was only moderately successful. It was the combination of the fourth album, Cash's death, a music video, and a movie that incompletely remade and fudged the Cash-Carter love story that brought Cash his fourth audience—the one that made two of his later albums number 1. Rubin presented Cash's comeback to a variety of audiences, using traditional forms of media. But it was received in a variety of ways and by a number of different audiences—first on radio then in the culture at large. I argue that Rubin and Cash used Cash's story and the notion that he was authentic, combined with a media and promotion campaign that played up traditional ideas of authenticity, to sell Cash to a new generation.

PRELUDE: THE JOHNNY CASH FAN CLUB

The most prominent display of fandom during Cash's more quiet years was the Johnny Cash and June Carter Cash International Fan Club. Started in 1971, it published one to three Cash-related offerings a year until it disbanded in 2002. First headed by Virginia Strohler, an elementary school teacher in Indiana, and later by two North Carolinians, its newsletters show devoted fans fervent in the belief that Cash's next big success was right around the corner. But of course it was not. The central irony of the organization was that it overlapped with the worst period of Cash's professional career, which produced only one charting hit from 1976 to the new millennium. But anyone reading the fan club publications over a thirty-year period would not have thought this was a fallow period for him. Though there was little editorializing about what the future might bring, the heads of the fan club matter-of-factly continued to gather information about Johnny Cash and June Carter and spread it to their devotees as if Cash's star had not dimmed.

The geographical distribution, which remained essentially unchanged over the life of the periodical, confirms that Cash's devotees were not just southerners; in fact, they were not only geographically diverse but more concentrated in the Midwest than in any other part of the country. In 1989, the club had fewer than 1,000 members, about half as many as in the 1970s.[10] A small sample of a geographical breakdown from the late 1980s: Michigan had 94 members, California 65, Minnesota, 54, Illinois 50, Iowa 46, Nebraska 43, Pennsylvania 39, New York 34, Tennessee 20, Texas 17, Florida 16. What we do not know, even if we posit that many fans were country music fans, is whether they were rural, suburban, or urban dwellers.

The club members, like those of many fan clubs, apparently enjoyed a perceived intimacy with Cash. As members, they often got to meet him backstage, and they searched out albums and merchandise for each other. They also gave Cash and Carter gifts, including popcorn makers, denim jackets, and backgammon sets.[11] This intimacy was played out in the newsletters by listing the gifts sent, copying notes from Cash and Carter, and providing instructions on how to contact Cash's management to arrange to meet him backstage after a particular show. Most of the information from the fan club was practical: how to send in material, offers of Cashanalia, apologies from the editors when the publication was late, and so on. Sometimes, though not very often, they published testimony about why readers liked Johnny Cash. One such excerpt from young fan Tommy Hunter suggests that they saw him in a dual role as a hero and an intimate: "I first turned on to Johnny Cash when I turned on to Jesus Christ. I had no idea that a man like Johnny Cash, with everything he has would even bother with religion. But then I talked to him and learned more about him. I found that's he's different . . . he's real. Johnny Cash is man enough to admit that he hit rock-bottom, and was brought back up to where he is to-day, by the power of Jesus Christ . . . here is a truly humble man."[12] Clearly, authenticity through humbleness or religious devotion was Hunter's criterion. Rarely did anyone address Cash's appeal so directly.

But most important, in the age before the Internet, the fan club was an easy way for fans to give one another what was probably most valuable to them—information about their hero—and to share what everyone was saying about him. Articles its members sent in reveal the waxing and waning comeback, the glory of the local concert, and the enduring appeal of Cash. The journal itself provides a brief history of the strange combination of permanence and irrelevance unique to someone famous but no longer culturally central. In all, it represents a fascinating account of fallowness, a chronicle of moderate success and fading hopes, ultimately turned triumphant.

THE LAUNCH: THE REINTRODUCTION OF JOHNNY CASH

There was not much fanfare in the fan club when Cash signed with Rubin. Members had seen similar optimism before. But this relaunch of Johnny Cash was different from his other comebacks; and that was because Rubin was adept at promoting and producing artists in the new era of multiple genres and mini-genres. The main point of the reintroduction was to move Cash away from the country music establishment he had been tied to for thirty years and toward the more uncertain, overlapping genres of alternative-country (alt-country) and Americana, which authenticants were embracing. It also had a mythos aimed at projecting authenticity, the May-December producing romance, the bearded hippie and the Man in Black. Few questioned the sincerity of either party or the process of song production, even though Cash often did not sing his own songs, and Rubin was a master of marketing and buzz.[13] And although Cash had

had a legion of *authentikos* producers, they had been celebrated mostly in retrospect. Authenticants immediately took note of Rubin as producer, thus enabling his easier promotion of Cash's new work. Wrote one reviewer, "*American Recordings* is perfect marketing. It also is brilliant song-making. Producer Rick Rubin wanted to introduce Cash to the MTV audience that went Tony Bennett–crazy last year."[14]

But Rubin was also to add two devoted audiences, college radio listeners and NPR aficionados, by the time Cash died in 2003, in addition to the classic country audience that had never stopped listening to him. What all three of these audiences shared was a love of authenticity. Indeed, the places where Cash's music was played on broadcast radio— his early material on "classic country" programs and later material on college or free-form radio—were the venues that celebrate the real over most other qualities. Yet they could not be more different in their overall musical preferences and politics. The second celebrates the newly signed and raw, the first the long-standing, winnowed royalty of a genre most popular in the 1940s, 1950s, and 1960s.

Cash knew he had various audiences. In 1994, months after Rubin reintroduced him, a December concert at the Frank Erwin Center, a large venue, in Austin, Texas, featured only six (of some thirty) songs from the *American Recordings* album.[15] But his late summer schedule in 1994 featured appearances at Woodstock 94, Carnegie Hall, and the Fillmore in San Francisco, all geared toward the new audiences. In the same period he taped an appearance on *Dr. Quinn, Medicine Woman* (a show that skewed demographically senior), played two dozen times at the Shenandoah South Theater in Branson, Missouri (another regional and older demographic venue), and appeared at a Billy Graham Crusade.[16] The difference in these venues and events show how various Cash's audiences really were. Still, the new and old audiences often overlap in the qualities they share: they both prefer rawness (the performers they listen to often have limited production quality, though college radio's is often more deliberate); and both are relatively narrow. And although they see in Cash different qualities, both audiences also care about tradition; they just choose to view this tradition through different lenses—one seeing it as a shared experience and the other as an embodiment of the iconic timelessness to which they are drawn.

In appealing to college radio and classic country listeners, Cash embodied a paradox: he was an established artist whose classic country canon was not going to grow through the release of new material, but if he wanted to appeal to new audiences, he had to find a way into their ears. As a member of the music world for almost forty years, Cash's marketable authenticity could not come by the same means as that of newer artists, whose supposed innocence often stands in for realness; being unsigned and playing at small venues but being hugely popular in those venues is one way we mark authenticity in new artists. In reintroducing Cash, however, Rubin did employ a version of this method of launching new artists, even though Cash's stature made such a process more complicated. He reemerged in the world of critical music media at the South by Southwest (SXSW) music festival and conference in Austin in 1994. Both the conference—which remains a crucial place for new bands to showcase their work in front of the music industry—and Austin itself were cool. And Austin was cool not only because of its music scene but also because of its technology sector and a city council that was becoming increasingly green.[17]

Of course, Cash did not come unknowledgeable into this new phase: he had, presumably, kept up with developments in music through his touring, and his relationships with his daughter, Rosanne, his two former sons-in-law, the performers Rodney Crowell and Nick Lowe, and his son, with whom he attended a Metallica show. That he could rely on Tom Petty and Rosanne for advice shows the network Cash had access to, even as someone who had not been an active presence in modern music for quite some time. (And he was not completely inactive; he had recorded "The Wanderer" for U2's 1993 release, *Zooropa*.)

And Cash did not enter the SXSW conference as a new artist would have. He first talked to the conference about the music industry and played a little for these music professionals; then that night he played at Emo's, a club widely known at the time for its punk lineup. Emo's is a place that breathes authenticity with its deliberate DIY vibe. Although it has played host to any number of bands who went on to become well known or already were (such as Mudhoney or the Butthole Surfers, who both played there), it only lists Cash in the history section of the bar's website: "We were even lucky enough to have the legendary, immortal man in black, Johnny Cash, play a set on one of our stages back in 1994, and you can still see the barstool on which he planted his ass hanging from the ceiling."[18] Note that Emo's itself trades on Cash's authenticity by both embracing the legend—"immortal man in black"—and slightly diminishing it through the direct reference to his "ass."

For a long time, SXSW has prided itself on being a crucial player in the music industry. Back then, the conference had a reputation as a place where music scouts could find new talent, and that may still happen, but SXSW has matured in much the same way the Sundance Film Festival has. At the time, *Entertainment Weekly* reporter Nisid Hajari observed that what the music industry came for was "to discover what's hip, and the overwhelming scope of this year's SXSW—thankfully tempered by Austin's laid-back spirit—provided plenty of that." But what better way to reintroduce Cash to the people Rubin would need the most—the young hipster music critics with the all-access passes, who wrote for both college and NPR audiences—than to have him first speak to them and then play that night. Suddenly, through Rubin, SXSW, and his appearances at Johnny Depp's Viper Room and Emo's, Cash had reclaimed some measure of his early authentic vibe by showing his new stuff—singer-songwriter material in new outlets, where Cash admitted later he felt nervous. Hajari named his appearance as "best performance": "Hands down, the unbilled half-acoustic, half-electric set by Johnny Cash. Five new unplugged numbers balanced humor and portentousness, and a rockabilly backup band transformed the elder statesman into a whooping cowpunk, playing the jaded-yet-rapt crowd like a revivalist preacher."[19] One wonders about all the adjectives in that sentence, including whooping, jaded-yet-rapt, and revivalist, but I would argue all were needed to build the narrative that something in the relationship between Cash and the music industry had changed.

That 1994 appearance at SXSW gave Cash a fresh start on the road to critical authenticity, but it was only part of a larger effort by Rubin. He also rewrote Cash's perceived authenticity through production practices and then through highlighting the mere fact of his aging. Besides Austin, the other reentry points for Cash were New York and Los Angeles, none of which is associated with country music, though Austin has a vibrant music scene that embraces almost every possible genre; if we count the valleys that surround Los Angeles, it has a country tradition too. But neither Austin nor Los Angeles was Nashville, which signaled that Cash had likely turned away from country music as a genre. Such a move was not surprising, given the fact that he had been unsigned in Nashville when Rubin inked him.

He had enjoyed *authentikos* status before the comeback, but his new genres made enjoying him easier for authenticants, who often shun mainstream country music. Critic Chuck Klosterman riffs on the way music fans and alt-country musicians alike will say that they like anything but country music:

> The most wretched people in the world are those who tell you they like every kind of music "except country." People who say that are boorish and pretentious at the same time. All it means is that they've managed to figure out the most rudimentary rule of pop sociology; they know that hipsters gauge the coolness of others by their espoused taste in sound, and they know that hipsters hate modern country music. And they hate it because it speaks to normal people in a tangible, rational manner. . . . Now, obviously this hipster distaste doesn't apply to *old* country music, because everybody who's cool *loves* that stuff (or at least claims to).[20]

Klosterman also quotes Lucinda Williams, who feels alienated from country music: "I definitely don't feel a part of what I call the straighter country music industry of Nashville. I'm definitely not connected with that world. Nashville is so straight. I guess I'm sort of considered an outlaw here with Steve Earle. They used to write grittier stuff. It's gotten so puritanical. . . . I don't want to be identified with the stuff that's on country radio now. Country music to me is Hank Williams and Loretta Lynn."[21] Like Cash, Williams can be considered alt-country and Americana, and just as Cash's albums were popular in Austin in the 1990s, so was Williams's *Car Wheels on a Gravel Road* a staple in Austin eating and drinking establishments then. Klosterman identifies the reverent authenticant attitude toward Cash, which gets Cash, Williams, and Earle outside of country music but not so much that authenticants do not get credit for being open-minded about genre—a key tenet of authenticant codes.

And so the Rubin appeal to this audience would not have worked had Cash not been country but pushed aside by the country music establishment during the 1980s and 1990s. In the new calculus, he benefited from being both in the country establishment and outside it at the same time—many of the signifiers associated with country music, including steel guitars, fiddles, and lyric staples such as broadly comical double entendres—were often not present in Cash's music. And yet, his country and non-country audiences alike linked Cash's voice and his subject matter to country music: the voice was unmistakably southern, and the content engaged subjects that resonate with traditional southern audiences (and others as well). Lyrics about farm life, coal mining, traveling the open road, and the nuances of family appeal to the country listeners.

But those subjects can appeal also to folk aficionados or, as the band Uncle Tupelo demonstrated, to alt-country fans. Uncle Tupelo, one of the originators of the alt-country genre (which combines a more rock-oriented sound with some of the lyrics normally associated with country), made it a point to cover songs like "No Depression," the classic folk/country tune by the Carter Family. It also happens to be the name of the late fanzine associated with the genre, which itself seems deliberately unstable—the slogan on the magazine, after calling itself alt-country, read "Whatever That Is." The tension of alt-country to some degree derives from its power—as Cash himself proved, genre confusion can be compelling. Rubin had some alt-country connections through producing the Jayhawks, another *authentikos* of alt-country. But it is not clear that Cash's first album with Rubin was supposed to belong to a particular genre. In covering songs by other artists and seemingly making them his, Cash put an emphasis on how the songs were performed, not just on how they were written.

It is also clear, however, that the reintroduction of Cash was supposed to imitate the introduction of new artists. The first clubs he played were small—the Viper Club and Emo's are both venues of 500 or fewer—like the first outlets that struggling new songwriters play. The comeback was authentic; it was true that Cash had believed his career as a recording artist was over and then it suddenly was not. But the model of production wasn't particularly "authentic": the chosen mode of production for the first volume, *American Recordings*, was no more real than the production of the second, *Unchained*. The former supposedly had Cash in a room playing songs for Rubin, who with two microphones got it down on tape. The latter featured Tom Petty and the Heartbreakers with such other Cash stalwarts like Marty Stuart. Each mode of production was "real," but the idea of a man and his guitar (sort of like a man and his gun, one of the visual symbols on the cover of *Love, God, Murder*) had more romantic parlance than a band does, though the second mode of production, involving an established band, also has authentic overtones—showing how problematic the idea of authenticity is.

One of the most remarkable aspects of the Cash-Rubin partnership was that many music writers acknowledged it, perhaps because of both Cash's and Rubin's recent history: the producer, much more recently successful than the artist, must be responsible for the artist's success. Rubin even marketed the work that way. In the liner notes to *Unearthed*, Sylvie Simmons speaks of the "remarkable music that came about through one of music's most remarkable relationships. This is the story of what happened when the man with the beard met the Man in Black." Later in the notes, Tom Petty, whom Rubin also produces, says, "You can't praise him enough for what he did with John's later career and what a genius idea it was to say, 'Johnny, I just want to break you down to one guitar and a voice and do an album.'"[22]

But collaboration on these multiple levels—the producer taking credit, artists singing others' songs, marketing as part of music making—works against the traditional view that music is artistry that can be produced only by serious artists. The privileging of the real—the chestnut of accepted wisdom from the growth of album-oriented rock in the 1960s—was being challenged not only by Cash but also by listeners whose loyalty was to their own listening pleasure, not to externally created norms for musical seriousness.

Mary Harron notes that for artists such as Bruce Springsteen, who she says owes his success to perceived authenticity, such a reputation is inherently unstable:

> For a performer like Springsteen the more he tries to detach his image from that sales process, the more artificial his image becomes— if only because the maintenance of his integrity requires a continual watchfulness and involvement in overseeing his own marketing process. It is as self-conscious as his decision—as a multimillionaire rock star—to always appear publicly in humble working man's clothes.

Madonna, with her unabashed artificiality and calculation, is actually presenting a more genuine image of herself and her position
than Springsteen, and finds her image easier to control.[23]

Cash's legacy as a songwriter and performer was long assured after his
1950s work, not to mention the prison concerts and thematic albums of
the 1960s. When he collaborated with Rubin in the 1990s, he was exploring
ways to become relevant again. No one could seriously accuse him of selling out, nor could one blame him for wanting to be listened to. And *American Recordings* is as good as any work he ever did.

Despite the novelty of the comeback, his first three American Recordings albums sold well, but not spectacularly, which I attribute to a genre
problem—the first one won a Grammy for best contemporary folk
album and the second for best country recording. Most critics prefer
American Recordings (everyone has it on their essential Cash list and
Unchained is on no one but music critic Bill Friskics-Warren's) because
of its comeback aspect but also probably because of the "man and his
guitar" motif so favored by authenticants.

In the end, one of the remarkable aspects of the *American Recordings*
sessions is the way Cash manages to take songs by other artists and put
them into his own vocal context. But so do Madonna and Britney Spears.
Again, the partnership shows the importance of performance: Cash
covering someone else's music, as opposed to Madonna and Spears, was
perceived as inventive and serious, while their work was often dismissed
as imitative.

AMERICAN RECORDINGS: A CLOSER LOOK

There is little context for Cash's achievement in the 1990s; no one has
ever reinserted himself so completely and so successfully into mainstream music after a long career and a significant drop-off. The only
other artists who come to mind are Bob Dylan and Willie Nelson, whose
long careers have gone through a number of distinct phases. Aerosmith's
comeback in the 1990s also bears some resemblance to Cash's situation,
and so does Tony Bennett's, though his was more a curiosity than a full-
fledged return to mainstream recognition. And Nelson's and Dylan's
careers were more consistent and turned more quickly into albums than

Cash's. But Cash had never had two studio albums as unified and strong as *American Recordings* and *Unchained*.

A number of factors make this so. First, the record culture during which Cash produced his early hits was a singles culture, not an album culture. That takes "Folsom Prison Blues" and "I Walk the Line" as well as "Hey, Porter" and "Cry, Cry, Cry" out of the realm of albums. Cash used the change in culture to produce his groundbreaking, if not as listener-friendly, thematic albums such as *Bitter Tears*, *Ride This Train*, and *Ballads of the True West*. The albums that he produced in the early and middle 1960s and in the 1980s were interesting but not necessarily great; *Ride This Train* and *Bitter Tears*, though fascinating, feel like experiments rather than fully realized works. Before the 1990s, only the prison albums achieved greatness.

When Cash asked Rubin how the partnership would work, Rubin said Cash would be "just him and his guitar" playing the songs he wanted to play. The first album was just that—a mix of songs with the man and his guitar on a tour through Cash's career. It kicked off with "Delia's Gone," which he first recorded in 1961; as a first statement in a revived career, it suggested that the dark Cash had returned. About a man who kills his lover, it sings unflinchingly of his murderous rage against Delia. Other songs were less violent but just as powerful, playing on themes both common and uncommon in Cash's career. "Let the Train Blow the Whistle" and "Down There by the Train" are two of his patented train songs. "The Beast in Me" and "Bird on a Wire," covers of songs by Nick Lowe and Leonard Cohen, both capture the edginess of Cash's music persona—a man caught within the limits of himself and society. "Why Me Lord?" "Thirteen," "Down There by the Train," and "Redemption" explore Cash's religious proclivities. "Like a Soldier" shows the fallout from the Vietnam War; "Oh, Bury Me Not" reworks the Western classic; and two songs, "Tennessee Stud" and "The Man Who Couldn't Cry," touch on Cash's humorous legacy.

Dan Durchholz's review hits the same notes: "If the duo's purpose was to construct an archetypal Cash album, they've succeeded. There are train songs ('Let the Train Blow the Whistle' and 'Down There by the Train'), traditional numbers that Cash puts his stamp on ('Tennessee Stud' and 'Oh Bury Me Not'), songs of salvation ('Like a Soldier' and 'Redemption'), outlaw songs ('Delia's Gone' and 'Thirteen') and even a wise ass ditty that takes on genuine pathos in Cash's treatment ('The Man Who Couldn't Cry')."[24]

According to Cash, "this was the dream album I always wanted to do—just me and my guitar singing songs for you. It was the first time I had truly expressed myself artistically. But when I listened to it, I realized a lot of the songs are very dark. I don't like to dwell on the past, but it can slip back up on you, I guess."[25] It was also savvy as a musical statement—not only revisiting all his music legacies but also making them feel fresh and current. Even though some critics accused Rubin of distorting Cash's legacy to highlight his violent side—the video for "Delia's Gone" with Kate Moss as the vanquished Delia providing the most fodder for that opinion—Rubin neglected no side of Cash's career in this and the other American Recordings albums. Still, a review by Amy Linden shows one example of the focus on Cash's black-hattedness:

> Guns, murder, blunts and booze: Move over Tupac, there's a new OG in town. Actually, make that an old Original Gangsta, 'cause Cash was singing about shooting men in Reno just to watch 'em die back when gangsta rappers were mere pups. And some things never change: The country star's first album in three years kicks off with "Delia's Gone," an unflinching morbidly funny tale of murder sung without a hint of irony. Delia's is only the most overt example of Johnny's grizzled gangsta-cowpoke vibe: Cash as Icon is the unspoken theme of American Recordings. The singer and his producer Rick Rubin (Red Hot Chili Peppers, LL Cool J) straddle a fine line between artful exploitation of the Man in Black legend (a mournful version of Leonard Cohen's "Bird on a Wire") and lame parody (schlock-satanist Glenn Danzig's "Thirteen").[26]

This review, while highlighting Cash's connection to rap music, focuses almost exclusively on the darkness of the album's content, hitting many of the notes that Rubin undoubtedly wanted but not seeing the more subtle aspects. Another review does the same:

> On his first album for the same record company that's given us Slayer and the Black Crowes, the Old Man in Black opts for a pretty punky move—singing a mix of country ballads and contemporary singer-songwriter meditations, accompanied only by his own strummed guitar. Even with such austere arrangements, though, Cash can't help being himself—namely, country's most subtly

deranged gonzo. He's equally at home with sexual innuendo, a sung prayer, ranch-hand songs, an ode to Vietnam vets, and a novelty about shooting his cheatin' woman dead.[27]

One can see in these two reviews how successful Rubin was at planting in critics' minds the idea that this was the same rebellious Johnny Cash they knew, a little bit older but with the same wicked ethos.

What was likely surprising to listeners was that there were more albums after *American Recordings*; comebacks are usually one and out. Indeed, when talking recently to a musician familiar with Cash both early and late, I found that he thought Cash had made only the one comeback album, unaware that four were released while he was living, and several posthumously.

Rubin abandoned the singer-songwriter mode for *Unchained*, which features Tom Petty and the Heartbreakers as a backup band and longtime Cash collaborator Marty Stuart as well. The lyrical content is as wide ranging as that of the first album, but because of the band involved, the music varies more. The album begins with Beck's "Rowboat," "Sea of Heartbreak," and Soundgarden's "Rusty Cage," whose over-the-top lyrics meld nicely with Cash's ability to sell apocalyptic vision. The album contains a number of spirituals, including the title track plus "Kneeling Drunkard's Plea"; a finished version of Cash's "Mean Eyed Cat"; and two fun covers: "I've Never Picked Cotton" (another life-gone-wrong story) and the travelogue "I've Been Everywhere." Although *Unchained* won a Grammy for best country album—a fact Rubin used on the famous Bird ad—it's clear that Rubin hoped it would reach a more general audience; the combination of Petty and the Beck and Soundgarten covers as well as the cover of "I've Been Everywhere" were meant as a means to cross over. Yet sales were modest.

The other two albums released before he died, *Solitary Man* and *The Man Comes Around*, do not pack quite the same punch. *Solitary Man*, named after a Neil Diamond song, is probably the weakest of the four albums but does contain a few strong songs, including "I Won't Back Down"—a cover of a Tom Petty song—and the title track. But it does not have the same energy as the first two, which is not surprising, given the state of Cash's health at this point. *The Man Comes Around* is a stronger album, paced by two great songs, the title track and "Hurt." Its originality comes not so much from the content as from its presentation of an author who seemed frail and old. American Recordings demonstrates that aging does not mean being irrelevant, and it does so in two artistic mediums that are generally considered the bailiwicks of young people: music and writing.

As Cash aged both in appearance and in our ears, we learned or relearned how powerful voices can be when stripped of sentiment. His voice reveals his age, especially as the American Recordings series progresses, and yet it's a voice that always reminds us of the Cash of the 1950s and 1960s. That's why Rubin's marketing, down to the reprinting of the bird photo as an ad, was so brilliant: it allowed us to think of Cash in a number of different ways all at once. The same concept was at work in the "Hurt" video, where we see the aging Cash in real time but also see the montages mixing with all the notions about Cash we have brought with us. Even more important was Cash's artistic statement itself, made in his sixties and seventies: he gave us an inadvertent model for how best to age with artistic vibrancy and a lack of self-consciousness but full self-awareness.

And yet success in finding audiences to listen to such powerful expression was elusive. Country music radio did not play Cash. Rock and roll radio did not play Cash. The clever marketing approaches and the appearances on MTV and shows like David Letterman's helped promote the first album, but one can go to that well only so many times. So although Cash's career continued and he had a producer committed to his work, his best-selling albums and most reliable audience remained those of classic country.

PRODUCT PLACEMENT: JOHNNY CASH AND RADIO

Radio is where we revisit Cash's audiences. His comeback was covered in national magazines, newspapers, and on television—his appearance as a guest of David Letterman (available on YouTube along with some 19,000 other entries about Cash) is one stunning reminder of the man's power before age started to ravage him in the middle of his comeback. In the light of inventions like iPods and the other ways of distributing new music, radio play no longer seems relevant, especially to those of us who have seen the importance of radio as a cultural arbiter diminish during our listening lives. Yet radio remains important in terms of basic music promotion—more than 230 million people listen in a particular week.[28] In one sense, as Michele Himes and Jason Lovigilio point out, "when music, news, and talk can be heard via the Internet, satellite, and MP3 sound files, and movies and television programs can be accessed via video-on-demand technologies, the future of radio as a distinct medium, and of broadcasting as a technological mode, is no longer certain."[29] This uncertainty is audience related; it's difficult to imagine wanting to listen to what others decide you want when programming one's own list via iPod and mixed CDs is so easy. And radio's curatorial functions have diminished. But radio is still the way music companies try to get their music into the homes (and cars) of listeners. Even today the *Billboard* charts base at least part of their rankings on radio play.

As for mainstream country radio, by the 1990s, Cash's time had passed. Even Columbia/Sony, in trying to promote his seventieth birthday, made this concession: "Johnny is one of the most enduring artists on classic country radio," and "Columbia's College radio staff will service college radio, where Johnny enjoys a tremendous cult status."[30] While both formats are widespread, they typically play on low-wattage stations or stations with relatively small listening audiences. According to Ed Shane, a programing consultant with many years of experience as program director, "You are probably not going to hear any more Johnny Cash on the radio"; radio needs its artists to fit into particular categories; and "country programmers didn't know what to do with the Johnny Cash album (nor the Loretta Lynn.)" Shane added that this was a problem Cash had had for almost his entire career, but in the end it likely helped rather than hurt him: "Johnny never fell into a clear category. Johnny never quite fit . . . he was the wrong size for the hole. I think that's what sustained him."[31] As a "Veteran Music Row exec" said: "Nashville turned its back on Johnny Cash, and country radio was their partner in crime. Younger deejays, program and music directors and consultants all refused to play his stuff on country radio. They've done it to all country stars over age 40—George Jones, Willie Nelson, Waylon Jennings, Johnny Paycheck, Merle Haggard. They can't get played on country radio."[32] In a sense, Rubin used country radio as a straw man in 1998 when he put out the bird ad, which presupposed a world where a Nashville establishment was the cultural arbiter for the type of music Cash made.

I can confirm that classic country and free-form or college radio still play Cash, and their context says a lot about his ideal and implied listeners. Just outside of Memphis on my way back to Nashville, I heard a remarkable stretch of music on a local AM station dubbed IPIG—it was the third time I had heard Cash on this road trip, but the first time I'd heard anything from later than 1970. "I Never Picked Cotton" from *Unchained* played, then Steely Dan's "My Old School," and then Elvis Costello—all safely within the "adult alternative" genre. IPIG was a low-power station that disappeared once I was ten miles out of Memphis, and likely was a free-form radio station, which Kathleen O'Malley defines as "an approach to radio programming in which a station's management gives the DJ complete control over program content."[33] Free-form radio exists in small pockets, at WFMU in the New York area (and on the Web) as well as in college radio. In such places, Cash is a staple. (Indeed, as I was typing this in a house in Amenia, New York, I heard "One Piece at a Time" from a small free-form station in Sharon, Connecticut, WKZE, near the New York border.) According to Rita Houston, music director and midday air personality at Fordham University's WFUV New York, speaking in reference to *Unchained*: "Only Johnny Cash could open his album with a Beck tune and four songs later be doing a country standard."[34] The iPod stations that play "everything" (being defined as broadly pop including rock, power pop, disco, and very little country) are a new source for Cash listening. On "Mike FM," a Boston-based station, "I Walk the Line" played right before a Prince song. It was one of three country songs I'd heard in eight months of steady listening to Mike—Glen Campbell's "Rhinestone Cowboy" and Garth Brooks's "Friends in Low Places" were the other two.[35]

Finally, Cash became a staple on National Public Radio, where Rubin's clever and often subtle ways of promotion had its desired effect on programers and listeners. The literate way that NPR publicizes music—through story as well as performance—serves Cash well. John Sutton, a consultant who has worked extensively with NPR, said the first reason it took to the Cash comeback was the "transcendent appeal of Johnny Cash. . . . "Public radio loves its icons." But there was something deeper going on, Sutton added: "One of the things people who listen to public radio are interested in is cultural anthropology"—meaning that the cultural stories told about Cash on the show serve to make him more interesting—which comes "from non-music programming. The real power is in *Morning Edition* and *All Things Considered*," he said. So on a program that likes to consider "all things," Cash's new status had real appeal.[36]

The NPR audience is highly affluent and educated; as one station's media kit states: "Public radio attracts an audience most notably distinguished by its education excellence and professional success. Listeners are affluent, active consumers, business leaders, and involved in their communities. Nearly 70% of all listeners are ages 25–54 with a median age of 42." More specifically, compared with the general public, "87% are more likely to have a bachelor's degree" and "326% more likely to have read *The New Yorker* in the past 6 months."[37] So what's interesting is that Cash's work over time, his performance in the folk field, his prison albums combined with a life that was, well, interesting, found their ideal audience among rich, well-educated viewers, some of them attracted by the same possibilities of genre-visiting that the *New York Times* embraced but others by the combination of an artist who said, sang, and did compelling things. And perhaps they were not crossing over so much as finding a new genre. As Jack Clement said, "It's impossible to put him in a genre. Maybe in a broad way, folk. He wasn't rock and roll. He's Johnny Cash; he's in the Johnny Cash genre, his own genre."[38]

RETELLING THE STORY: "HURT" AND *WALK THE LINE*

The video uses collage, someone else's song, and an acting performance by Cash himself. The movie involved close consultation with Cash and Carter. The latter covered two hours and the former four minutes. There's an argument to be made that "Hurt" does a better job of helping us understand Cash than does *Walk the Line*. Yet it was the film that helped bring the fourth audience—beyond college, classic country, and NPR—that Cash and Rubin sought.

"Hurt" (2003) is the video of Cash's recorded song of the same name, written by Trent Reznor and first recorded by Reznor's band, Nine Inch Nails. In the song a narrator reflects back on a life of pain he has caused himself and others, beginning with the stark line "I hurt myself today / to see if I could feel." The song's subject seemed appropriate and autobiographical for Cash and was amplified in the video by the expert mixing of images by director Mark Romanek. Romanek says he got the job because of his relationship with Rubin, "one of his closest friends": "I had pestered him for 8 years to allow me to make a video for John. He played me the rough mixes of Hurt and a few other tracks and I said, 'I'm doing a video for that song. Period.' Without Rick's entree, I could never had made such an intimate piece. Rick very graciously said to John, 'Just trust this guy. He's a true fan.'"[39]

In "Hurt," Cash looks frail, not long for this world, and discontented. As Virginia Heffernan describes, "the video is loosely and beautifully made, and, by running the stark song up against set pieces and still-lives of trinkets, it manages to make perishing kitsch stand in for end-of-life regrets."[40] The video begins with a shot of a bust of Jesus, a statue of a cowboy on a horse, a bowl of fruit, and hands strumming a black guitar; then it moves to Cash, dressed all in black, visibly aged beyond our iconic idea of him. He's balding, puffy, with white hair, an indistinct body in black. The video continues to cut quickly between video of Cash playing guitar and piano, and sitting at a saturnalian feast; images from outside and inside the House of Cash; archival footage from a number of different sources, including the documentary *The Man, His World, His Music* and *The Gospel Road* film, both directed by Robert Elfstrom; footage from performance on television shows, both other people's and his own; and shots from other documentaries, including the Granada-produced one about San Quentin. The video is fast paced, with over 150 cuts in less than four minutes. The effect of these multiple perspectives, both current and past, fictional and documentary, along with lyrics that seem to match our idea of Cash's life, is to make us feel we're watching something that is true, that is Cash. In Streissguth's words, the video "turned Reznor's 'Hurt' into documentary on Cash's mortality."[41]

What the video did was combine our ideas of what Cash is—dark, troubled, southern, connected with prisons, married to June Carter, a celebrity, and (for those with a little more familiarity with Cash) religious and obsessed with trains—with new information. Romanek said he made the video based on what he encountered when he met Cash:

As a fan (and as a human being) I certainly would've been happier had Mr. Cash's health been more robust. However, upon meeting him I saw that he appeared frailer than the vital and virile persona we're used to seeing on stage or TV. Additionally, when I saw that the Cash Museum was in a state of some neglect and disrepair, a theme of "impermanence" started to emerge for me as a film-maker. That said, though I was emboldened by Mr. Cash's example of candor in his own work, I was extremely concerned that what-ever we created over those two days as filmmakers would remain respectful to Mr. Cash and his astonishing artistic legacy.[42]

The truth came through the literal presence of the House of Cash, plus awareness that his career had not always gone well and, most important, that he had aged more rapidly than viewers might have known. The fas-cinating combination of footage, which is all performance (in other words, done in front of *someone's* camera), mixed with current video (also performance), somehow gives us a sense that we are rediscovering Cash. Romanek called it "a more direct, almost documentary expression" compared with previous videos he had done. The stark views of Cash aging along with the premise of a life full of regret anchors the video. Romanek said such an arrangement essentially came by happenstance:

> We stumbled onto this archival material at the House of Cash Museum. There was no preconceived intention of putting archival material into the video. Our filming time with Mr. Cash was lim-ited, and when we got back to Los Angeles to edit, our suspicions were confirmed that we didn't really have enough of our own material to make the video feel rich and varied enough.
>
> It felt incomplete. We started experimenting with the archival material, and this stark contrast (between the old and new foot-age) was immediately impactful and moving. I'm not sure if we could've put it into words at the time, but in retrospect, we (my editor Robert Duffy, and myself) were chilled by the shock of time's passing and the apparent cruelty of our mortality that these cuts seemed to express.

But as Romanek himself says, the video was not reality. For one thing, he says Cash was not really as mournful, infirm, destitute, and regretful or "quite as frail as he appears in the video. The song is slow and somber and it required a subdued and serious performance. In between takes, he was a lot more spirited and frisky (making jokes, etc.) than he appears on camera. So, the video is, in some ways, by necessity, not really a fully accurate account of his actual state of health at the time. He was a bit infirm, but not that infirm." And though there had been financial setbacks, the disrepair of the House of Cash was probably not as literally symbolic as it seemed. Romanek diminishes the Cash connection to religion, too, by intersplicing *Gospel Road* images, to make them seem ancillary images to the stark lyrics of "Hurt."

Still, the realness of Cash's age anchors the video, and we learn something about him that neither Rick Rubin's record covers nor public images have told us: Romanek connects the iconic image of Cash forged by rockabilly and San Quentin with a sensibility that Rubin presents. Romanek is a little hesitant to hang the word authenticity on either Cash or his work but acknowledges that it was one of principles behind both his own work and Cash's:

> Authenticity in art, I suppose, whether fine art or popular art, is something that one senses in one's gut. You watch and/or listen and deem the artist either sincere or not. I feel certain in my own soul that Mr. Cash's work was unquestionably sincere. Though the art of music-video is often more akin to marketing, I've always tried to render short music films that were a sincere expression of my feelings about the artist and my love of both cinema and popular music. In the case of Hurt, those feelings ran quite strong in me. Mr. Cash was one of our greatest American artists.

When a video works, as "Hurt" certainly does, it is a piece of informed simplicity—the concept standing in for a greater "truth." In other words, it becomes metaphor, a smaller piece representing the whole, as these small fragments of performance, primary and secondary, stand in for the life of Cash. Leigh Edwards concludes that, "the video captures significant recurring themes in Cash's oeuvre, given its attempt to summarize his entire career."[43]

On the other hand, *Walk the Line*, though an entertaining movie with a fantastic performance by Reese Witherspoon as June Carter and a more than adequate one by Joaquin Phoenix, tells us only what we think we know about Cash. Director James Mangold chose the right period to focus on—before the success brought by the prison albums—and there was nothing wrong with emphasizing the love story of Carter and Cash. Indeed, the film succeeded in underscoring Cash's troubled life in the 1960s. In an interview, Mangold said he did not consider the movie a biopic but rather "a true-life story. . . . We did it in deep consultation with Johnny and June. The movie is filled with their love. It's a clean, classical story in that way." Mangold said it "was all about authenticity. That trumped everything."[44] But authenticity here simply meant reinforcing the story commonly told, and a clean, classical story is often one that avoids greyness and subtlety. For a younger generation, the information presented in the movie may or may have not been new, but for anyone familiar with the Johnny Cash story, it reconfirmed much of what we thought we knew about him—the darkness, the relationship with June Carter—and perhaps added some information about familial relations with his father and his brother. It has some timeline issues (particularly with June Carter's penning of "Ring of Fire") and conflicts with Streissguth and Vivian Liberto on the origin of "Hello, I'm Johnny Cash." Most important, it leaves out the intellectual and artistic work Cash performed in the 1960s, focusing instead on the more tabloid-like material that only partially defined him. No one can deny that the bad behavior Mangold portrayed in the movie was based on reality; Cash himself confirmed it, and Marshall Grant and John Carter Cash detail some of it in their books. The problem is one of emphasis: in a 136-minute movie, there was room and opportunity for a more nuanced Cash.

Walk Hard: The Dewey Cox Story (2007), in parodying *Walk the Line*, shows exactly the problem with the original—that it retells not only the Johnny Cash story as commonly told but as *many* rock-and-roll and music stories are told. The movie does triple duty as it mocks *Walk the Line* (it begins with an aged Dewey Cox thinking in the dark about his "whole life," just Joaquin Phoenix did in as *Walk the Line*, and features a homewrecking June Carter clone, Darlene Madison), music biopics in general, and the lives of musicians. It's particularly tough in lampooning the father-son relationship and the stupidity of the main singer (my strongest complaint about *Walk the Line*). But it's also tough on Cash specifically, as the title spoofs his famous hit and his genre experimentation. It also shows how clichéd the rock-and-roll life seems—the travel, the sex, the comebacks, and so on all seem familiar—and why Rubin took such pains to reintroduce Cash in a different way. And the parody also demonstrates the limitations of authenticity-based myth building and music criticism; what we think of as authentic is really very narrow. Todd Martens says of the movie, "If 'Walk Hard: The Dewey Cox Story' teaches us anything, it's that authenticity in rock 'n' roll is largely just a myth, and one that's ripe for laughs."[45]

Unfortunately, the parody does work as legitimate criticism. *Walk the Line* did little but reinforce the darkness narrative that Cash himself helped create. Some of this had to do with Cash himself, whom Mangold interviewed for the screenplay, but its weakness came in merely reinforcing the story that Johnny Cash told over his career rather than doing much to complicate it. "Hurt" did some of the same work, telling a similar story, but it also provided a commentary of sorts by splicing the popular images of Cash into a video that seemed to present Cash as a more mature version of the incomplete one in *Walk the Line*. The diversity of images and the complex version of the aging patriarch offered a meta-narrative that suggested a much deeper, if similarly troubled, version of the Cash presented in the movie. The video did not give a more complete version of Cash, nor did it give us much more than visual and iconic information about his past. Rather, it derived its power from the juxtaposition between past glory and present regret. More important, "Cash" appeared on screen; though it's all performance, "Cash" played Cash with his age on display.

Still, both texts did what Rubin alone could not: they brought Cash beyond the small critical audiences he attracted with American Recordings. "Hurt" appeared on *The Man Comes Around*, the fourth album in the series, and the only one to go platinum (a million albums sold); *A Hundred Highways*, the fifth album in the series, released posthumously, was the only other one to reach gold (500,000).[46] In sales, they still competed unfavorably with his older music—many compilations also went platinum during the same period.

Of course, it was not just *Walk the Line* and "Hurt" that led to Cash's newfound success—it was his death as well. A famous person's dying leads to both predicable and unpredictable reactions. With Johnny Cash, the predictable included tributes from artists of all stripes, increased attention to his life and work, and attempts to classify him in familiar, iconic ways. Because his passing was inextricably linked with the deaths of several people—his late wife, Elvis, and John Ritter, who died the same day—the coverage was a little surreal. Two stars died in one day—one who received coverage because of his immediate impact on American culture (in the loss of a television show, *Eight Simple Rules for Dating My Daughter*) and one whose already legendary status was permanently lodged in the American psyche.

The range of interpretations of Cash upon his death went from working-class hero to a child of the government, a rebellious icon, and/or a country king—none of which got him wrong, exactly. It's clear that commentators understood him on some level, but the interpretations—save for Daniel Menaker's brief mention in the *New Yorker*'s "Talk of the Town," which described his indeterminacy—failed to recognize the depth of his life and his commitment to the business of songwriting. At this point, it should have been clear who Johnny Cash was, given the sheer amount of available information about him and by him. The books, the videos, the songs and performances, the arrests, the merging of a family with an icon—we should know a lot about him. And in some ways, we do—he seems familiar, stately, knowable.

Yet Cash continued to add identities as he aged. In the last set of interpretations, he was the joyful wounded patriarch who died of a broken heart. Such an interpretation was bolstered by the musical material released after his death. The box set *Unearthed,* a five-CD set of outtakes and other material from the American Recordings series supposedly planned before his death, felt like a coda but sounded freshly made, a prime example of the informed simplicity that Cash seemed to seek and Rubin understood. There were more songs about God, a few beautiful outtakes (including an orchestral version of "Bird on a Wire" and the Sun-like version of "The Man Comes Around"), and a carefully chosen greatest-hits disc. The accompanying book was also a tribute to Cash, featuring interviews with those who had worked with him. The package itself was all in black, with the newly traditional Cash-brand label rendering his name in white. The black packaging has triple meanings—of rebellion, of cool, and now of mourning. There also have been his two posthumously best-selling albums, *American Recordings V: A Hundred Highways* and *The Legend of Johnny Cash*. His estate also released *Per-*

sonal File, a collection of materials recorded in the 1970s, and Columbia has methodically re-released remastered versions of his albums, including the two prison concerts.

The release of the box set seemed to posit a death that was tragic but not unexpected. In his younger days, Cash's death would have been viewed as pure tragedy. But "Hurt" and the frequent trips to the hospital, not to mention June Carter's death, made his passing almost expected. Still, for someone like Cash there is no concrete end to his story. Like Elvis and Tupac and Kurt Cobain, Cash will continue to generate material, whether it's his own unreleased music, music criticism, or scholarship. But Mangold, Romanek, and Rubin began his last chapter. Retelling the Johnny Cash story required not only a paean to authenticity and to Cash's past but also a way to make him relevant to the present. Rubin laid the groundwork by getting Cash to play an *authentikos* game, getting himself recognized as a vibrant creative force. But he needed larger forces outside the music industry to make it work in full, forces that Romanek and, finally, Mangold were able to provide.

CODA

Rosanne Cash's recent album *The List* comes from a moment she and her father shared in 1973, a moment she described in a number of media outlets (including NPR and the *New York Times*). Cash was sober at the time (Rosanne makes note in the *Times* that her father was an "addict"), and Rosanne was just beginning to perform. After asking if she knew a particular song, which she did not, Cash was chagrined. So he compiled a list of "100 Essential Country Songs," of which twelve appear on *The List*. The album is wonderful, but the list's significance goes beyond that. It means that Cash believed there was a country-folk-pop canon; the songs range from prerecording folk ("Motherless Children") to Dylan ("Girl from the North Country") to iconic pop (the Hal David/Paul Hampton penned "Sea of Heartbreak") to country (Merle Haggard's "Silver Wings").

Rosanne's was not the only list Cash made. Produced just before his death, *Artist's Choice: Johnny Cash* was a compilation album (presumably) put together by Cash for Starbucks. It includes Hank Williams ("Lovesick

Blues"), Eddy Arnold ("I'll Hold You"), Johnny Horton ("North to Alaska"), and Glenn Campbell ("Witchita Lineman'), all country—classic country—staples. But it also includes two songs by Kris Kristofferson and one by Linda Rondstadt, country/folk tweeners like Cash, and songs by Roberta Flack ("The First Time I Ever Saw Your Face"), Mahalia Jackson ("His Eye Is on the Sparrow"), Bruce Springsteen ("Highway Patrolman"), and Bob Dylan ("The Times They Are A-Changin'"). The mix of iconic country, pop, folk, gospel, and rock musicians, black and white, women and men, seems perfectly balanced—one designed to introduce the patrons of Starbucks to music outside their own jukebox but with some familiar names thrown in.

More significant, however, list making is done by authenticants; indeed, one of the primary sports of *High Fidelity* is the characters' list making. The Rob character even calls his burgeoning label "Top Five Records." List making turns the personal into the published, even if only in the immediate sphere, which is why *High Fidelity* characters argue so strenuously about each others' choices. In the end, as his daughter shows, Cash was an authenticant as well as an *authentikos*.[47]

CASH CHOOSES SOTHEBY'S

Almost a year to the day after Johnny Cash died, Sotheby's held an auction for his estate, an elaborate affair that featured not only the sale of Cash and Carter's possessions but also an accompanying exhibit. Cash was not the first celebrity to have his materials auctioned off at Sotheby's, the most famous perhaps being Jacqueline Kennedy Onassis in 1996, whose sale became a national story.[1] Unlike Jackie O, however, whose son and daughter arranged for her auction after she passed away, Johnny and June Carter Cash had planned to hold theirs before they died, hoping to sell off a lifetime of shopping and accumulation of artifacts of many kinds. Their son, John Carter Cash, said preparations had not progressed very far before they died, suggesting that an additional reason for the auction was Cash's grief about losing Carter: "He seemed determined to remove from the house everything that reminded him of her, though he would barely begin the process before he passed."[2] Still, the choice to auction off his materials was easy—Cash and Carter had accumulated an enormous amount of material and selling it would benefit the estate.

Cash likely chose Sotheby's because of its prominence. That it was in New York, was not a problem as he and Carter visited their daughter, Rosanne Cash, there quite often, and they liked frequenting old bookstores and antique shops. Although New York seems vast, in actual distance, many of Cash's familiar places in the city were close to one another. His favorite hotel in New York, the Plaza Athenee near Central Park, was less than a mile from Sotheby's, which itself is only a few miles from the East Village, where I took the photographs of Cash T-shirts. It's not far either from the New York headquarters of Sony, the parent company of Columbia, where Cash recorded for almost thirty years, nor from the Ed Sullivan Theater, where Cash performed on its namesake show in the 1960s and on the David Letterman show some thirty years later. Sotheby's is close to Carnegie Hall, where Cash played a few times. And the Upper East Side, long called the "silk stocking" district, known for its wealth and prestige, is also home to an entertainment and business world that artists encounter all the time.[3]

New York revels in its culture, but it also remains the financial capital of the world, and only Los Angeles rivals its nexus of finance, culture, and media. In particular, Sotheby's, Letterman, Sony, and the East Village shops all helped negotiate the transactional relationship between Cash and his audience, though their commodities vary widely: Letterman and the record companies essentially sell experience; Sotheby's and the East Village sell affiliation. When we watch Letterman, we see a performance similar to what we hear when we buy an album (though authenticants like Rob in *High Fidelity* often fetishize the physical album as much as the performance). Buying a T-shirt at a souvenir shop and wearing it shows an audience that the wearer feels some connection to the artist displayed, though the reasons for such feelings differ.

The Sotheby's auction had similar emotional roots, though on a much grander scale—purchasers would be buying a more intimate idea of affiliation. In his book about Sotheby's, Robert Lacey suggests that identity is somehow consonant with ownership: "It is the assumption of most people today that they can be defined by their material possessions. Fine things display a fine person."[4] For Cash's fans, the fine things that he put up for auction would be relatively unremarkable had Cash not owned them. The exhibit at the auction displayed artifacts of importance—Cash's guitar, Mother Maybelle's guitar, gold records, a Grammy—juxtaposed with items that were specifically Cash-oriented, as well more everyday items; in fact, the exhibit was a lot like the House of Cash in the "Hurt" video. The arrangement of the auction lots was eclectic—awards mixed with canceled checks; turquoise dresses and lavender hats; black suits of different styles; two busts of Cash and one of June Carter and John Carter Cash; three full rooms of furniture, including a beautiful four-poster bed; a glass case containing twenty harmonicas; photographs; a Remington statue; and part of a display from the House of Cash museum. "Hurt" played on a television set in a Victorian dining room, and there was a moment when the bust of Cash appeared on the screen as well as on the dining room table in front of me. Its suggested price was $500.

The objects showed the lives of Cash and Carter in a way that both glamourized them and normalized them. It displayed his fashion hiccups—for example, a "Sea Island" snap-button shirt with raised flowers on it. The quantity of silver flatware and furniture, the Remington, and dozens of guitars made it clear how wealthy they were. But seeing the everyday elements also made Cash and Carter seem more normal. And the exhibition was set up so that we could in essence walk through a version of their house, diminishing the difference between us and them. It's the irony of celebrity that we want to know that they are ordinary. We want to know that they collect their awards, wear ugly clothes, and pay their taxes.

The auction room itself had seats like a theater, with an auctioneer, and a supporting cast that helped field phone and computer orders and provided other assistance. The day I attended the auction did not bring a full house, though, given the options of phone and Internet bidding, not to mention that the auction was held over several days. In fact, there were only five or ten people there when I arrived, in an auditorium that could probably have seated 320, and at its height, the auction had about sixty people. Projection computers shot the image of each item up for sale on two huge screens, while the actual items rotated out on a little tan carpeted platform that reminded one of *Let's Make a Deal*.

Bidders paid the highest single-item price of $187,000 for a Grammy given for *The Class of '55* album featuring Cash, Carl Perkins, Jerry Lee Lewis, Roy Orbison, Sam Phillips, Rick Nelson, and Chips Moman. A limited-edition Black Martin guitar that Cash helped design went for the second highest price of $131,200. A lucky bidder paid only $180, the lowest winning bid, for a set of envelopes devoted to musical figures (including the Carter Family) which was owned—but not signed—by Cash. Overall, 773 lots brought the Cash estate more than $3.98 million.[5]

Audience participation made the auction successful in much the same way that audiences help produce hit records. Auctions require audiences to participate in the setting of prices. In the live auction, members of the crowds indicated bids by raising a paddle, but they were competing with the aforementioned off-site bidders. To some extent, it mirrors the process in which the audience participates in making meaning out of cultural production, whether live or recorded. A fan who purchased an album or went to a concert got something that Cash in part made, with the help of the producers and record companies who brought what Cash produced to market. At the auction, fans or collectors purchased items that Cash himself had purchased but that had become transformed by his very ownership. The auction can be broken down into smaller categories: some things were obviously marked by Cash's imprimatur, such as a canceled check or a guitar, a bust or a painting of him, or the badges given to him by sheriff's departments all over the country. But what about the shirt Cash wore while fishing or the furniture from his home? When they were made, they had nothing to do with Cash, but he purchased them, used them, and changed them by his very touch. What do they mean now that Cash has owned them? That's a calculation that audiences and auctioneers have to make.

These parties calculate not only retail value but also intrinsic value based on a notion of authenticity, built on intimacy. This idea of authenticity involves the notion of historical genuineness. When selling art, auction houses hire experts to make sure paintings are real. Authenticity means "the real thing"—buyers do not want to buy a fake Rembrandt; they want a painting done by the artist himself. When selling celebrity collectables, too, an auction house might need expert help, but in a sense, that authenticity comes from the subject of the auction. Selling art and auction materials that are not celebrity-related follows some of the same guidelines as selling Cash records—auctions determine in a small market what the prices are. But when it comes to Jackie O or Johnny Cash, those calculations are based not on production but on association. And so auctions seem to be selling authentic associations.

If I bid on Johnny Cash cuff links (one of the only things I could possibly afford in the 300-page catalog), what am I buying? A chance to say, "Johnny Cash owned these." If you are a guest in my house, because I would likely display them rather than keep them in a jewelry box for ordinary use, you might say, "Those are cool." And then you might ask me to calculate: "How much are they worth?" I might tell you how much I paid. And then we might come to some conclusion as to their value. But outside of a commodity value, what are Johnny Cash's cuff links worth to me? They suggest an intimacy, and one reason I never did bid on the cuff links was that I needed to reject this intimacy if I planned to write about Johnny Cash. They certainly have little utility, and I would be unlikely to wear them very often, if ever. Did owning such cuff links make a fan's relationship with Cash more real? Did it give depth to his understanding of Cash? Was the transaction purely monetary, the cuff links up for resale as soon as purchased (and given the popularity of the movie and the last few albums, ultimately a tidy profit)? Did it make the buyer more cool or of a higher status? Did the item reflect what he thought of as the "real" Cash?

So what we are purchasing at celebrity auctions is a bit of intimacy, intimacy authenticated by the connection between us, the artist, and the auctioned item. But this is not the only issue of authenticity here; there are two others that are related—was the auction, and its catalog and display, showing the real Johnny Cash? And when we watch the auction, are we looking at Johnny Cash the person, the celebrity, or the artist?

An auction that included only old records and musical instruments and songwriting notes would have been one devoted to Cash as a musician. One that comprised rendered images of him and keepsakes related to his performance and life outside the studio would have been related to his celebrity. Of course, there is overlap here, since he was a celebrity *because* he was a musician. But the actual auction goods were more oriented to the way he lived his life outside his albums. And finally, there were items that he lived with or used in his daily life, the sort of things that almost all of us would own and use. There was no need to establish Cash as a real person, as we all know that the ontological idea of authenticity applies to each of us: because we exist, we are real. But in presenting everyday items in an auction, were the organizers trying to appeal to the audience by means of Cash's ordinariness? And if so, what purpose did it serve to do so?

Cash and his estate and the auctioneers seemed to be making this appeal. Not that his legacy was in any danger, but part of the Johnny Cash story is that he was "down to earth," honest, and real; therefore, to sell only musician or celebrity goods would have played against the idea of Cash as a real person. It would also have been ineffective as an auction, since most of the things for sale were the thousands of items that

Carter and Cash accumulated in their everyday lives. According to Rita Forrester, a member of the Carter family, what John Carter Cash did was add elements of Cash as the celebrity and musician back into the auction by including such items as the Grammy.[6]

Cash the real person was a construction in another way. In thinking about him as a "real person," we are really thinking about Cash acting in such a way that makes him seem unchanged by his celebrity. We are thinking of him as humble, able to initiate small talk, and tolerant of small inconveniences and difficulties. Such a portrait emerged when I went to Hiltons, Virginia, site of the Carter Family Fold, to look around. As a matter of luck, I was able to talk with Flo and John Wolfe and Rita Forrester, all of whom stressed Cash's ordinariness. (Flo and Rita are both grandchildren of A.P. and Sara Carter and cousins to June Carter.) Flo Wolfe stressed that Johnny Cash "was down to earth" with stories that reinforced such a notion; they focused on everyday matters—casseroles and coffee. Forrester talked about Cash's grief after the loss of June.[7] But the conversation had a subtext; he was ordinary in the context of being a celebrity. In other words, they were stressing *his* resistance to being thought of as or acting like a celebrity, but it was also clear that *they* thought of him as a celebrity.

It was, in a way, a performance of ordinariness in the same way that juxtaposing ugly Sea Island shirts with a Remington sculpture worked as a performance. He was already a real person but this myth is a crucial part of being a beloved celebrity. A noncelebrity being himself is not interesting to us. We want a celebrity who does not act as if the celebrity should be treated differently—the paradoxical relationship that country musicians especially have to have with their fans. It mirrors the injunction to them to "act naturally" when performing, when we know that the performer is performing. But perhaps a celebrity and a performer *are* acting normally when they perform and act like celebrities. We know how we and our friends act, but we are curious about celebrities. It's somehow comforting to know that while celebrities may think and talk about "celebrity things" (just as professors talk about professor things, and supermarket workers talk about supermarket things), celebrities have not lost their basic human functions. And indeed, one of the powers of "Hurt" was that it humanized Cash and Carter: no matter what celebrity images and artifacts were displayed on the screen, Cash had aged, as we all do. Is that why "Hurt" was played at the auction? To remind us of his frailty? Or to remind us of his celebrity? Both?

So the stakeholders in this decision—Cash, intermediaries, and audience—all brought their own ideas to the auction. Whereas the audiences for the movie, video, and new work by Cash are relatively easy to determine, an auction seems to me to be geared especially toward devoted fans, ones who are also collectors. It seems less likely that college radio audiences and NPR audiences were purchasers, and the large audience had not quite developed yet. What the auction showed was a different way for audiences to participate in telling a story about Johnny Cash, one seemingly commercial but intimate as well.

THE CATALOG AND ITS COHORTS

In a sense, the real storytelling of the Sotheby's auction was done in its catalog. The narratives and tributes published there gave an excellent context not only for the items themselves but also for the careers of Cash and Carter and serve as sort of a collage-biography: Cash's and Carter's stories told through the accumulation of artifacts, organized thematically and chronologically.

The publication of the auction's glossy, picture-laden catalog coincided with the publication of several other photo books that aimed to give readers an idea about what Cash was "really like." Such books are part of the larger effort to get a "true" picture of Johnny Cash, a quest that will ultimately be fruitless because who Johnny Cash was varies with who the viewers are, what part of Cash they are looking at, and what their agenda is. There is no doubt that Cash was a real person with strengths and frailties like everybody else. But "Johnny Cash" is a complicated construction of desire, familiarity, performance, visual images, sounds, actions, and words, given to his public by people like me, who know Cash only in part. And the books, because they allow us to see him over time, work on this level.

Bill Miller's book, *Cash: An American Man*, is an uncomplicated love letter to both Cash and his fans. It draws on and enhances the bond between Cash and us as it transfers "real-life" documents and photographs into a glossy book that cannot help but engage our sympathetic response to Cash's death—Miller's loss seems to mirror our own. It is a beautiful book that features, for example, a photograph of Cash with the notes he wrote from the "Manila Hilton" superimposed; on another page is a photograph of his passport, stamped "Canceled." Another spread has documents from his television shows, including a script, a cover from *TV Guide* (the photo on the cover became the cover of the Sotheby's auction catalog), and a picture of Cash and Dylan. Still another spread includes just photographs of checks or what can best be called Johnny Cash commemorative cash—er, money (two separate dollar bills with Cash's face instead of Washington's, a commemorative coin, a $1,000 bill with Cash and Carter in the middle). The checks include those made out to Carl Perkins for $300, to Marshall Grant for $491.04, to "Clem Ruh Chev C." for $1,211.15.[8]

A *Rolling Stone* book devoted to Cash is also hagiographical in nature. Here we get Cash as musical superstar, the classical narrative of rags to riches to rehab and, ultimately, to renewal; the narrative still is tinged with a sadness for someone who had gone too soon, despite the perception that he would, indeed, go soon. And despite its excellent narrative written by Mikal Gilmore, the funny and touching story by his daughter Rosanne about her father teaching her to water-ski, and many other gorgeous touches, the book is firmly rooted in 2002, when Cash had finally restored his position as a contemporary, not only classic, musician. The Cash of 2002, however, is only one facet of him. It was the right book for the time, but it feels a little like a cheat, as if something crucial is missing, some deeper element—which is, of course, the post–San Quentin period when Cash became more seriously committed to his religion: the *God* part of Cash's three-record anthology, *Love, God, Murder.* One cannot fault *Rolling Stone* or its writers for their presentation, because it is a rock-and-roll magazine, doing its best to give us the perspective of Cash as rock and roller first and man of his time second. The catalog does not do any better at recreating this element, though the many artifacts do give the sense of Cash in this period—roaming around, wearing ugly shirts, paying taxes, and making music.[9]

The catalog is organized as basic narrative of Cash and Carter.[10] It contains picture after picture of them alone and with friends, beginning with an iconic photo on the cover: Carter is looking at Cash, who is looking down, silhouetted in black. The first lot for sale also provides a biography of June and the rest of the Carter Family, and the first few pieces are Carter memorabilia, all with explanations of their origins. Lot 1 is Carter's childhood shoes, with a projected bid of $300 to $500; lot 2 is a photograph of the original Carter Family—Maybelle, A.P., and Sara ($300 to $500); lot 3 is Maybelle's and June's Oscar Schmidt Double Neck Guitar ($1,000 to $1,500). These artifacts give one a sense of some of the history behind the Cash-Carter pairing. But what the catalog does best is provide an understanding of the trappings of being a music celebrity, the sheer quantity of tributes one receives. For example, pages 158 and 159 (lots 358 to 365) show the painting of Cash commissioned by the Country Music Hall of Fame ($1,000 to $1,500) and the wooden shoes made to celebrate his silver anniversary ($200–$400). The right shoe has "Johnny 1955" over a carved guitar, and the left shoe has "Cash 1989" over a guitar. (What wooden shoes had to do with any of Cash's identities—they would seem to have little relevance either an Arkansas farmboy or a music superstar—one can only speculate.) Lot 488, in a two-page spread (196–97), features the "patchwork denim and tan suede long duster worn by Johnny Cash on the cover of *Johnny Cash Is Coming to Town*" ($2,500 to $3,500). Even material from an album that did not sell well—and a pretty ugly coat to boot—was still expected to fetch more than $2,000.

Some of the tributes seemed ironic but probably were not intended to be. Page 136 of the catalog (lots 299 to 305) feature all the honorary police badges Cash received—one each for deputy sheriff of Jefferson County in Kentucky, of Shelby County, Tennessee, of Coweta and Spaulding Counties in Georgia; a Dodge City (Kansas) marshal's badge; one for honorary police chief of Port Richey, Florida (where the Carter Family had a home); a director of Memphis police badge; and a detective badge for Greenville, South Carolina. With suggested auction prices ranging from $500 to $1,200, the badges are arranged over a red background that features a photograph of Cash wearing a police hat. What to say about such a display? Given Cash's bad behavior in the 1960s, it could be seen as ironic. But it does not feel that way; it feels like another trapping of celebrity.

Other items, while seemingly superfluous, celebrated more specific aspects of his celebrity. Lot numbers 534 to 539 (pages 218 to 219) reveal an even more random assortment: an unpublished song about drug addiction, "Going Going Gone," which the catalog quotes, revealing that Cash spelled inventory "envetory"; handwritten commercials for "Cash Country," the Branson, Missouri (home to many country-oriented musical venues) destination that never happened; a "June Carter Cash Roberto Cavalli Outfit"; shooting scripts from the television show *Dr. Quinn, Medicine Woman* and a "Lee jean jacket with embroidery on the chest reading right 'Johnny' and left 'Dr. Quinn, Medicine Woman'"; and baseball jackets for Carter and Cash, hers "embroidered left, 'June Carter Cash' and on the back 'Highwaymen,'" Cash's country supergroup. Prices ranged from $300 to $500 for the baseball jackets to $2,000 to $4,000 for the handwritten lyrics.

Antiques were also on display. Lots 143 to 145 featured a "Jacobean style carved walnut tester bedstead," purchased when Cash and Carter were newlyweds ($4,000 to $6,000); a "baroque style walnut mirror" ($1,000 to $1,500); a "pair of Louis XIV style walnut fauteuils a la reine" ($2,500 to $3,500). Seeing the monetary worth of an item owned by a celebrity is a way of providing context; one can only characterize such a listing as display by accumulation. The catalog serves as a tribute to celebrity stuff, both attached to Carter and Cash and accumulated by them.

Cash gave some indication of the end he would choose by the way the auction catalog closes. The last four items (lots 766 to 769) are handwritten lyrics to "A Long Time Ago" (commissioned for a Ford ad, which hasn't appeared yet in either an ad or an album); lyrics for "Like the 309," a song about trains that serves as a metaphor for his own death— "the second to last song Johnny wrote"; the proposed song list for *American V*; and a "Hello! I'm Johnny Cash" display from the House of Cash museum (766—$1,500 to $2,500; 767—$800 to $1,200; 768—$2,500 to $3,500; 769—$1,000 to $1,500). The writing in the lyrics and the list is shaky but clear.

What ties the two books and the catalog together is their emphasis on the visual—they are beautiful books, that seem to bring out the texture of Cash's life. Their visual content seems appropriate given the way Cash traded on visual content in his career, particularly in his use of black. He knew he was a text; he explained why he was wearing black in a song; he reused his own photograph for an antiestablishment ad; he quoted his first autobiography in his second autobiography.[11] He was a casual postmodernist in that his self-referentiality was an essential part of living as a celebrity and artist in the twentieth and twenty-first centuries. Choosing an auction, a public letting-go of possessions, may also have been a way of paying debts and leaving something for his heirs.

The auction itself stands in for the indeterminacy Johnny Cash brought to almost all public iterations. That his artifacts became a measurable, variable form of commodity seems a metaphor for an entire career that begins in the cottonfield and ends with movies, auctions, videos, and T-shirts, all items to be bought and sold. But to call them commodities belies the emotional response we have to our possessions, the same sort of emotional tie Cash and Carter must have had to theirs. Prices can be measured in what auctioneers call as the final bid or a clerk announces at the checkout of a Wal-Mart. But our emotional ties, our reception of artists and their productions (and in this case their possessions) remains a murkier business, given the difficulty of understanding even our own emotional responses, let alone the emotional trajectories of authorial intent.

But we can understand, at least to some degree, Cash's decision-making. He never chose for one reason only, for art *or* commodity. He did not shy away from complexity, indeterminacy, or, as Leigh Edwards notes, contradiction. And he did not seem to mind that complex reasons for making decisions would result in complex responses; this contradiction was certainly part of his appeal.[12] But a larger indeterminacy, especially of genre, tested our own conceptions of how we viewed music. Given permission by authenticants and musical tastemakers and their own emotional responses, millions of people around the world who said they were not country music fans became Johnny Cash fans. That appeal has to go beyond indeterminacy; it comes from our engagement with something that seems simple yet sets off a complex response—an elemental response. The reason "Hurt" works is that it seems to mimic Cash's own response to the world: the power of a man playing in front of a prison, made doubly complex by his own bad behavior and a falsity attached to his criminal career.

In looking at the auction and the hagiographies, one can see only parts of what made Cash such an American icon. As all major artists have done, he will continue to produce long after his death, as things he recorded are released, albums are rereleased, compilations are constructed, and so on. But Cash is no longer in control of his destiny or decision-making; that is now the province of the Cash estate and family, record companies, and cultural arbiters of every variety, including moviemaker James Mangold and video director Mark Romanek. And most important, perhaps, are the audiences, who ultimately decide what Cash's legacy will be. When I was in Norway speaking about Cash as part of a Fulbright grant, I was faced with many Norwegians who had already made their own version of Cash, based mostly on Mangold's movie. In one setting where I invited audience response, two students eagerly asked me question after question beginning with "Isn't it true that . . ." and ending with a "fact" that *Walk the Line* had portrayed. I was being asked to confirm for Norwegians the veracity of a movie that I fault for its interpretation.

But I understood it too. We want to learn what is true about Johnny Cash and what is false and, more important, what is fake and real. Such a task is ultimately an ongoing one. What the auction did was take what was tangible about Cash and Carter—their possessions—and interpret those items by highlighting their qualities, organizing them, presenting them in public, giving them a monetary value, and offering them for sale. The audience, in the form of the market, was ultimately responsible for making a decision as to what these possessions were worth and, after taking possession, what they meant.

In that sense, this book and others like it are only the beginning of the effort to understand a man whose complicated life and art make categorization a multifaceted and multistep process. The search, like Cash's own searches, can at best bring only partial success. Cash's familiarity, his embrace of tradition and quest for the new, seem to have echoed in our own experiences, whether young or old, authenticist or postmodernist, believer or agnostic.

I end with one more photograph, taken in the small farming school at Tomb in Norway. Tomb was a religious school, decidedly against the norm in that country. After giving one of my longer presentations, I was approached by a student who revealed a tattoo of Cash on his leg. There probably is a way to break this down further—the presence of Cash in a religious institution (though that was probably not the reason for the tattoo), the inking of an icon on a body, the literal possession of the icon— but to me, it simply states what we already know about Johnny Cash. He lives in many places and in many forms for many different people.

NOTES

INTRODUCTION

1. There is some dispute as to where the phrase was first uttered. Michael Streiss-guth says it was invented to begin recording his famous concert at Folsom Prison (*Johnny Cash at Folsom Prison The Making of a Masterpiece* [New York: Da Capo, 2004], 88); Vivian Liberto, Cash's ex-wife, says it was at the first prison concert in the 1950s (*I Walked the Line*, with Ann Sharpsteen [New York: Simon & Schuster, 2007]).

2. Michael Streissguth, *Johnny Cash: The Biography* (New York: Da Capo, 2006), xiv. A recent work by Rodney Clapp suggests that Cash is the nexus for many American contradictions, a formidable argument. Where I disagree is in his use of Cash as an American symbol—I think the complications as well as Cash's own agency make his career work against him as a usable symbol. Rather he is many symbols, overlapping and contradictory and, more important, to be read like a Rorschach blot (in black) rather than a defined symbol. Clapp, *Johnny Cash and the Great American Contradiction: Christianity and the Battle for the Soul of a Nation* (Louisville, KY: Westminster John Knox, 2008).

3. Leigh Edwards, *Johnny Cash and the Paradox of American Identity* (Blooming-ton: Indiana University Press, 2009), 1. Edwards focuses more on American identity, whereas I focus more on the conception, production, and reception of Cash. There is overlap in our books, especially on his intellectual aims, authentic-ity, some aspects of gender, and the texts we examine, and her examination of Cash's masculinity is a brilliant reading in a field that always needs more attention.

4. Daniel Menaker, "Nashville Postcard: Cash on Tape," *New Yorker,* November 24, 2003, 38.

5. Quoted in Christopher Wren, *Winners Got Scars Too: The Life of Johnny Cash* (New York: Dial, 1971), 220.

6. Though I discuss the influence that Cash, his producers, and the media may have had on audiences, I side with scholars such as Janice Radway and Stuart Hall, who generally affirm the power of fans. In country music, Diane Pecknold and Bruce Feiler, among others, affirm the power of audiences. I also side with reader-response theorists and semioticians who suggest that meaning-making takes places outside of authorial intent. This book as a whole consciously balances

between the idea of authorial intent and audience participation suggesting that authors in this case do have agency but that audiences make their own decisions about an artist, despite the artist's intent. Where marketing is concerned, I tend to agree with Toby Miller, who writes that "the life of any text is a passage across space and time, a life remade again and again by institutions, discourses, and practices of distribution and reception—in short, all the shifts and shocks that characterize the existence of cultural commodities, their ongoing renewal as the property of productive workers and publics, and their contingent status as the property of unproductive business people." Miller, "The Reception Deception," in *New Directions in American Reception Study*, ed. Philip Goldstein and James L. Machor (New York: Oxford University Press, 2008), 361.

7. Marie-Laure Ryan, *Narrative across Media* (Lincoln: University of Nebraska Press, 2004), 298.

8. The poem is more complex than that, but its popular interpretation is not.

9. Jonah Lehrer, in discussion with the author, April 24, 2009. Also see Lehrer, *How We Decide* (Boston: Houghton Mifflin, 2009).

10. *High Fidelity* (DVD) dir. Stephen Frears (Dogstar Films, 2000). Nick Hornby's novel (set in London) does not contain this reference.

11. Jody Rosen, "Johnny Cash, Cornball: Can Pop Music Be both Great Art and Shameless Kitsch?" *Slate*, August 15, 2006.

12. Richard Peterson. *Creating Country Music: Fabricating Authenticity* (Chicago: University of Chicago Press, 1997), 220.

13. The statement reads "The goal of man and society should be human independence: a concern not with image of popularity but with finding a meaning in life that is personally authentic." Port Huron Statement, available at *The Sixties Project*.http://www2.iath.virginia.edu/sixties/HTML_docs/Resources/Primary.html/.

14. Marshall Berman, *The Politics of Authenticity: Radical Individualism and the Emergence of Modern Society* (New York: Atheneum, 1970), xiv.

15. Peterson, *Creating Country Music*, 211.

16. Simon Frith, *Sound Effects: Youth, Leisure, and the Politics of Rock'n'Roll* (New York: Pantheon, 1981), 36–37.

17. Derek Scott, "Postmodernism and Music," in *The Routledge Companion to Postmodernism* (New York: Routledge, 2001), 129.

18. Edwards, *Johnny Cash and the Paradox*, 27–28.

19. Indeed, I would have to call myself a recovering authentican.

20. Diane Pecknold, *The Selling Sound: The Rise of the Country Music Industry* (Durham, NC: Duke University Press, 2007), 2–8.

21. Richard Crawford, *America's Musical Life: A History* (New York: Norton, 2001), 228.

22. Miles Orvell, *The Real Thing: Imitation and Authenticity in American Culture, 1880–1940* (Chapel Hill: University of North Carolina Press. 1989), xv, xvi. One could certainly write here about Theodore Adorno and the Frankfurt School's dismissal of mass culture, some of which seeps into modern authenticants' critiques.

23. Edwards, *Johnny Cash and the Paradox*, 10.

24. Alessandro Portelli, "The Many Autobiographies of a Coal Miner's Daughter," in *Caverns of Night*, ed. William B. Thesing (Columbia: University of South Carolina Press, 2000), 248.

25 Aaron A. Fox, *Real Country: Music and Language in Working-Class Culture* (Durham, NC: Duke University Press, 2004).

26. Kelefa Sanneh, "The Rap against Rockism," *New York Times*, October 31, 2004.

27. Rubin quoted in Sylvie Simmons, liner notes for *Unearthed* by Johnny Cash (Nashville: Lost Highway Records, 2003), 9; Bob Johnston, in discussion with the author, March 24, 2006.

28. Barry Mazor, in discussion with the author, July, 29, 2004; Frith, *Sound Effects*, 11.

29. Michael Coyle and Jon Dolan, "Modeling Authenticity," in *Reading Rock and Roll: Authenticity, Appropriation, Aesthetics*, ed. Kevin J. H. Dettmar and William Richey (New York: Columbia University Press, 1999), 33.

30. David Sanjek, "All the Memories Money Can Buy," in *This Is Pop: In Search of the Elusive at Experience Music Project*, ed. Eric Weisbard (Cambridge, MA: Harvard University Press, 2004), 171–72.

31. Anthony DeCurtis, *In Other Words: Artists Talk about Life and Work* (Milwaukee: Hal Leonard, 2005), 5.

32. Such participation is crucial to the idea of artist authenticity, as Lionell Trilling notes, "The artist seeks his personal authenticity in his entire autonomousness—his goal is to be as self-defining as the art/object he creates. As for the audience, its expectation is that through its communication with the work of art, which may be resistant, unpleasant, even hostile, it acquires the authenticity of which the object itself is the model and the artist the personal example." Trilling, *Sincerity and Authenticity* (Cambridge, MA: Harvard University Press, 1972), 100. Trilling's idea that the audience participates in the making of authenticity is crucial in Cash's case; the diversity of his audiences suggest an audience actively choosing Cash in hopes of discovering part of his identity.

33. Mark Romanek, e-mail message to the author, August 22, 2008.

34. Jason Gay, "The Clean Teen Machine," *Rolling Stone*, August 7, 2008, 73–74.

35. Larry Linderman, "Johnny Cash: The *Penthouse* Interview," *Penthouse*, August 1975, 66; in Frist Library and Archive at Country Music Hall of Fame and Museum clip file (hereafter (CMHF clip file)).

36. Edwards, *Johnny Cash and the Paradox*, 62.

37. Ibid., 2.

38. Ibid., 27.

39. DeCurtis, *In Other Words*, 9. Jack Clement, in discussion with the author, March 22, 2006.

40. Johnny Cash, *Cash: The Autobiography*, with Patrick Carr (San Francisco: Harper San Francisco, 1997), 66.

41. In my research notes, I cite this as Johnny Cash, interview, WIXK (New Richmond, WI), October 21, 1996, reprinted in Johnny Cash and June Carter International Fan Club, *Our Kinda Cash*, but I have not since been able to verify the reference. The newsletter is archived at the Country Music Hall of Fame Frist Library and Archive.

42. Robert Hilburn, "Johnny Cash: The Rolling Stone Interview," in *The Rolling*

Stone Interviews: 1967–1980; The Classic Oral History of Rock and Roll (New York: St. Martin's Press, 1989), 274.

43. Quoted in Simmons, liner notes for *Unearthed*, 9.
44. DeCurtis, *In Other Words*, 42.
45. Cash, *Cash*, 48–49.
46. Carrie Brownstein, "More Rock, Less Talk," in Weisbard, *This Is Pop*, 318–24.
47. Johnny Cash, *Man in Black* (Grand Rapids, MI: Zondervan, 1975), 13.
48. Edwards, *Johnny Cash and the Paradox*, 48. She too discusses the extensive nature of his identity construction (48–54).
49. Ibid., 186.
50. These figures come from a Lexis-Nexis search done in early 2009.
51. "I Liked Johnny Cash BEFORE the Movie," *Facebook*, http://www.facebook .com/group.php?gid=2212099770&ref=ts.
52. Edwards, *Johnny Cash and the Paradox*, 11.
53. Ibid., 45, 46.
54. Matthew Frederick, *101 Things I learned in Architecture School* (Cambridge, MA: MIT Press, 2007), 45.
55. Robert Sullivan, *The Thoreau You Don't Know* (New York: HarperCollins, 2009).
56. This discussion synthesizes material from Wren, Cash, and Streissguth.

1. CASH CHOOSES MEMPHIS

1. Johnny Cash, *Cash: The Autobiography*, with Patrick Carr (San Francisco: Harper San Francisco, 1997), 65.
2. Jennifer Senior, "Alone Together," *New York*, November 23, 2008.
3. Leigh Edwards, *Johnny Cash and the Paradox of American Identity* (Bloomington: Indiana University Press), 28.
4. Benedict Anderson, *Imagined Communities: Reflections on the Origins and Spread of Nationalism*, rev. ed. (New York: Verso, 1991), 6. Though Anderson's theory is geared more toward the way nations imagine themselves and each other, the theory does work here because we often imagine America as a series of small towns, though in reality it is more urban.
5. It is also true that in America people often live in many places throughout the course of their lives, and become fond of multiple genres of music (one could even generalize abut the tendency to live in more urban places and listen to louder music when younger, more suburban areas and more sedate music when older).
6. Nicholas Dawidoff argues that Cash's travels bespeak a man who is restless and that this restlessness led to a weakening of talent. But Cash knew that the road was also a sign of his genuineness, a part of his existence that could not be excised from his music and career. Dawidoff, *In the Country of Country: A Journey to the Roots of American Music* (New York: Pantheon, 1997).
7. Dorren Massey, *Space, Place, and Gender* (Minneapolis: University of Minnesota Press, 1994), 121.
8. Robert Sullivan, *Cross Country: Fifteen Years and Ninety Thousand Miles on the Roads and Interstates of America with Lewis and Clark, a Lot of Bad Motels, a*

Moving Van, Emily Post, Jack Kerouac, My Wife, My Mother-in-law, Two Kids, and Enough Coffee to Kill an Elephant (New York: Bloomsbury, 2006), 4–5. Of course, places are more than geographical locations. As Michael Godkin notes, "The places in a person's world are more than entities which provide the physical stage of life's drama. Some are profound centers of meanings and symbols of experience. A such, they lie at the core of human existence." We read places as symbols because they stand in for and contribute to our feelings about times and people, and the combination of the two: whether we visit a place where we used to live or one we never have been to before, we attach meanings to those places. Godkin, "Identity and Place: Clinical Applications Based on Notions of Rootedness and Uprootedness," in *The Human Experience of Space and Place*, ed. Anne Buttimer and David Seamon (New York: St. Martin's Press, 1980), 73.

9. Christopher Wren, *Winners Got Scars Too: The Life of Johnny Cash* (New York: Dial, 1971), 36.

10. Johnny Cash, "Five feet High and Rising" in *Songs of Our Soil* (Columbia 1959).

11. Bruce Feiler, *Dreaming Out Loud: Garth Brooks, Wynonna Judd, Wade Hayes, and the Changing Face of Nashville* (New York: Avon, 1998).

12. Aaron A. Fox, *Real Country: Music and Language in Working-Class Culture* (Durham, NC. Duke University Press, 2004), 28, 29.

13. Everett J. Corbin, *Storm over Nashville: A Case against Modern Country Music* (Nashville: Ashlar Press, 1980), 34. It is also important to recognize here that there are at least two other contexts that matter: race and gender. As Nolan Porterfield notes, "If there is any sociocultural constant in country music, it surely lies in the almost total absence of racial plurality throughout its history." Porterfield, "The Day Hank Williams Died: Cultural Collisions in Country Music," in *American's Musical Pulse: Popular Music in Twentieth-Century Society*, ed. Kenneth J. Bindas (Westport, CT: Greenwood Press, 1992), 180. And despite the presence of country stars such as Kitty Wells, Patsy Cline, and Cash's future wife, June Carter, most country artists were indeed men. While Cash has little to say about either race or gender in his two autobiographies (save for a note abut racial politics in the army in *Cash*), it's clear that he benefits within the country genre from being a white male, not to mention a tall one.

14. *Johnny Cash: The Man, His World, His Music*, dir. Robert Elfstrom (Verite, 1969).

15. See Richard Butsch, *The Making of American Audiences: From Stage to Television, 1750–1990* (New York: Cambridge University Press, 2000).

16. Wren, *Winners Got Scars*, 54.

17. Cash, *Cash*, 81.

18. Feiler, *Dreaming Out Loud*, 89.

19. Clive Davis, *Clive: Inside the Record Business* (New York: Morrow, 1974), 228.

20. Edwards, *Johnny Cash and the Paradox*; Dawidoff, *In the Country of Country*, 19.

21. Wren, *Winners Got Scars*, 54.

22. Michael Streissguth, *Johnny Cash: The Biography* (New York: Da Capo, 2006), 35, 47.

23. Stephen Greenblatt, *Will in the World* (New York: Norton, 2004), 41. I am making the case not that Cash was just like Shakespeare but that childhood work is often the genesis of much later and more profound work, and that holds true for Cash.

24. Cash, *Cash*, 93. See also Charles Reagan Wilson, introduction to Larry E. McPherson, *Memphis* (Harrisonburg, VA: Center for American Places, 2002).

25. Pete Daniel, *Lost Revolutions: The South in the 1950s* (Chapel Hill: University of North Carolina Press for Smithsonian National Museum of American History, 2000), 7.

26. Robert Gordon, *It Came from Memphis* (Boston: Faber and Faber, 1995), 3, 6, 9.

27. Lewis Mumford, *The City in History: Its Origins, Its Transformations, and Its Prospects* (New York: Harcourt, Brace & World, 1961), 517.

28. Cash, *Cash*, 93.

29. One is reminded of Greenblatt's conception of London in the 1600s: "In all such moments, of course, sheer genetic accident is at work, but there are always institutional and cultural circumstances that help the accident make sense." *Will in the World*, 199.

30. Peter Guralnick, *Last Train to Memphis: The Rise of Elvis Presley* (Boston: Back Bay Books, 1994), 38.

31. Cash, *Cash*, 95. He also differed from Elvis in that he was a musical migrant and thus had more in common with Elvis's parents, who had migrated to Memphis (from East Tupelo, Miss.) for some of the same reasons as Cash did: to find a better way of life. And when arriving in Memphis, Cash had a family, but Elvis was single. Cash's search for a musical career becomes more remarkable because of his conventional side—we hear of very few rock or country musicians who "make it" after they become "settled."

32. John Schorr, in discussion with the author, November 2008.

33. This discussion synthesizes materials from Wren, Cash, and Streissguth.

34. Schorr, in discussion.

35. Peter Guralnick, *Lost Highway: Journeys and Arrivals of American Musicians* (Boston: Back Bay, 1999 [1979]), 2, 3, 5.

36. Wren, *Winners Got Scars*, 119–31.

37. Johnny Cash, *The Fabulous Johnny Cash* (Columbia 1958), album.

38. Edwards, *Johnny Cash and the Paradox*, 13.

39. John A. Jackle., Keith A. Sculle, and Jefferson S. Rogers, *The Motel in America* (Baltimore: John Hopkins University Press, 1996), 327.

40. Adam Gopnik, "The In-Law: Willie Nelson Has a Song for Everyone," *New Yorker,* October 7, 2002, 56+.

41. Curtis Ellison, *Country Music Culture: From Hard Times to Heaven* (Jackson: University of Mississippi Press, 1995) 37, 240–41.

42. Cash *Cash*, 63.

43. Feiler, *Dreaming Out Loud*, 111.

44. "Johnny Cash Amoco Commercial 1972," http://video.google.com; Cash, *Cash*, 368.

45. Wren, *Winners Got Scars*, 122.

46. Joan Didion, "Some Dreamers of the Golden Dream," in *Slouching towards Bethlehem* (New York: Farrar, Straus, and Giroux, 1968), 3–4.

47. Cash, *Cash*, 66.

48. Johnny Cash, "I Still Miss Someone, " *Live at San Quentin* (Columbia 1969), album.

49. Quoted in Lisa Robinson, "Johnny Cashes in on His Dream," *New York Post*, May 27, 1994; reprinted in Johnny Cash Fan Club, *Our Kinda Cash*, Summer 1994, 11.

50. Dan Daley, *Nashville's Unwritten Rules: Inside the Business of Country Music Machine* (Woodstock, NY: Overlook Press, 1998), 18.

51. Bill C. Malone, *Country Music, U.S.A.*, 2nd rev. ed. ([1968, 1985] Austin: University of Texas Press, 2002), 209–10. Although I focus more on the way Cash tried to *transcend* country music for most of his career, Malone's work was enormously helpful in giving me background on the history of country music and a pleasure to read.

52. *Nashville Chamber of Commerce*, "Nashville's Music Industry Worth $6.38 billion," January 10, 2006, www.nashvillechamber.com.

53. Daley, *Nashville's Unwritten Rules*, 27–29, 337.

54. Peter Taylor, *A Summons to Memphis* (New York: Random House, 1986), 23–26.

55. Robert Oermann, in discussion with the author, August 3, 2004.

56. Wren, *Winners Got Scars*, 161.

57. Feiler, *Dreaming Out Loud*, 88, 95–96.

58. Brian Mansfield, in discussion with the author, August 3, 2004; Oermann, in discussion.

59. Cash, *Cash*, 339.

60. Edwards discusses the ad in *Johnny Cash and the Paradox*, 42–43.

61. Johnny Cash Fan Club, *Our Kinda Cash*, second quarter, 1980, 7.

62. Simon Frith, *Sound Effects: Youth, Leisure, and the Politics of Rock'n'Roll* (New York: Pantheon, 1981), 26.

63. R. J. McGinnis, ed. *The Good Old Days: An Invitation to Memory* (New York: Harper, 1960), 9. A more sociological and historical accounting of rural nostalgia is *A Vanishing America: The Life and Times of the Small Town*, ed. Thomas C. Wheeler (New York: Holt, Rinehart and Winston, 1964), with an introduction by Wallace Stegner, who calls it "an unabashed invitation to nostalgia." Stegner writes that "a good part of our affection for the past is the other side of an angry repudiation of the life that industrial urbanism has shaped for us. Addicted though we probably are to the products of technology, we may find spiritual satisfactions harder to come by than they used to be; we concede to natural activities, honest materials, and simple pleasures a poetic possibility that we do not find in mechanized entertainment and mass-produced gadgets" (9).

64. Edwards, *Cash and the Paradox*, 33.

65. Dave Hoekstra, "Johnny Cash: The Man in Black Lives Close to the Earth," *Chicago Sun-Times*, September 11, 1988; reprinted in *The Legend*, December 1988, 48. A newsletter of a Johnny Cash fan club, *The Legend* is archived at the Country Music Hall of Fame Frist Library and Archive.

66. Karen Schoemer, "Pop View; Johnny Cash, An Enduring American Icon," *New York Times*, May 3, 1992.

67. Joel Baldwin, in discussion with the author, September 1, 2009.

68. J. B. Jackson, *Discovering the Vernacular Landscape* (New Haven: Yale University Press, 1984), xii.

2. CASH CHOOSES COLUMBIA

1. Johnny Cash, *Cash: The Autobiography*, with Patrick Carr (San Francisco: Harper San Francisco, 1997), 136.
2. Leigh Edwards's discussion of Cash, class, and folk music is extensive and insightful in *Johnny Cash and the Paradox of American Identity* (Bloomington: Indiana University Press, 2009), 140–54.
3. "Cash Launches Radio Show on Folklore," *The Tennessean*, May 14, 1986, reprinted in *The Legend*, December 1986, 25.
4. "Johnny Cash—Awards," *Country Music Television*, www.cmt.com/artists/az/cash_johnny/awards.jhtml.
5. Jack Clement, in discussion with the author, March 22, 2006.
6. Recounted in *No Direction Home: Bob Dylan*, dir. Martin Scorsese (Spitfire, 2005).
7. Patrick Parsons, "The Business of Popular Music: A Short History," in *America's Musical Pulse: Popular Music in Twentieth-Century Society*, ed. Kenneth J. Bindas (Westport, CT: Greenwood Press, 1992), 137.
8. Simon Frith points out that an industry lies between a song and its listener: "While in live musical experiences the musicians and their audiences are joined by the immediacy of sound, in recorded music they are linked by an elaborate industry. Between the original music and the eventual listeners are the technological processes of transferring sound to tape and disc and the economic processes of packaging and marketing the final product." *Sound Effects: Youth, Leisure, and the Politics of Rock 'n' Roll* (New York: Pantheon, 1981), 5.
9. Geoffrey Stokes, *Star-Making Machinery: The Odyssey of an Album* (Indianapolis: Bobbs-Merrill, 1976), 2–3.
10. Nolan Porterfield, "The Day Hank Williams Died: Cultural Collisions in Country Music," in Bindas, *America's Musical Pulse*, 177.
11. Steve Chapple and Reebee Garofalo, *Rock 'N' Roll Is Here to Pay* (Chicago: Nelson-Hall, 1977), 1–8.
12. Ibid., 6.
13. Parsons adds: "As a result, the number and diversity of record labels and companies expanded radically through the early 1960s, breaking down the dominance the majors had held over the industry after World War II. By 1963, the top four firms accounted for only 26 percent of the year's Top 10 hits, and the total number of record labels making the Top 10 had increased from ten in 1951 to fifty-two." Parsons, "The Business of Popular Music," 140–41.
14. Quoted in Chapple and Garofalo, *Rock 'N' Roll Is Here to Pay*, 47.
15. Clive Davis, *Clive: Inside the Record Business* (New York: Morrow, 1974), 6.
16. Steve Perry, "Ain't No Mountain High Enough: The Politics of Crossover," in *Facing the Music*, ed. Simon Frith (New York: Pantheon, 1988), 51, 68.
17. Robert Gordon, *It Came from Memphis* (Boston: Faber and Faber, 1995).
18. Cash, *Cash*, 101.
19. Johnny Cash, *Man in Black* (Grand Rapids, MI: Zondervan, 1975), 74.

20. Colin Escott, *Good Rockin' Tonight* (New York: St. Martin's Press, 1992), 100; Vivian Liberto, *I Walked the Line*, with Ann Sharpsteen (New York: Simon and Schuster, 2007), 183.

21. Cash, *Man in Black*, 90.

22. John L. Smith, *The Johnny Cash Discography, 1984–1993* (Westport, CT: Greenwood Press, 1994), 111–12, 113; Peter Lewry, *I've Been Everywhere: A Johnny Cash Chronicle* (London: Helter Skelter, 2001), 18–21.

23. Jack Clement, in discussion with the author, March 22, 2006.

24. Anthony DeCurtis, *In Other Words: Artists Talk about Life and Work* (Milwaukee: Hal Leonard, 2005), 15.

25. Don Law, recording logs (Columbia, 1958–1967).

26. Smith, *Johnny Cash Discography*, 114–16, 117, 118, 199–20, 143; Law, recording logs.

27. Review of *I Walk the Line*, *Billboard*, July 4, 1964, 60.

28. The ad appeared in *Billboard* on October 17, 1964.

29. Smith, *Johnny Cash Discography*, 145–47, 155, 158, 165.

30. Michael Streissguth, *Johnny Cash: The Biography* (New York: Da Capo, 2006), 195–97.

31. Agnes de Mille, foreword to Oscar Brand, *The Ballad Mongers: The Rise of the Modern Folk Song* (New York: Funk and Wagnalls), 1962.

32. Jacques Vassal, *Electric Children: Roots and Branches of Modern Folkrock*, trans. Paul Barnett (New York: Taplinger, 1976 [1971]), 46.

33. Ibid.

34. Bruno Nettl, *Folk Music in the United States: An Introduction*, 3rd ed., revised and expanded by Helen Myers (Detroit: Wayne State University Press, 1976), 159.

35. Frith, *Sound Effects*, 32.

36. David E. James writes that "like 'the folk,' the concept of folk music is a politically charged Romantic fabrication; we inherit the traditions of putatively authentic songs either from the eighteenth century via bourgeois antiquarians like Cecil Sharp and Francis Child, whose aesthetics bore little relation to the cultural program of the modern working class, or from Communist attempts deliberately to construct a proletarian music in the 20s." James, "The Vietnam War and American Music," in *The Vietnam War and American Culture*, ed. John Carlos Rowe and Rick Berg (New York: Columbia University Press, 1991), 231, is referring to the folk revival of the 1930s, which had a distinct political bent and sometimes was explicitly communist. And the question of authenticity was even more vague: "Today, much of the appeal of professional folk music in the Untied States comes because these songs remind us of the past, of less complicated times in which there was still a rural culture. But in order to find out about the true heritage of song in the United States we must go into the field, to the folk singer for whom songs are not only entertainment but also the expression of a way of life." Nettl, *Folk Music in the United States*, 156, 20–21.

37. "These are artificial but not arbitrary points; by general agreement they mark the boundaries between which a long-standing folksong movement, with elaborate political and social affiliations, emerged out of relative obscurity to become an immensely popular commercial fad, only to be swallowed by a rock-and-roll revo-

lution whose origins, ironically, it shared." Robert Cantwell, *When We Were Good: The Folk Revival* (Cambridge, MA: Harvard University Press, 1996), 20–21.

38. "The Jukebox: Write Is Wrong," *Time*, February 23, 1959.

39. Johnny Cash, interview by Goddard Lieberson on *Playback*, 1959; included in *Johnny Cash's 70th Birthday* (Sony Music, 2001), video.

40. For example, see Bill Sachs. "Folk Talent and Tunes," *The Billboard*, July 30, 1955, 20.

41. Johnny Cash, liner notes, *Ride This Train* (Columbia, 1960; Sony, 2002).

42. Ibid.

43. Arthur Levy, liner notes, *Ride This Train*, 10.

44. Leigh Edwards, *Johnny Cash and the Paradox*, 118–25, discusses the way the album works as social protest, the way Cash uniquely uses nationalist claims and "merges European ballad forms with the oral storytelling of American Indians, Euro-American folk song traditions with American Indian chanting styles" (122). Antonino D'Ambrosio in *A Heartbeat and a Guitar: Johnny Cash and the Making of Bitter Tears* (New York: Nation Books, 2009) explains the context of how the record got made. He posits the battle between Cash and his record company with help from producer Bob Johnston, as one between the commercial concerns of Columbia versus the political and artistic ideas of Cash. My take is complicated by my belief that Cash was a more savvy reader of commercial versus artistic concerns by the time he put out *Bitter Tears*. But nonetheless, D'Ambrosio's nuanced context of Cash and *Bitter Tears* stakes out new ground in putting Cash in context.

45. High Cherry, liner notes, Johnny Cash, *Bitter Tears (Ballads of the American Indian)* (Columbia, 1964; Sony, 1994).

46. "Country Spotlight: *Bitter Tears*," *Billboard*, November 7, 1964, 54.

47. Johnny Cash, letter (in Ira Hayes ad), *Billboard*, August 22, 1964, 31.

48. Johnny Cash, liner notes, *Johnny Cash Sings the Ballads of the True West* (Columbia, 1965; Sony, 2002), 5.

49. Johnny Whiteside, ibid., 10.

50. Edwards, *Johnny Cash and the Paradox*, 115; Cash, liner notes, *Johnny Cash Sings Ballads*, 6.

51. Streissguth, *Johnny Cash*, 122; Cash, liner notes, *Johnny Cash Sings Ballads*, 6.

52. Whiteside, liner notes, *Johnny Cash Sings Ballads*, 10.

53. Vassal, *Electric Children*, 50.

54. Ibid.

55. Peter Doggett, *Are You Ready for the Country: Elvis, Dylan, Parsons and the Roots of Country Rock* (New York: Penguin, 2000), 295–98.

56. David Hadju, *Positively 4th Street: The Lives and Times of Joan Baez, Bob Dylan, Mimi Baez Farina, and Richard Farina* (New York: North Point Press, 2002), 193.

57. Doggett, *Are You Ready*, 18–19.

58. Ibid., 15.

59. Streissguth, *Johnny Cash*, 123.

60. Robert Christgau, *Any Old Way You Choose It: Rock and Other Pop Music, 1967–1973* (Baltimore: Penguin, 1973), 100–101.

3. CASH CHOOSES PRISON

1. I followed the path from Gordon Jenkins to Little Brother Montgomery (and confirmed it) through a link provided by anonymous comment in an Internet forum. In fact checking, I could no longer locate that link but confirmed it independently by listening to all three albums.

2. "Crane Wilbur," Internet Movie Database, www.imdb.com.

3. Review of *Inside the Walls of Folsom Prison* (film), *New York Times*, May 28, 1951.

4. Gordon Jenkins, "Crescent City Blues," *Gordon Jenkins' Seven Dreams* (Decca 1954), album.

5. Sylvie Simmons, liner notes, *Unearthed* by Johnny Cash (Nashville: Lost Highway Records, 2003), 48.

6. Leigh Edwards notes that the saint-sinner contradiction she chronicles served his prison concerts well. *Johnny Cash and the Paradox of American Identity* (Bloomington: Indiana University Press, 2009), 92–95.

7. Johnny Cash, *Cash: The Autobiography*, with Patrick Carr (San Francisco: Harper San Francisco, 1997), 76–77.

8. "Folsom: Cash and the Comeback," featurette on *Walk the Line* two-disc special ed. DVD (Fox, 2006).

9. Susie Hopkins, in discussion with the author, August 2, 2009.

10. Scott Christianson, *With Liberty for Some: 500 Years of Imprisonment in America* (Boston: Northeastern University Press, 1998).

11. Prison reform became a national issue because of prison riots. Whether they were matters of protest or rebellion, the outcome of the riots that hit American prisons in the 1950s was reform. Riots in Walla Walla, Wash; Trenton, N.J.; Jackson, Mich.; Concord, Mass.; Soledad in California; a Georgia road camp; Charlestown, Mass.; Columbus, Ohio; and elsewhere led to reevaluation of procedures on everything from inmate treatment to architectural changes. Blake McKelvey, *American Prisons: A History of Good Intentions* (Montclair, NJ: Patterson Smith, 1977), 322–48. Prisoners began to file more lawsuits in the 1960s to get more rights; Black Muslims sued successfully for access to the Koran in their cells as well as the right to follow the dietary requirements of Islam. Prisoners had received a number of improvements by 1980, including "access to the courts," "living conditions that meet certain minimum standards of cleanliness and safety," "medical attention for serious health problems," "freedom to practice any religion as long as it does not disrupt institutional routines or threaten institutional safety," and the right to "present their side when facing punishment for violating prison rules." Nicole Hahn Rafter and Debra L. Stanley, *Prisons in America: A Reference Handbook* (Santa Barbara, CA: ABC-CLIO, 1999), 13–15.

12. R. Theodore Davidson, *Chicano Prisoners: The Key to San Quentin* (New York: Holt, Rinehart and Winston, 1974), 21.

13. John Sloop, *The Cultural Prison: Discourse, Prisoners, and Punishment* (Tuscaloosa: University of Alabama Press, 1996), 88.

14. Christianson, *With Liberty for Some*, 312.

15. Cash and Johnston quoted in Simmons, *Unearthed*, 44, 46–47.

16. Quoted in David Ragan, ed., *The Great Johnny Cash* (New York: Macfadden-Bartell, 1970), 31.

17. Flannery O'Connor, "A Good Man Is Hard to Find," in *The Complete Stories* (New York: Farrar, Straus and Giroux, 1971), 117–33; Albert Camus, *The Stranger*, trans. Matthew Ward (1946; New York: Vintage, 1989).

18. Johnny Cash, interview, WIXK, October 21, 1996; reprinted in Johnny Cash Fan Club, *Our Kinda Cash*.

19. Informally, it's a much different story; as Guy Logsdon's "*The Whorehouse Bells Were Ringing" and Other Songs Cowboys Sing*, (Champaign: University of Illinois Press, 1995), suggests, unpublished songs were often graphic.

20. Scott McCloud, *Understanding Comics* (New York: HarperCollins, 1993), 63–69.

21. Quoted in Barry Dickins, "The Man in Black," *Melbourne Age*, November 18, 1995; reprinted in Johnny Cash Fan Club, *Our Kinda Cash*, Winter 1995.

22. Richard Schechner, *Between Theater and Anthropology* (Philadelphia: University of Pennsylvania Press, 1985), 118.

23. Andrew Tolson, "'Being Yourself': The Pursuit of Authentic Celebrity," *Discourse Studies* 3, no. 4 (2001): 445.

24. Simmons, *Unearthed*, 44–49.

25. Michael Streissguth, *Johnny Cash: The Biography* (New York: Da Capo, 2006), 150. Also see *Johnny Cash at Folsom Prison* DVD (Sony, 2008).

26. Christopher Wren, *Winners Got Scars Too: The Life of Johnny Cash* (New York: Dial, 1971), 87.

27. Edwards, *Johnny Cash and the Paradox*, 48.

28. Eldridge Cleaver, *Target Zero: A Life in Writing* (New York: Palgrave Macmillan 2006), 58.

29. Carrie Brownstein, "More Rock, Less Talk," in *This Is Pop: In Search of the Elusive at Experience Music Project*, ed. Eric Weisbard (Cambridge, MA: Harvard University Press, 2004), 319, 324.

30. Johnny Cash, "San Quentin," *At San Quentin* (Columbia, 1969; Sony, 2006).

31. Simmons, *Unearthed*, 48.

32. Michael Streissguth, *Johnny Cash at Folsom Prison: The Making of a Masterpiece* (Cambridge, MA: Da Capo, 2004), 89.

33. Simmons, *Unearthed*, 48 and, quoting Rubin and Johnston, 49.

34. The concert finally solves the issue of why Johnny Cash urges Perkins to stay and play with him on "A Boy Named Sue." Perkins had just finished a version of "Blue Suede Shoes."

35. Susan Brownmiller, *Against Our Will: Men, Women, and Rape* (New York: Simon and Schuster, 1975), 258, 256.

36. Helen Eigenberg and Agnes Baro, "If You Drop the Soap in the Shower You Are on Your Own: Images of Male Rape in Selected Prison Movies," *Sexuality and Culture* 7, no. 4 (2003): 56–89; Gordon James Knowles, "Male Prison Rape: A Search for Causation and Prevention," *Howard Journal* 38, no. 3 (1999): 267–82.

37. In his *Concert behind Prison Walls* (Eagle Rock, 2004) DVD, Cash does his own beeping of "son of a bitch."

38. Carter is particularly prone to repeating the same joke—in both the San Quentin concert and in a network recording of *The Johnny Cash Show*, she utters (not udders) a particularly unfunny joke about a cow.

39. In *The Cultural Prison*, 3, Sloop talks about why the images of prisoners in mass media matter: "Mass mediated representations of prisoners function as a public display of the transgression of cultural norms; as such, they are a key site at which one may investigate the relationship of the individual to culture in general, as well as the cultural articulation of 'proper behavior.' Hence, the cultural articulation of the prisoner and the punished teaches everyone, convict and law-abiding citizen alike, his or her position relative to cultural institutions that constitute the culture at large."

40. Bo Lozoff, *We're All Doing Time: A Guide for Getting Free* (Durham, NC: Prison-Ashram Project, 1987). The book is a metaphorical and spiritual examination of prison.

41. Michel Foucault, *Discipline and Punish: The Birth of the Prison*, trans. Alan Sheridan (New York: Vintage, 1995 [1975]).

4. CASH CHOOSES JUNE CARTER

1. Johnny Cash, *Cash: The Autobiography*, with Patrick Carr (San Francisco: Harper San Francisco, 1997), 212–13. This story also appears in *Will You Miss Me When I'm Gone: The Carter Family and Their Legacy in American Music*, by Mark Zwonitzer with Charles Hirschberg (New York: Simon and Schuster, 2002), 346; this book does a wonderful job of recounting the Carter legacy, focusing chiefly on Maybelle Carter and the family itself, especially how the Carter Family seemed to touch all of American musical history from the 1920s on: its early, groundbreaking recording sessions with Ralph Peer in 1927; the rise of the Grand Ole Opry in the 1940s and 1950s; a fateful extramarital courtship (with gunshots fired) by Hank Williams of Anita Carter; the growth of Chet Atkins's importance in Nashville; Elvis's relationship with the family; and the "rediscovery" of the Carter Family by the folk revivalists of the 1960s.

2. Anthony DeCurtis, *In Other Words: Artists Talk about Life and Work* (Milwaukee: Hal Leonard, 2005), 24–25.

3. Ibid., 25.

4. Leigh Edwards extensively discusses Cash though the lens of gender in *Johnny Cash and the Paradox of American Identity* (Bloomington: Indiana University Press, 2009), 65–80.

5. Benjamin Kunkel, "Sam I Am: Beckett's Private Purgatories," *New Yorker*, August 7 and 14, 2006, 87.

6. Michael Streissguth, *Johnny Cash: The Biography* (New York: Da Capo, 2006), 218.

7. David Ragan, ed. *The Great Johnny Cash* (New York: Macfadden-Bartell, 1970), 50.

8. Filmmaker Robert Elfstrom stayed with Cash while editing a film, and said June Carter would serve him breakfast: "June would be in a housecoat with breakfast in

bed," he said. "She was a real saint. Everybody loved June, especially John." Elfstrom, in discussion with the author, November 12, 2009.

9. "Ring of Fire: The Passion of Johnny and June," featurette on *Walk the Line* two-disc special ed. DVD (Fox, 2006).

10. *Neighborhood Playhouse School of Theater*, 2008, www.neighborhoodplayhouse. org/acting.html.

11. Cash, *Cash*, 314.

12. DeCurtis, *In Other Words*, 8. Marshall Grant says in *I Was There When It Happened* (Nashville: Cumberland House, 2006), 177, that Cash did not get off drugs until his son John Carter was born in 1970.

13. See Mary A. Bufwack and Robert K. Oermann for a wonderfully extensive history of women and country music: *Finding Her Voice: Women in Country Music* (Nashville: Country Music Foundation Press and Vanderbilt University Press, 2003).

14. My choice is to refer to June Carter Cash as "Carter" to avoid confusion with "Cash."

15. Cash, *Cash*, 196, 296.

16. Ibid., 77.

17. Sharon Waxman, "The Secrets That Lie beyond the Ring of Fire," *New York Times*, October 16, 2005, Arts and Leisure, 13.

18. Larry Linderman, "Johnny Cash: The *Penthouse* Interview," August, 1975 (CMHF clip file).

19. Cash, *Cash*, 163.

20. Bill Friskics-Warren, "June Carter, 1929–2003," *Nashville Scene*, May 22, 2003, 25.

21. Waylon Jennings with Lenny Kaye, *Waylon: An Autobiography* (New York: Warner Books, 1996), 108.

22. Anthony DeCurtis, "Johnny Cash Won't Back Down, " *Rolling Stone*, October 26, 2000, 64.

23. Cash, *Cash*, 124.

24. Karla B. Hackstaff, *Marriage in a Culture of Divorce* (Philadelphia: Temple University Press, 1999), 213.

25. Ibid., 2.

26. The 1960s and 1970s led to such legal milestones as the Civil Rights Act of 1963; Title IX of the Education Act, which forced schools to fund "women's athletics and other programs"; and the 1973 U.S. Supreme Court ruling that women had the right to receive an abortion. More particular to marriage, "legislators across North America and Western Europe repealed all remaining 'head and master' laws and redefined marriage as an association of two equal individuals rather than as the union of two distinct and specialized roles." Culturally, "surveys from the late 1950s to the end of the 1970s found a huge drop in support for conformity to social roles and a much greater focus on self-fulfillment, intimacy, fairness, and emotional gratification." Stephanie Coontz, *Marriage, a History: From Obedience to Intimacy, or How Love Conquered Marriage* (New York: Viking, 2005), 255, 258.

27. Eugene Robinson, "*The View* Meets the Unvarnished," *Washington Post*, July 4, 2006, A15.

28. Steven Nock, *Marriage in Men's Lives* (New York: Oxford University Press, 1998), 40. June Carter Cash, *Among My Klediments* (Grand Rapids, MI: Zondervan, 1979), 40.
29. Johnny Cash, *Man in Black* (Grand Rapids, MI: Zondervan, 1975).
30. Dorothy Gallagher, "Johnny Cash: I'm Growing, I'm Changing, I'm Becoming," in *Ring of Fire: The Johnny Cash Reader*, ed. Michael Streissguth (Cambridge, MA: Da Capo, 2002), 109–23 (originally published in *Redbook*, August 1971, 113). *Look* photographer Joel Baldwin said that what he observed was a real romance, especially on Cash's part: "He was totally in love with his wife. He totally felt she had saved him." He was totally panicked at airports. He would yell out her name." Baldwin, in discussion with the author, September 1, 2009.
31. Carter Cash, *Among My Klediments*, 94.
32. Ibid., 101.
33. Michael G. Lawler, *Family: American and Christian* (Chicago: Loyola, 1998), 87.
34. Herbert G. May, and Bruce Metzger, eds., *The New Oxford Annotated Bible with the Apocrypha*, rev. standard version (New York: Oxford University Press, 1977 [1973, 1962]) Eph. 5: 22–30.
35. Carter Cash, *Among My Klediments*, 110–12.
36. Cash, *Cash*, 315.
37. June Carter Cash, *Among My Klediments*, 112, 97
38. Ibid., 97; Hackstaff, *Marriage in a Culture of Divorce*, 3.
39. Christian Smith, *Christian America? What Evangelicals Really Want* (Berkeley: University of California Press, 2000), 160, 189.
40. Cash, *Cash*, 313.
41. Ibid., 314–16.
42. Bill C. Malone, *Country Music, U.S.A.* 2nd rev. ed. (1968, 1985; Austin: University of Texas Press, 2002), 64.
43. Ibid.
44. Rita Forrester, Flo Wolfe, in discussion with the author, July 12, 2008.
45. Friskics-Warren, "June Carter," 1929–2003, 25.
46. Alicia C. Levin, "Audience, Authenticity, and the Man in Black: How Johnny Cash Joined the Carter Family Circle" *IASPM*, Charlottesville, VA, October 15, 2004.
47. Edwards, *Johnny Cash and the Paradox*, 29.
48. Johnny Cash, letters to Vivian Liberto in *I Walked the Line*, by Vivian Liberto with Ann Sharpsteen (New York: Simon and Schuster, 2007), January 14, 1952, 50; March 3, 1952, 58; July 16, 1952, 88; August 13, 1954, 180; July 26, 1952, 226.
49. Liberto, *I Walked the Line*, 287.
50. Ibid., 290, 312.
51. Ibid., 312.
52. John Carter Cash, *Anchord in Love: The Life and Legacy of June Carter Cash* (Nashville: Thomas Nelson, 2007), 130–35, 167.
53. Liberto, *I Walked the Line*, 294.
54. Quoted in Brian Mansfield, "June Carter Cash, Country Music Legend, Dies," *USA Today*, May 15, 2003.

55. Friskics-Warren, "June Carter, 1929–2003," 23.
56. Patricia Pender, "*Mea Mediocritas:* Mary Sidney and the Early Modern Rhetoric of Modesty," in *What Is the New Rhetoric?* ed. Susan E Thomas (Newcastle, UK: Cambridge Scholars, 2007), 104–25.
57. Jon Pareles, "Johnny Cash and Family, " *New York Times*, August 29, 1988, C20.
58. "Johnny's Angel," *People*, June 2, 2003, 89.

5. CASH CHOOSES (NOT TO CHOOSE) VIETNAM

1. Johnny Cash, "Last Night I Had the Strangest Dream," *At Madison Square Garden* (Columbia, 2002), album.
2. Jesse Walker references this story in an obituary in *Counterpunch*. Cash called the remark stupid in his interview with Larry Linderman, "Johnny Cash: The *Penthouse* Interview," *Penthouse*, August 1975 (CMHF clip file).
3. Leigh Edwards, *Johnny Cash and the Paradox of American Identity* (Bloomington: Indiana University Press, 2009), 132.
4. Cash, "Man in Black," *Man in Black* (Columbia, 1971), album. The single was released first.
5. An interesting question is to what extent Cash reflects the political radicalism of the period, especially in his antiwar politics. His radicalism was audience-dependent, indeterminate, and generally changeable—a lot like the definition of radicalism itself, and probably reflective of a large portion of the country. As Timothy Patrick McCarthy and John McMillian explain in their anthology of American radical writing: "'Radical' has always been an elusive adjective—a contested and fluid concept that owes no allegiance to any particular movement, ideology, or period. Radicalism must always be understood, therefore, within specific historical contexts. It is also a painfully subjective concept: One person's radicalism is often another person's reform." McCarthy and McMillian, eds., *The Radical Reader: A Documentary History of the American Radical Tradition* (New York: New Press, 2003), 3.

There is also a perception that "radical" in this period means the New Left, which historian Doug Rossinow and others have said was mostly led by college students, focusing on antiwar concerns." Rossinow, *The Politics of Authenticity: Liberalism, Christianity, and the New Left in America* (New York: Columbia University Press, 1988). As Stanley Aronowitz notes, the war united a number of disparate groups under the antiwar banner: "By the late 1960s, the anti-war forces had developed into a multi-tendency popular movement, which extended far beyond its initial student and pacifist base." Aronwitz, "Toward Radicalism: The Death and Rebirth of the American Left," in *Radical Democracy*, ed. David Trend (New York: Routledge, 1996), 92. Cash certainly was part of that new base. On his 1971 release, *The Man in Black*, Cash's "Singing in Vietnam Talking Blues" relates the story of his trip to Vietnam and calls for the return of the troops. Nevertheless, in its focus on the troops, the song does not really engage the politics of U.S. involvement, as, for example, does Phil Ochs's "Talking Vietnam Blues."

6. Tom Smucker, "Johnny Cash, 1932—2003, Cowboy and Indian, Sinner and Believer, Patriot and Protester, the Man in Black Walks His Final Line, " *Village Voice*, September 12, 2003.

7. Catherine McNicol Stock, *Rural Radicals: Righteous Rage in the American Grain* (Ithaca, NY: Cornell University Press, 1996).

8. Mark Steele covers some of this material and the Native American connection in his March 2006 column in the *Socialist Review,* "A Country Divided against Itself."

9. David Ragan ed., *The Great Johnny Cash* (New York: Macfadden-Bartell, 1970), 21–22; Christopher Wren, *Winners Got Scars Too: The Life of Johnny Cash* (New York: Dial, 1971), 166–67.

10. Edwards, *Johnny Cash and the Paradox*, 109–12.

11. Gregg. L. Michel, "Building the New South: The Southern Student Organizing Committee," in *The New Left Revisited*, ed. John McMillian and Paul Buhle (Philadelphia: Temple University Press, 2003), 48–66.

12. Dewey W. Grantham, *The South in Modern America: A Region at Odds* (Fayetteville: University of Arkansas Press, 2001), 273.

13. Johnny Cash, "Man in Black," in *Johnny Cash: The Songs,* ed. Don Cusic (New York: Thunder's Mouth Press, 2004), 297.

14. These numbers come from doing a Boolean search on Johnny Cash on the *New York Times* website.

15. Arthur Gelb, *City Room* (New York: Berkley, 2003), 325, 319.

16. Tom Dearmore, "First Angry Man of Country Singers," *New York Times Magazine*, September 21, 1969.

17. Robert Shelton, "Johnny Cash Sings to Full House," *New York Times*, October 24, 1968, 51; Dearmore, "First Angry Man."

18. Michael Lydon, "Ain't Nothin' Too Weird for Me," *New York Times*, March 16, 1969, D27.

19. The author also incorrectly predicted that Cash was "much too sensible to ape the rock-'n'-rollin' musical delinquents." "The Jukebox: Write Is Wrong," *Time*, February 23, 1959.

20. William Kloman, "Dylan, Cohen, Hardin—Poets for Our Time," *New York Times*, April 27, 1969.

21. Dearmore, "First Angry Man."

22. Merle Haggard has suggested at various times that his lyrics were meant as a joke or to portray his father's beliefs. Like Cash's, his politics were murky—he played the song both at the White House and on the liberal *Smothers Brothers* show. Robert Hilburn, "Merle Haggard's String of Country Classics Captures the Common Man with Uncommon Grace," *Los Angeles Times: CalenderLive.com*, June 20, 2004.

23. Johnny Cash, "What Is Truth?" (Columbia, 1970, a single, subsequently rereleased on numerous albums).

24. Nan Robertson, "Cash and Country Music Take White House Stage," *New York Times*, April 18, 1970, 33. The *Times* also printed two articles from wire services: "Johnny Cash Loath To Sing 'Cadillac' at the White House," March 31, 1970, 43; and "Nixon Is Criticized for Song Request, 'Welfare Cadillac,'" March 28, 1970, 24.

25. Linderman, "Johnny Cash: The *Penthouse* Interview," 108, 110.

26. Willie Morris, *North toward Home* (New York: Vintage, 1967, 2000), 319, 412, 413.

27. Grantham, *The South in Modern America*, 312.

28. Robert Oermann, in discussion with the author, August 3, 2004.

29. Bill Bell, "Cashing in at Carnegie," *Daily News*, September 16, 1994; reprinted in Johnny Cash Fan Club. *Our Kinda Cash*.

30. Edwards, *Johnny Cash and the Paradox*, 136–38.

31. Robert Elfstrom, in discussion with the author, November 12, 2009; Chris Willman, *Rednecks and Bluenecks: The Politics of Country Music* (New York: New Press, 2005), 250, 253.

32. Bill Flanagan, "Johnny Cash, American," *Musician*, May 1988; reprinted in *The Legend*, December 1988, 25.

33. Peter Cooper, "Hello, This Is Johnny Cash," *The Tennessean*, October 22, 2000; reprinted in Johnny Cash Fan Club, *Our Kinda Cash*, February 2001, 2–3.

34. Geheimbundler,"DefendingJohnnyCash@theRNC,"*DailyKos*,August22,2004, Arlingtonian comment, www.dailykos.com/story/-2004/8/22/142419/096.

35. Johnny Cash, interview by Lev Grossman, *Time*, September 23, 2003.

36. Rosanne Cash, "August, 27, 2004," *Mrs L's Monthly Archives*, rosannecash.com/monthly/column_archive.html.

37. Edwards, *Johnny Cash and the Paradox*, 133–40, features an interview with the organizer of the protest against the RNC.

6. CASH CHOOSES TELEVISION

1. Chance Martin, in discussion with the author, March 22, 2006.

2. Bill Friskics-Warren, *I'll Take You There: Pop Music and the Urge for Transcendence* (New York: Continuum, 2005), 157.

3. Rodney Clapp, *Johnny Cash and the Great American Contradiction: Christianity and the Battle for the Soul of a Nation*, (Louisville, KY: Westminster John Knox, 2008), 17.

4. "Johnny Cash," *Internet Movie Database*, imdb.com.

5. Richard A. Peterson, *Creating Country Music: Fabricating Authenticity* (Chicago: University of Chicago Press, 1997).

6. Robert Oermann, in discussion with the author, August 3, 2004.

7. Michael Streissguth, *Johnny Cash: The Biography* (New York: Da Capo, 2006), xiv.

8. Joel Baldwin, in discussion with the author, September 1, 2009.

9. Michael Lydon, "Ain't Nothin' Too Weird for Me," *New York Times*, March 16, 1969, D27. Greil Marcus famously writes about American culture and its relationship to music in *The Old Weird America: The World of Bob Dylan's Basement Tapes* (New York: Picador, 2001). His definition of weird comes in relationship to listening to Harry Smith's *Anthology of American Folk Music* as a way of tracing Bob Dylan's evolution.

10. David Kamp, "Letter from Nashville: American Communion," *Vanity Fair*, October 2004, 200+.

11. *Time*, September 23, 2003.

12. Elfstrom said the project was the brainchild of Arthur Baron, who received partial funding from Public Broadcast Labs, a precursor to PBS; it also first aired on the station. Robert Elfstrom, in discussion with the author, November 12, 2009.

13. *The Man* is somewhat at odds with James Mangold's *Walk the Line*, which focuses on the love story between Cash and June Carter. A possible reason why Mangold's vision is darker than Elfstrom's is that the video takes place after the movie, when Cash had found some peace and prosperity after the difficulty Mangold displays. Elfstrom said that Arthur Baron wanted to focus on Cash's drug use, something he resisted: "He was most interested in substance abuse. I thought it was irrelevant to the film. When I first met him [Cash], it was a wonderful period in his life. He was clean; he wasn't doing any sort of substances as far as I know." Like Joel Baldwin, Elfstrom found Cash to be cooperative and open to thematic suggestions. He describes the project as a "kind of love affair": "He opened the door completely. He felt very comfortable with my presence. I don't think that I threatened him in any way." Ibid.

14. If *The Man* looks familiar when viewed now, that's because Mark Romanek made extensive use of the footage in the video for "Hurt," including scenes on the bus, the scenes in Dyess, a cross arch from Wounded Knee, and some concert footage. Elfstrom noted that "there is quite a bit of my stuff there. I thought it was a nice piece." But he also noted that no one had contacted him about using the footage: "I had reservations about it." He said he did not investigate legal action because the work he had done with Cash was "very special" and he did not want to "contaminate it." Ibid.

15. John L. Smith, *The Johnny Cash Discography* (Westport, CT: Greenwood Press, 1985), 166–73; Friskics-Warren, *I'll Take You There*, 157.

16. Marc Weingarten, *Station to Station: The History of Rock 'n' Roll on Television* (New York: Pocket Books, 2000), 144.

17. Blaik Kirby, "The Country King Has a Cause," *Globe and Mail*, October 18, 1969 (CMHF clip file).

18. Albert Govoni, *A Boy Named Cash: The Johnny Cash Story* (New York: Lancer Books, 1970), 12–13, 16–17; Kirby, "The Country King."

19. Cleveland Amory, "*The Johnny Cash Show*," *TV Guide*, April 4, 1970, 34. (CMHF clip file).

20. Mark Jacobson, "New Adventures of the Man in Black," *Esquire*, August 1994; reprinted in Johnny Cash Fan Club. *Our Kinda Cash*, Winter 1994.

21. Johnny Cash, *Man in Black* (Grand Rapids, MI: Zondervan, 1975), 110; Larry Linderman, "Johnny Cash: The *Penthouse* Interview," *Penthouse*, August 1975 (CMHF clip file).

22. Johnny Cash, *Cash: The Autobiography*, with Patrick Carr (San Francisco: Harper San Francisco, 1997), 274, 275.

23. Cash, *Man in Black*, 199.

24. Hal Erickson (writer), "Swan Song." *Columbo*, March 3, 1974. Available at www.allmovie.com/work/columbo-swan-song-129333.

25. I interviewed two of the writers of *Beavis and Butt-Head*, Jeff Goldstone and Guy Maxtone-Graham, who, while admitting that they may have worked on

the Cash video, said their method of writing was so improvisational that they could shed little light on how this particular dialogue came about.

26. Waylon Jennings, *Waylon: An Autobiography* (New York: Warner Books, 1996), 111.

27. Margy Holland, "Johnny Cash Sues Retail Chain over T-Shirts," *Yahoo! Music*, April 26, 2001.

28. Desmond Morris, Peter Collett, Peter Marsh, and Marie O'Shaughnessy, *Gestures: Their Origins and Distribution* (New York: Stein and Day, 1979), 81.

29. David McNeill, introduction to *Language and Gesture*, ed. David McNeill (New York: Cambridge University Press, 2000), 6.

30. As Keith Thomas says, "Gestures tend to be polysemous and their meaning can only be determined in context. "Introduction to *A Cultural History of Gesture*, ed. Jan Bremmer and Herman Roodenburg (Ithaca, NY: Cornell University Press, 1992), 4.

31. Because semiotic analysis often focuses on the process of interpretation rather than the product, according to Mieke Balaban and Norman Bryson, it often puts the audience or viewer in focus: "Standing somewhat to one side of the work of interpretation, semiotics has as its object to describe the conventions and conceptual operations that shape what viewers do." In other words, a semiotic reading is concerned with how signs work, which necessarily includes how they act on audiences. Balaban and Bryson, "Semiotics and Art History," *Art Bulletin* 73, no. 2 (1991): 174–208. The type of analysis I'm doing here will not provide a specific meaning but meanings, which is especially appropriate for a sign that has been reimagined any number of times. As Roland Barthes says, semiotic investigation "will not teach us what meaning must be definitively attributed to a work; it will not provide or even discover a meaning but will describe the logic according to which meanings are engendered." Barthes, *Criticism and Truth*, trans. and ed. Katrine Pilcher Keuneman (Minneapolis: University of Minnesota Press, 1987), 79.

32. Johnny Cash, liner notes, *At San Quentin* (Columbia, 1969; Sony, 2000); Simmy Richman, "Marshall Law: He Is Hailed as Rock'n'Roll's Greatest Photographer," *Independent on Sunday*, December 12, 2004; "Cash Flipping the Bird," *Marshall Photo*, www.marshallphoto.com/collection/detail/image/1062; Jim Marshall, in discussion with the author, October 2004.

33. Mary E. Ballard, Shavonda Green, and Caroline Granger, "Affiliation, Flirting, and Fun: Mock Aggressive Behavior in College Students," *Psychological Record* 53 (2003): 34–35.

34. Oermann, in discussion.

35. American Recordings advertisement, *Billboard*, March 14, 1998.

36. Oermann, in discussion.

7. CASH CHOOSES HIS FAITH

1. Chorus: "Who was it, everybody? (It was Jesus) / Who was it, everybody? (It was Jesus) / Who was it, everybody? (It was Jesus) / It was Jesus Christ our Lord." *Johnny Cash: The Songs*, ed. Don Cusic (New York: Da Capo, 2004), 4.

2. Leigh Edwards, *Johnny Cash and the Paradox of American Identity* (Bloomington: Indiana University Press, 2009), 170. Though I engage the same texts, Edwards focuses more on how Cash's religious history is contextualized within country music and southern traditions.

3. Rodney Clapp, *Johnny Cash and the Great American Contradiction: Christianity and the Battle for the Soul of a Nation* (Louisville, KY: Westminster John Knox, 2008), 48.

4. Christian Smith, *Christian America? What Evangelicals Really Want* (Berkeley: University of California Press, 2000), 1–19.

5. Randall Balmer, *Mine Eyes Have Seen the Glory: A Journey into the Evangelical Subculture in America* (New York: Oxford University Press, 1989), 229.

6. Stephan L. Carter, *The Culture of Disbelief: How American Law and Politics Trivialize Religious Devotion* (New York: HarperCollins, 1993), 4.

7. Balmer, *Mine Eyes Have Seen the Glory*, 228–29.

8. Johnny Cash, *Man in Black* (Grand Rapids, MI: Zondervan, 1975), 213.

9. Cusic, *Johnny Cash: The Songs*, 48.

10. As Martin Marty says, "From the First Great Awakening to recent evangelicalism the impulse to choose has been strong. Billy Graham most successfully calls for decision for Christ by voluntary agents and characteristically calls his magazine *Decision*." *Religion and Republic: The American Circumstance* (Boston: Beacon Press, 1987), 279.

11. Quoted in Hollis Landdrum, "Cash: Sad Songs Are Fun to Sing," *Jackson Daily News*, November 8, 1973 (CMHF clip file).

12. Cash, *Man in Black*, 74–75.

13. Ibid., 142, 177.

14. Quoted in Charles Paul Conn, *The New Johnny Cash* (Old Tappan, NJ: Revell, 1973), 34.

15. Cash, *Man in Black*, 209.

16. Conn, *The New Johnny Cash*, 34. I have not yet discovered anything in his own words that describes being "born again," though that is indicated by his answering the altar call.

17. Johnny Cash, *Cash: The Autobiography*, with Patrick Carr (San Francisco: Harper San Francisco, 1997), 274, 275.

18. Stephen Prothero, *American Jesus: How the Son of God Became a National Icon* (New York: Farrar, Straus and Giroux, 2003), 145.

19. Robert Elfstrom, in discussion with the author, November 12, 2009.

20. Billy Graham, *Just as I Am: The Autobiography of Billy Graham* (San Francisco: HarperCollins, 1997), 417.

21. Edwards, *Johnny Cash and the Paradox*, 177, and 175–77 for a more extensive reading on the movie. Elfstrom noted that Cash did not express his religious

beliefs that openly. "He didn't lay it on you"—even though he did bring his own clergy to Israel. Elfstrom in discussion.

22. There was an initial outline, Elfstrom said, but the movie was actually made in day-to-day editing: "We never really had a script. All in all, "it's a mediocre

movie," Elfstrom admitted. But "it was good enough for John, he loved it. He thought it was one of the best things he did in his life." Elfstrom, in discussion.

23. Gary Heinlein, "Cash 'Countrifies' the Gospel," *Des Moines Tribune*, October 23, 1973 (CMHF clip file).

24. Richard Mial, "'The Gospel Road' Called Boring," *Delaware State News*, October 25, 1973 (CMHF clip file).

25. George Vescey, "Cash Says Religion Made the Difference," *Beaumont Enterprise*, December 23, 1973 (CMHF clip file).

26. Quoted in Bill McAllister, "Cash Stands Up for His 'Man' at Revival," *Fort Worth Star-Telegram*, June 29, 1974 (CMHF clip file).

27. Cash, *Man in Black*, 224.

28. Rita Forrester, in discussion with the author, July 12, 2008.

29. Yet it was a popular book, in Austin, where I lived; many of those who rediscovered Cash seemed to have a copy of it. I do not think they read it.

30. Bruce Ryskamp, "Welcome to Zondervan," Zondervan: The Leading Christian Communication Company, www.zondervan.com/desk/about.asp.

31. Larry Linderman, "Johnny Cash: The *Penthouse* Interview," *Penthouse*, August 1975, III (CMHF clip file).

32. Johnny Cash, with Billy Zeoli and Al Hartley, *Hello, I'm Johnny Cash* (Old Tappan, NJ: Revell, 1976), 5–7, 9, 13. The publisher, Spire Christian Comics, also put out Archie comics, as well as a comic religious biography of Dallas Cowboys coach Tom Landry.

33. Don Cusic, "Cash Discusses Christianity and the Gospel Message," *Cash Box*, June 14, 1980, C–10+.

34. Cusic, *Johnny Cash: The Songs*, 13.

35. Quoted in Marshall Frady, *Billy Graham: A Parable of American Righteousness* (Boston: Little, Brown, 1979), 370.

36. Edwards, *Johnny Cash and the Paradox*, 178–82.

37. Jim Lewis, "Man in Black Explains Book 'Man in White," *Denver Post*, June 20, 1986, reprinted in *The Legend,* December 1986, 35.

38. Andrea Chambers, "Johnny Cash Changes His Tune—From *A Boy Named Sue* to a Saint Named Paul," *People*, November 3, 1986; Mary Campbell, review of *Man in White*, in *Daily Sentinel*, November 2, 1986; both reprinted in *The Legend,* December 1986, 49 and 50.

39. I talked to the assistant manager in August 2004. Lifeway and other religious publishers and distributors have an enormous presence in Nashville.

40. Johnny Cash, preface to Arthur A. Smith, *Apply It to Life* (Nashville: Thomas Nelson, 1991) n.pg.

41. Jimmie N. Rogers and Stephen A. Smith, "Country Music and Organized Religion," in *All That Glitters: Country Music in America*, ed. George H. Lewis (Bowling Green, KY: Bowling Green State University Popular Press, 1993), 270.

42. Quoted in Ken Briggs, "Gospel according to Johnny Cash," *Rochester (NY) Democrat and Chronicle*, January 5, 1974. (CMHF clip file).

43. Quoted in Jennifer Jacobs, "For Laughs, Hospital Nets $235,000; Few Escape

Bob Newhart's Barbs at Crouse Hospital Foundation's Tribute Evening," *Syracuse (NY) Post-Standard*, November 4, 2001.

44. Kelefa Sanneh, "The Rap Against Rockism," *New York Times*, October 31, 2004.

45. Aaron A. Fox, *Real Country: Music and Language in Working-Class Culture* (Durham, NC: Duke University Press, 2004), xv, 21. See also Cecelia Tichi, *High Lonesome: The American Culture of Country Music* (Chapel Hill: University of North Carolina Press, 1996).

46. Even Norman Greenbaum's "Spirit in the Sky," which mentions having a friend in Jesus, is not really an expression of faith; Greenbaum, who is Jewish, admits that he made the insertion of Jesus because it might sell better. "Happy Birthday, Norman Greenbaum," *PopWatch*, November 20, 2007.

47. Rogers and Smith, "Country Music and Organized Religion," 270.

48. Barbara Ching, *Wrong's What I Do Best: Hard Country Music and Contemporary Culture* (New York: Oxford University Press, 2001).

49. Cusic, *Johnny Cash: The Songs*, 1–53.

50. Arsenio Orteza, "From the Other Side: Gospel Music from 'Secular' Artists Who Have Come to Faith," *World Magazine*, January 25, 1997.

51. Bruce Lincoln, "Bush's God Talk," *Christian Century*, October 5, 2004, 22.

52. Dan Gilgoff, "Winning with Evangelicals: How the 2004 Presidential Race Turned on Religious Outreach," *U.S. News and World Report*, February 25, 2007.

53. "Business Data for The Passion of the Christ," Internet Movie Database, June 22, 2005, imdb.com.

54. In Beverly Gaddy's opinion, "Nearly a half-century of research has confirmed that religious belief is indeed associated with intolerance—with, as far as I have been able to find, no evidence to the contrary." Gaddy, "Faith, Tolerance, and Civil Society," in *Faith, Morality, and Civil Society*, ed. Dale McConkey and Peter Augustine Lawler (Lanham, MD: Lexington Books, 2003), 160.

55. Johnny Cash, interview at Fan Fair, Johnny Cash Fan Club, *Our Kinda Cash*, second quarter, 1977, 7–8.

56. *Meet the Press*, transcript, November 28, 2003, MSNBC.com.

57. Sufjan Stevens, "All the Trees Will Clap Their Hands," from *Seven Swans*, www.lyricsmode.com.

58. Randall J. Stephens and Delvyn Case, "Hidden under a Bushel: Sufjan Stevens and the Problem of Christian Music," *Christianity Today*, November–December 2006.

59. Nick Sylvester, "Like Other Religious Artists before Him, Sufjan Stevens Puts His Faith in Craft," *Village Voice*, August 8, 2006.

60. Quoted in Andree Farias, "Sufjan Stevens: *Seven Swans*," *Christianity Today*, 2004.

61. Sylvester, "Like Other Religious Artists."

62. Farias, "Sufjan Stevens."

8. CASH CHOOSES RICK RUBIN

1. Paul Zollo, *Conversations with Tom Petty* (New York: Omnibus Press, 2005), 149–50.

2. Quoted in Sylvie Simmons, liner notes, *Unearthed* by Johnny Cash (Nashville: Lost Highway Records, 2003), 7.

3. David Kamp, "Letter from Nashville: American Communion," *Vanity Fair,* October 2004.

4. Indeed, when growing up, I had no idea that Crystal Gayle, Helen Reddy, Anne Murray, Linda Ronstadt, and Charlie Rich were considered country. Barry Mazor, in discussion with the author, July 29, 2004.

5. Jack Clement, in discussion with the author, March 22, 2006.

6. Louis Black, "Bob Johnston Discography: A Work in Progress," *Austin Chronicle,* December 7, 2007.

7. Quoted in Alan Light, *The Skills to Pay the Bills: The Story of the Beastie Boys* (New York: Three Rivers Press, 2005), 21.

8. Michael Streissguth, *Johnny Cash: The Biography* (New York: Da Capo, 2006), 254.

9. Bill Shaw, "Easing Back with Johnny Cash," *People,* July 11, 1994, 100–102.

10. Johnny Cash Fan Club, *Our Kinda Cash,* August 1989.

11. In 1978, other gifts included a *People's Almanac* and *Star Wars* force beam swords for John Carter Cash; in 1986, a hurricane lamp and a genie bottle. Ibid., first quarter 1978, 6; April 1986, 17.

12. Ibid., Spring 1975.

13. A straw-man model of authenticity is a singer or band writing and singing about things she or they care about, unconcerned about reception, production, or marketing of their work. Authentic bands play in intimate clubs and have a small committed fandom that worships them. And authentic bands live only in a moment of time; they face the path either of obscurity (and remain authentic in the eyes of a few) or of popularity (where they necessarily sell out).

14. Bill Eichenberger, "Cash's Greatest Assets Are Simple; His Voice, Lone Guitar, Great Song," *Columbus Dispatch,* May 12, 1994 (CMHF clip file).

15. Johnny Cash concert, Austin, Tex., Frank Erwin Center, December 8, 1994.

16. *Our Kinda Cash,* Summer 1994, 23.

17. Voters in the city itself had passed an ordinance restricting development in an area of town increasingly popular for development and in the aquifer of a stream that led to a landmark pool, Barton Springs.

18. Emo's, www.emosaustin.com.

19. Nisid Hajari, "Generation Tex," *Entertainment Weekly,* April 8, 1994, 54.

20. Chuck Klosterman, *Sex, Drugs, and Cocoa Puffs: A Low Culture Manifesto* (New York: Scribner, 2004 [2003]), 175.

21. Ibid., 177.

22. Simmons, *Unearthed,* 3; Petty, *Unearthed,* 8.

23. Mary Harron, "McRock: Pop as a Commodity," in *Facing the Music,* ed. Simon Frith (New York: Pantheon, 1988), 213.

24. Daniel Durchholz, "The Last American Hero?" *Request,* June 1994, 25+.

25. Quoted in Shaw, "Easing Back with Johnny Cash," 100.

26. Amy Linden, review of *American Recordings, People,* May 16, 1994 (CMFH clip file).

27. David Browne, review of *American Recordings*, *Entertainment Weekly*, April 29, 1994 (CMHF clip file).

28. Katy Bachman, "Study: Radio Listeners Up, despite Industry Doldrums." *Mediaweek*, December 10, 2008.

29. Michele Himes and Jason Loviglio, introduction to *Radio Reader: Essays in the Cultural History of Radio* (New York: Routledge, 2002), xiv. Though they concede that in some ways radio is returning to power, Himes points out that, "the four largest companies together [Chancellor (parent company of Clear Channel), CBS, ABC, and Emmis] control over 75% of the radio audience in the ten largest US metropolitan areas." She adds that "the local scene appears fairly diverse, supplemented as it is with public, community, and a few holdout locally owned stations. In most cities there are more radio stations operating today than ever before, giving an impression, at least, of something for everyone" (12). But though each geographical or metropolitan area does have its own mix of stations, some places having more rock than country stations, what is played on those stations from place to place is remarkably similar, governed by similar playlists.

30. "Johnny Cash: 70th Birthday," unattributed marketing plan from Sony/Columbia, 2002, 5 (CMHF archives).

31. Ed Shane, in discussion with the author, August 19, 2004.

32. John Turner, "'Thanks for Nuthin': Johnny Cash Blasts Nashville Bosses with Sassy Ad!" *Examiner*, April 7, 1998, 9 (CMHF clip file).

33. Kathleen M. O'Malley, "LCD 21/A Brief History of Freeform Radio," WFMU, 1999, www.wfmu.org/freeform.html.

34. Quoted in Paul Verna, "Johnny Cash Courts Young Fans; American Icon Backed by Petty and Band," *Billboard*, October 12, 1996 (CMHF clip file).

35. What I like about iPod stations is that they prove how similar to one another different types of music are. When almost everything they play is three to four minutes, with choruses and bridges and so on, and yet are supposedly in different genres, it seems clear that the distinctions we make are arbitrary.

36. John Sutton, in discussion with the author, November 2008.

37. "How Do NPR Listeners Compare to the Average American?" WUOT, August 2002, sunsite.utk.edu/wuot/h/underwriting/demographics.html.

38. Clement, discussion with the author.

39. Mark Romanek, e-mail messages to the author, August 22 and September 4, 2008.

40. Virginia Heffernan, "In Black: Johnny Cash's Bleak New Video," *Slate*, February 26, 2003.

41. Streissguth, *Johnny Cash: The Biography*, 277.

42. The following Romanek quotations are all from his e-mails to the author.

43. Leigh Edwards, *Johnny Cash and the Paradox of American Identity* (Bloomington: Indiana University Press, 2009), 61; she also reads the video extensively (59–61).

44. *Walk the Line*, dir. James Mangold, (Fox 2000 Pictures, 2005), film. My interview with Mangold was done for the *Telluride Film Watch* in August 2005.

45. Todd Martens, "'Walk Hard' Live and Kicking," Extended Play, *Los Angeles Times*, December 4, 2007.

46. Information taken from the Recording Industry Association of America's listings of gold and platinum records. See http://www.riaa.com/goldandplatinum .php for a searchable artist database.
47. Rosanne Cash, *The List* (Manhattan Records, 2009); *Artist's Choice: Johnny Cash* (Hear Music, 2003); Deborah Solomon, "Daddy Sang Base: Questions for Rosanne Cash," *New York Times*, October 4, 2009.

9. CASH CHOOSES SOTHEBY'S

1. For example, see Shawn Sell, "O, For a Little Piece of Camelot," *USA Today*, April 23, 1996.
2. John Carter Cash, *Anchored in Love: The Life and Legacy of June Carter Cash* (Nashville: Thomas Nelson, 2007), 190.
3. Michael Streissguth, *Johnny Cash: The Biography* (New York: Da Capo, 2006), 265.
4. Robert Lacey, *Sotheby's—Bidding for Class* (Boston: Little, Brown, 1998), 15.
5. "Johnny Cash Auction Closes at $4 Million," *BBC News*, September 17, 2004.
6. Rita Forrester, in discussion with the author, July 12, 2008.
7. Forrester, Flo Wolfe, and John Wolfe, in discussion with the author, July 12, 2008.
8. Bill Miller, *Cash: An American Man* (New York: Pocket Books, 2004).
9. Editors of *Rolling Stone, Cash: A Tribute to Johnny Cash*, ed. Jason Fine (New York: Crown, 2004).
10. All catalog descriptions refer to *Cash: Property from the Estate of Johnny Cash & June Carter Cash* (New York: Sotheby's, 2004).
11. Johnny Cash, *Cash: The Autobiography*, with Patrick Carr (San Francisco: Harper San Francisco, 1997), 233–34.
12. Leigh Edwards, *Johnny Cash and the Paradox of American Identity* (Bloomington: Indiana University Press, 2009).

INDEX

JONATHAN SILVERMAN was born in Aberdeen, Maryland, and grew up in Connecticut. He received his BA in English from Dartmouth College and his PhD in American studies from the University of Texas at Austin. He is an assistant professor of English at University of Massachusetts Lowell and is the coauthor (with Dean Rader) of *The World Is a Text: Writing, Reading, and Thinking About Culture and Its Contexts.* (Prentice Hall, 3rd ed., 2008). He recently served as the Fulbright Roving Scholar in American studies in Norway. Silverman lives in Arlington, Massachusetts.